A Client Called Noah

ALSO BY JOSH GREENFELD

A Child Called Noah
A Place for Noah
Harry and Tonto
O for a Master of Magic
The Return of Mr. Hollywood

A
CLIENT CALLED
NOAH
A FAMILY JOURNEY
CONTINUED

Josh Greenfeld

A Harvest/HBJ Book
HARCOURT BRACE JOVANOVICH, PUBLISHERS
San Diego   New York   London

362.3
6812c
1988

Published by arrangement
with Henry Holt and Company, Inc.

Library of Congress Cataloging-in-Publication Data

Greenfeld, Josh.
    A client called Noah: a family journey continued/Josh Greenfeld.
      p. cm.
    Continues: A place for Noah.
    "A Harvest/HBJ book."
    ISBN 0-15-618168-1 (pbk.)
      1. Greenfeld, Noah Jiro, 1966—Mental health.
2. Brain-damaged children—California—Biography.
3. Brain-damaged children—California—Family relationships.
I. Title. [RJ496.B7G722 1988]
362.3—dc 19
[B]   88-17741

Printed in the United States of America

First Harvest/HBJ edition

A B C D E

For Noah

INTRODUCTION

In *A Child Called Noah* I described my son Noah in 1970 this way:

> At the age of four Noah is neither toilet-trained nor does he feed himself. He seldom speaks expressively, rarely employs his less-than-a-dozen-word vocabulary. His attention span in a new toy is a matter of split seconds, television engages him for only an odd moment occasionally, he is never interested in other children for very long. His main activities are lint-catching, thread-pulling, blanket-sucking, spontaneous giggling, inexplicable crying, eye-squinting, wall-hugging, circle-walking, bed-bouncing, jumping, rocking, door-closing, and incoherent babbling addressed to his finger-flexing right hand. But two years ago Noah spoke in complete sentences, had a vocabulary of well over 150 words, sang the verses of his favorite songs, identified the objects and animals in his picture books, was all but toilet-trained, and practically ate by himself.
>
> What was the matter with Noah? For the longest time it seemed to depend upon what diagnosis we were willing to shop around for. We'd been told he was mentally retarded; emotionally disturbed; autistic; schizophrenic; brain damaged; or that he was suffering from a Chinese box combination of these conditions. But we finally discovered that the diagnosis didn't seem to matter. . . . There was no single viable treatment immediately available for Noah, no matter what category he could eventually be assigned to.

In 1977, just as Noah was eleven, I wrote in *A Place for Noah*:

My son Noah was—and is—brain-damaged. He suffers from severe developmental disabilities and acute deprivation in his fine motor processes; he is definitely mentally retarded and naturally has a behavior problem. We have yet to discover the exact reasons—which area of the brain and what perceptional faculties are not functioning properly.

But encircling him with an Orwellian word such as *autism*—one that cosmeticizes rather than communicates—is no help. . . .

How is . . . Noah now? He is doing better than he has done, but not as well as I would have hoped. If I had once seen his malady as transient, I now know it to be permanent. But I still must deal with it on a transient—or existential—basis. I still both enjoy Noah and endure him. . . .

This book begins where *A Place for Noah* ended and chronicles our family life up until November 15, 1980, my wife Foumi's fiftieth birthday. I have not brought the time frame further up to date out of respect for the privacy of my older son, Karl. We all need the protective buffer of hang time, especially while we're still growing up. And if I had to worry about stepping on too many recent feelings and incidents it would have made complete candor impossible.

Because again I have tried to communicate as honestly as possible our family lives on a day-to-day basis, our confusions and muddles along with our dreams and hopes. Once more I have culled the pages of my journal and transcribed them in order best to recapture the immediacy of the experiences. And in concentrating on a briefer time frame, I hope I have rendered more faithfully the density—and intensity—of our trials. In order to protect the innocent and ward off the guilty, I have sometimes found it necessary to mask completely the real identities of certain people and places. The rest is truth.

At this remove, if I had to sum up *A Child Called Noah* in a single word it would be *denial.* And the one word for *A Place for Noah* would probably be *rage.* So it should almost follow, as a textbook example of the adjustment process, that perhaps the word that might best encapsulate this book is *acceptance* or *resignation.* However, either word implies a passivity that seems alien to both my past accounts and present recollections of the period limned. In fact, I never before, nor ever since, have felt so vibrantly alive.

When I last wrote about Noah he was still nonverbal. But somewhere I believed the spark to communicate still smoldered within him. His brother, Karl, a year and a half older, was then twelve years old, perched at the precarious edge of adolescence. Most of Foumi's energies were directed toward running a day-care center for the developmentally disabled that we had established. But she was also working on a novel in Japanese that she hoped to get published. And as for me, I was still writing for the movies and television, but like some traditional cliché character out of a tired old script was also trying to find the time to get a novel of my own done. We lived in Pacific Palisades, a section of Los Angeles that was then having its brief moment in the media sun because Ronald Reagan lived here. But he lived in another part of town and has long since moved away. We still live in our part of town.

A word about the title: *Client* literally means one leaning on another, usually for protection; the word *incline* comes from the same root. *Client* is also the official designation or description assigned to Noah by the governmental agencies responsible for the supervision of his care.

Pacific Palisades, California
May 15, 1986

A Client Called Noah

1

In my house the sound of reality is plop-plop-plop. Last night Noah shit everywhere: on the bathroom mat, the hallway carpet, his own bedroom rug. This morning Karl woke up complaining of nausea and diarrhea. While I don't like to see him sick I prefer his being ill to Noah's.

Next the dishwasher backed up and flooded the kitchen. I was able to fix that by cleaning out the clogged drainage pipe with a wire clothes hanger. But then the washing machine wouldn't agitate. I didn't know how to fix that so I called a repairman who has yet to come.

I spent the rest of this inaugural morning watching Jimmy Carter walk down Pennsylvania Avenue with his family to the White House and envied him. Not his presidency. But the fact that he doesn't have to worry about broken washing machines and sick kids. Just the fate of the nation instead.

And now I'm off to lunch with a producer. The yearn of the stage, the call of the screen, like shitting kids and malfunctioning machines, are but time-fiddling ways of avoiding writing. No wonder I am prey to them.

January 21, 1977

The repairman pronounced the washing machine dead upon his arrival. I rushed out and bought a new one, with the deal-breaker

1

being that it had to be delivered by five o'clock. We can't be without a washing machine for a single day. Meanwhile, thankfully, Noah is in a good mood and Karl feels better. I drove them both to school this morning.

January 22, 1977

Suddenly, it's summer—on a lovely Saturday. Foumi went with Noah to our day-care center. She is the director and she had to resolve a transportation problem for a new kid and meet a new parent. I took Karl to breakfast, to his soccer game, to lunch, and then to a movie with some of his friends where I gave the kids an open tab at the refreshment counter. They took advantage, too, knowing a real sucker father when they saw one.

January 23, 1977

Last night both Karl and I had different versions of our recurring dreams. His dream: "You die. And when you die Noah becomes normal. So Foumi closes the day-care center and tries to kill all the parents so their children can become normal too. But the police arrest her. And then Noah goes crazy again."

My dream isn't as well plotted: It always involves a little girl, a daughter, who precociously can crawl at two months and is not brain-damaged in any way.

January 24, 1977

Noah's school keeps a complete change of clothing on hand in case of a toilet accident. This morning when I drove Noah there I brought along a freshly laundered set. But I forgot the extra pair of socks. So I took mine off and left them there. Greater love hath no barefoot father.

January 25, 1977

Last night we squeezed out of Karl a report on Noah for his Health class assignment. The teacher had wanted the kids to do one of those copy-and-cull-from-the-encyclopedia reports. I can't stand that sort of academic rigmarole. I told Karl to write what

2

he knows. And, after much prodding, pushing, and tugging from me, he finally did. This morning, when I told him his report wasn't bad at all, he blithely replied, "I know. I put in some real catchy things."

The weather is warm, springlike, eternally hopeful. I miss winter until I read of the weather back East. I am happy to be here now, happy to be with my family. But there has to be a better way to top an evening than bathing Noah.

Or filling out forms. The day-care center devours time. Last night Foumi and I diligently completed our payroll tax and W-2 forms. And today we have another kid coming. A rubella kid who is barely toilet-trained and doesn't listen to commands. But somehow I think it's all worth the effort, that someday we'll remember our kitchen-table activities the same way Exxon recalls its first oil strike.

January 26, 1977

Karl's Health teacher questioned him about his report, asking him if Noah was "autistic." Karl tried to explain to her that there was no such thing as autism—the word means nothing—and that what his brother was suffering from was a form of brain damage. I hope the student was able to teach the teacher something.

Noah is in a good mood these days. And I am too until I realize he is almost ten and a half. Which puts me in a bad mood.

January 27, 1977

Karl received his report card. No A's. Just B's and C's. Nothing exceptional. But not too bad either. His Health teacher gave him only a C. She should be shot for that. He deserved a better grade on the basis of that report alone and I told him so. Suddenly tears began to cloud his eyes. I don't know whether he was going to cry over the injustice of his grade or the tragedy of his brother. But it didn't matter. At that moment I loved him for his vulnerability.

He also has good taste. Last night he went with us to see Truffaut's *Small Change* and giggled all the way through it.

I know behavior mod is not the complete answer when it comes to treating children like Noah. At the same time I think it's the best first step. So I can appreciate the dilemma of state hospitals although I don't agree with their solution. On the one hand they are supposed to keep the patients in control. On the other hand they are legally constrained from punishing them in any way. Except they are allowed to administer drugs—which ultimately are a silent, sanitized form of punishment anyway. We assume deterrents are necessary to keep unruly nations in check. Why not brain-dysfunctional people, too? The problem, unfortunately, like integration is too complicated for legislated answers alone.

I feel bad that the comedian Freddie Prinz is dead. Not that I knew him. I just relate everything to Noah, especially a death that comes too soon, out of the expected order of things. After all, Noah too died too soon. At the age of two when his brain gave out.

We experimented yesterday afternoon, leaving Karl in charge of Noah for three hours. It seemed to work. Noah had no untoward behavior, even though Karl did make the mistake of having his friend Erich over. Which meant that as they played together Noah was ignored. Noah does not like to be ignored. He reminded us of that fact at dinner by refusing to eat and having a tantrum.

Karl seems to be the subject of an experiment in school. He was in an English honors class he liked. Now he will be in an experimental class in which honor students are paired off with remedial students in a tutorial relationship. It doesn't seem to make much sense to me but I'll stay tuned. I might have to get him out of that class. I want him to learn a little more in school rather than for him to teach the little he knows, more or less. In terms of education, what to do with Karl remains as much a problem as what to do with Noah.

A footnote on the normalcy of the abnormal—or the abnormality of the normal: Foumi has observed that both Karl and Noah prefer using our bathroom to their own.

February 2, 1977

A bad day in Hollywood. As I left a lunch with my agent, a young producer, and an older actress, I realized anew that taking on a movie writing assignment is like volunteering for a rape.

February 3, 1977

Karl seems to like his remedial-honors class, Noah has been in a good mood lately, and Foumi is tired. But then she's always tired. So too is my compassion for her. I guess I'm as worn out as she is.

February 4, 1977

Today I bought a new typewriter that sounds at times like a titwillow in an electronically operated forest. At other times the Olivetti's squeaky chirps seem like a nervous, high-strung Italian landlady's constant demand for the rent. But mostly it reminds me of the "self-stim" of Noah, the meaningless sounds he singsongs to himself. My whirring electric typewriter is as autistic as my keening mysterious son.

February 6, 1977

Last night Foumi couldn't sleep. First, one of the social workers over at Family Service, where we rent the day-care site, was hinting that we would be asked to leave because it needed the space. Second, Reva Jones, our key worker, the infantry of our day-care center, announced that she is thinking of starting a day-care center of her own for children in the black ghetto. So Foumi was up all night wondering what to do, spinning out options in her head. I don't know what we should do either. But I could sleep. I have learned that with every setback there is a possible advantage. Except with Noah.

Noah is with me now. I brought him to my office this Sunday morning because otherwise sleepy Foumi would not have allowed me to get away. At first he objected coming here. I think he thought it might be the office of some new doctor I was taking him to. But now he's settled down to his usual routine. Doing nothing but bouncing up and down on my couch. While I perform my self-stim at this self-stimming typewriter.

February 7, 1977

Noah has bigger hands than Karl. Does that mean he'll become bigger than Karl? He also does not like to be teased. Yesterday I called him "a good boy" ironically. His response: He pulled Foumi's hair.

February 9, 1977

I went to a Writers Guild meeting last night and came home convinced that writers who always get screwed will find a way to screw themselves again. This morning at breakfast I told Karl there might be a writers' strike. "So what," said Karl. "It's not so terrible. It's not like they're farmers or something." "But it means," I said, "that after a while there'll be no new episodes of 'All in the Family,' 'Happy Days,' or 'M.A.S.H.'" "You mean just reruns?" Karl asked. "Just like summer?" "Yes," I replied. "Gee," Karl said, and poked his egg thoughtfully, "that's terrible."

I had the usual dream again, Noah talking. But this time it wasn't too difficult to wake up into reality. He only said two words throughout the dream: "You bet."

February 10, 1977

At dinner last night Foumi observed that both Karl and Noah eat more than either of us. I guess when the kids put down more food than the parents, it means the Oedipal weight is shifting.

February 13, 1977

The bad news: We got our walking papers from Family Service, our day-care landlord. The good news: They will not just evict us into the cold, we'll have ample time to find a new day-care site. The best news: Reva will stay with us.

February 14, 1977

Karl slept at his friend Erich's house on Saturday night and yesterday informed me that the trained rat belonging to Erich's kid brother, Maxie, was not that trained. It had bitten him, drawing blood. When I called our pediatrician to learn if there were any special precautions I should take, he asked how old Karl was. I didn't quite realize until I answered him that Karl was twelve.

Which means he's not so young anymore. Theoretically, in another six years he could be sent off into the world on his own. Certainly, in another nine or ten years I'm off the hook with him. With Noah, theoretically I'm off the hook at any time—and never.

February 16, 1977

I observed Karl from a distance as he was walking home from school. He looked lean and trim to me, someone who would grow taller and slimmer. I saw Noah from a distance as he was getting out of the car coming home from day-care. He looked fat, and like someone who would get even fatter. So this morning I made him go light on breakfast.

February 17, 1977

My health tests out good according to my doctor, but my genes continue to haunt me. My cholesterol is up to 301. I will take another test. And if it is still up, lean as I am, I'll have to go on some slim-trim-low-fat-no-taste diet.

February 20, 1977

A winter Sunday in Southern California, the sun shining in a clear blue sky, and I've come to my office to do a little work. I always think that whatever I accomplish on a Sunday is worth double an ordinary day. I've also come here to get away from the house. Karl and Foumi are arguing about drums: He wants to get a set and play them in the house.

And I feel guilty about the way I treated Noah last night. I struck him unnecessarily when he began to spit and claw at me. So he just did more of the same, reminding me that I have to be patient with him. I have to spend more time teaching him with rewards rather than just chastising him. But why oh why does the parent of a special child have to be more of a teacher and a tutor than the parent of a normal child?

February 21, 1977

We picked up a sign-language book. The sophisticated finger movements seem to me to be beyond Noah's range of motor skills. Perhaps we should try to teach him a simpler homemade language that he can use to communicate just with us. Like touching his throat when he is thirsty. Or a thump on his chest for when he wants to go outside. We could figure out a King Kong kind of language.

February 23, 1977

The family stayed home en masse today. It was one of those day afters that seem to come only after a holiday. What happened was this: Last night Noah had a loose stomach, the shit sliding down his leg. Foumi insisted on giving him a medication even though I argued that it would keep him up all night. And I was right. Then this morning Karl woke up vomiting.

So everybody is at home today with Noah the healthiest, Karl the sickest, Foumi the sleepiest, and me the laziest. But I do have a cold, which gives me the excuse to curl up with a book, Alma Mahler's life story. I love to read about old Vienna. I knew when I was stationed in Germany that there is a part of me that is Germanic. I only wish that I had been a better linguist. Perhaps Karl will be. He has a musical sense I never had.

February 24, 1977

Foumi and I decided that living well is not the best revenge. But that if one has health, if one has materials, the best revenge is living longer. An editor I know died at forty-nine playing tennis.

In three days I'll be forty-nine and the only thing I have going for me is that I don't play tennis. This morning I took another cholesterol test, after manfully abstaining from red meat all week. I'm rooting against a cottage-cheese future.

The weather is wintry, or as wintry as Southern California gets, and I like it. I like days on which there is no place where one would rather be than indoors. And I especially delight in watching Karl bury himself in a book. I love books. I would rather forsake movies and television for the rest of my life than have to surrender the enjoyment of books. Only reading gives me pleasure and makes me feel virtuous at the same time. Perhaps it will be the same with Karl.

February 25, 1977

A Noah night. He woke us twice and was up long before the dawn's early light. The result: I'm still sleepy and chilly.

February 26, 1977

We had some old friends over for dinner, a couple, both painters, from the East, who had sort of served as Foumi's surrogate parents the summer we met at MacDowell, the retreat for artists, writers, and composers in New Hampshire. He is seventy, she is sixty-seven, and they are still so alive. (Artists, Foumi reminded me, stay young.) Noah, embarrassed and shy, acted up. Karl, embarrassed and shy, took to his room to work on his model ships and planes and rockets. He really devotes a lot of time to them.

This afternoon I joined him and his friends and their father in a boyhood I never had, blasting off rockets from electronic launching pads, sending them high over the high school athletic field and watching their capsules parachute back down. I really enjoyed it. Until Karl told me that a kid in his class calls him "a harbor bomber" because of his Japanese heritage. Oh, that prejudice would be that easy to blast away.

February 27, 1977

Let's hear it for the kid. Today's my birthday. Forty-nine big ones. I celebrated the start of my jubilee year by making a quick getaway for the day. Driving Karl to a friend's. And leaving Foumi stuck with Noah. Hell, it's not her birthday.

February 28, 1977

The great day has passed without anything of moment happening. Except I did decide that even with a Noah in my life it is not yet a lost cause—just a long season with some serious slumps.

2

March 1, 1977

Noah has a tantrum each day when he comes home from school. And I feel like having a tantrum whenever I observe Karl doing—or not doing—his math homework. He doesn't understand negative numbers. But then neither did I. Still don't. It's a wonder I ever passed algebra. It'll be a wonder if Karl passes it. But when Karl and I were tossing a football around yesterday along the cliff, I noticed the kid throws a better pass now than I did when I was his age. In fact, he throws a better pass now than I do now. So he should be able to pass algebra.

March 2, 1977

In New York people would ask me if I've read anything good lately. In L.A. people ask me if I've seen anything good lately. Each city has its industry, but New York has the better tradition.

March 3, 1977

A woman who chauffeurs one of Noah's classmates to school turns out to be a self-styled miracle worker. This morning she told me that she had found Noah's classmate a "vegetable" but because he could "respond" to her she's made great progress with him and that Noah "responds" to her, too. And then she went on to babble about Bettelheim in a way that turned me off completely. She said I was being "negative"; I said I was being "realistic." But oh how I still dream of an intelligent Noah.

March 4, 1977

If Noah is sitting beside me when I'm driving he constantly puts his hand in my face. And if he is sitting behind me he reaches over and pokes me in the eye. Driving him home from school yesterday I became angry, stopped the car, pulled over to the side of the freeway, and whacked him one.

I don't like to whack Noah. I know that even dignifying the whack by calling it behavior mod is not the answer. No etiology is. But sometimes "the stick" is necessary to instill fear in Noah in order to control him. Of course, it should only be applied judiciously. The problem is that sometimes I get out of hand—or apply the hand too much. But yesterday was not the case. There is no way I could have gotten him to stop being dangerous with a "carrot" approach. Still I wish I didn't feel so goddamned guilty.

March 6, 1977

I spent a long afternoon at day-care filling in for our male aide. As I watched objectively the way the other parents treat their retarded children I realized I make the same mistake. We all treat our children as babies, so it is not surprising that they act like babies. I should not hug and kiss Noah so much. I should demand more of him.

March 8, 1977

I was wrestling with Karl last night and suddenly it stopped being playful. He was trying to hurt me and I responded with too much pressure. I have to be careful.

I can't wrestle with Noah. The kid's too fat anyway. Foumi tried to get him into a pair of Karl's old pants but couldn't.

March 9, 1977

When I came home this evening Foumi was crying. The great State of California has refused to fund one of our new day-care kids for the past month. It had made a clerical error but was not willing to pay for it. I told Foumi to stop crying because it was only money. But that wasn't why she was crying, she explained to me. It was because of the cruel coldness of the state workers, their utter inhumanity, and the certain knowledge that some day we will be placing Noah in the hands of such a bureaucratic mentality.

Instead of taking my ritualistic walk with Noah I tossed the football around with Karl. Karl needs a real brother, though. Someone to prod and guide and challenge him on his own level. He has only me to treat him as a sibling and I cannot slip in and out of the role that easily and without confusion.

March 10, 1977

I sometimes have to deal with the special problems of a disabled child rhetorically as well as actually, and it's a lot more satisfying. At least in terms of feedback. I was on the phone to Sacramento complaining about the peremptory manner in which one of our day-care kids wasn't being funded. And now I think Sacramento will reverse its decision.

March 13, 1977

I won the little day-care funding battle. The result: I've been inundated with paperwork this weekend. Perhaps it would have been better to let them not pay the two dollars.

March 14, 1977

I went out to the University of Southern California to participate in a symposium on screenwriting and enjoyed the students. I envied them their youth, their desires, and their dreams, but not the reality that lay ahead.

March 15, 1977

Noah gave me a hard time yesterday. He did not want to put on a jacket and cared even less about taking a walk. But I prevailed.

We attended a meeting of Family Service, our day-care-center landlords. One look at the faces there convinced me that we'll have to move out soon. After we returned home Foumi kept talking about the day-care-center problem, and I criticized her for her constant preoccupation with the subject. But she said we're like a couple with a "milk shop"—the Japanese equivalent of the old Brooklyn candy store—so we have to talk about it. And she's right.

The care of Noah is always the center of our lives. But at least our lives have a center. Which is more than I can say for a lot of lives about us.

Noah woke up hungry at five o'clock this morning. I think we'll have to give him his after-dinner fruit a little more "after" from now on.

Karl brought home his report—or progress—card. He is still talking too much in class and not doing well in math. He really is a lousy mathematician. I wonder what—if anything—he'll be good at.

Sunday with the Greenfelds: Noah was up before seven but I put on earplugs and managed to stay in bed until nine. Then I prepared breakfast for Noah, cleaned our room, vacuumed the house, gassed up the cars for the week, stopped off in my office for a little work, and picked up some deli sandwiches and brought them home for lunch. Karl had seen an ad for the movie *Mohammed* and wanted to go see it. He thought, until I informed him differently, it was about a boxer "just like *Rocky*." My only plans for the rest of the afternoon had been to walk Noah for an hour.

Foumi, however, decided it was a good day for all of us to go shopping. At the mall we wound up with Noah sitting in the car, refusing to get out of it, and Karl with a new pair of pants and two shirts.

In the evening Foumi tried to scrape together a meal of leftovers. But when Karl wouldn't eat curry, I wouldn't eat pizza, and Noah wouldn't eat anything, she was suddenly overwhelmed. And who wouldn't be? It's hard to deal with a family in our condition. Even on Sunday. Always on Sunday.

March 21, 1977

Foumi is writing a novel in Japanese dealing with the relationship between a mother and a daughter. She worries about its lack of plot. I don't know what to tell her. I feel so inadequate because of my inability to help in any way. How difficult it must be having a husband who literally can't speak your language.

March 24, 1977

Foumi is constantly bugging me that we need a new day-care site. I also wonder about looking for a new school for Noah. He hasn't made any discernible progress for a long time. He hasn't regressed either. But then he doesn't have that much leeway in that department.

March 26, 1977

Most people who want to write do not have a subject to write about. I have a subject but he keeps me from my writing.

March 27, 1977

I have a sick sense of humor. I was thinking about the severely handicapped, such as the paraplegics. How might society best employ them? And I thought of using them as psychoanalysts. Prospective patients could hardly feel sorry for themselves when they were confronted by paraplegics. Especially if they were hanging from baskets in their offices. You could even call the operation "Analysis in a Basket" and franchise it. As I say, I have a sick sense of humor.

March 28, 1977

Noah was in a good mood yesterday. He willingly went for a long walk with me. But Foumi was in a foul mood. She was on my case for not looking hard enough for another day-care site. Day-care site? Perhaps I should look for a marriage guidance center. Sometimes I think we're truly getting tired of each other. Sixteen years is a long time. But what probably disturbs us both the most is not each other but the decisions over which neither of us has any control. And most of these involve Noah.

March 29, 1977

Foumi is being very mean—she says it is I who am being mean—but lately I do not feel even a spark of like from her for me. Or am I looking for an excuse for the middle-age doldrums I sense in myself. I really do yearn to shake up my life. To stray—or stroll—down some new road. But then I think of the hostages, Karl and Noah, I would be leaving behind. For Karl it could be disastrous. When I play football with him he gets very temperamental when he drops a pass. He still simply cannot handle rejection or defeat of any kind. And, of course, that's how he would interpret any leave-taking on my part. For Noah it would not matter at all.

Meanwhile I talked with the pastor over at the Brentwood Presbyterian Church and there is a good chance they might provide a site for our day-care center. In any case I found him a lovely man.

March 30, 1977

I have always thought an interest in toy soldiers is the sign of a rejected child. And now Karl is a kid lost in military affairs. But it does bring him to books. Last night his head was dipped into a big fat biography of Patton that I had taken out of the library for him.

Noah was in a good mood. He slept well, getting up only once, and did not have a single tantrum all day.

But Foumi had severe menopausal menstrual pains. I should thank my lucky stars for being a man. I should be grateful for the state of grace in my life at this time. But I'm not.

March 31, 1977

Karl has to pick his electives for next semester. I feel we should tell him to take French. Because I know that whenever we defer to his choice we make a big mistake. A child does not know what is best for him. Still, he also has to be taught to make his own decisions. What to do?

April 2, 1977

We probably have a site over at the Brentwood Presbyterian Church, a large room of our own on the second floor. But we still looked at other churches. The only ones that held out real promise were the Presbyterians in West Los Angeles and in Santa Monica.

Both boys are off from school this week. Thank God we have day-care. Thank God for the Presbyterians.

April 3, 1977

I have been thinking about loneliness, the loneliness I knew as a young writer. I do not look forward to an old age when I would be alone. Without Foumi. Without Noah.

April 4, 1977

Noah hit the shit trail again last night, leaving a streak across the hallway floor. Then after going to bed he awoke at four and never went back to sleep, wheedling and keening into the morning. Otherwise, he has been behaving unusually well for a vacation period.

April 7, 1977

Rick Schaeffer and I drove Karl and the Schaeffer boys, Erich and Max, out to Mount Baldy. We wanted to take the kids frolicking in the snow. There was much driving, a little frolicking, and less snow. But there was enough for the kids to have fun sliding down Baldy on inner tubes. Karl didn't quite know how to break a fall with his feet. Once he went barreling head over heels into the leaves where the snow ended. But at least he did get to play in the snow.

April 9, 1977

We've temporarily lost our accident insurance at day-care. But we still have our liability, which is the important thing. And I will prepare a history of our organization and a summary of its purpose for the board at the Brentwood Presbyterian Church to review.

April 15, 1977

Foumi and I drove to Santa Barbara with the vague idea of buying a home there. We figured that if we could not get away from Noah for vacations we could at least get away with Noah. But oh how prices for a dream house have risen there! No real way I could swing it at this time.

April 21, 1977

I went to a meeting of "austistic" parents at Regional Center, the state agency that deals with the handicapped and developmentally disabled on a local level. I saw a twenty-one-year-old autistic for whom there is no program. He had come with his parents and I felt sorry for them. I felt sorry for him, too. And I felt sorry for Noah. Once more I dreaded the future.

April 22, 1977

Foumi thinks we've all become too lenient with Noah lately. She's right. But it takes so much energy on our part to get him to expend any energy on his part that most of the time it doesn't seem worth the effort. Still, I'll give him a few sessions of gung-ho conditioning.

April 28, 1977

Every evening I work with Noah. But, as always, with little result. I don't know who's worse. I'm a lousy teacher and he's a rotten pupil.

April 29, 1977

Hooray. We definitely have the church site for our day-care. The people there are wonderful. To use the current word, they really are most "supportive." And we can use a lot of support.

Karl is in the doldrums because we won't buy him drums. We have enough noise about the house. If he really wants to play drums he will have to find a place where he can practice.

May 1, 1977

Foumi's talking again about our buying a second home in Santa Barbara. But how to get away to look for one? We won't have a baby-sitter for the next three weeks.

Karl visited a local hospital with his class and was surprised it was "so good. Not like the ones on television." I'm delighted. Because it means he won't be afraid of hospitals if we ever have a problem in that area.

We do have a drum problem, though. It seems every time he goes for a lesson his teacher continues to pressure him into buying a drum. Which figures. It is a music store. Karl was tearful last night when we refused him again. But Foumi just will not let him have drums in the house. Both Noah and drums, she says, would just be too much for us.

I have been drilling Noah every night, trying to put him through a little P.T. His coordination is really bad. He cannot swing his hands alternately. Or even independently. What the left arm does the right arm has to do at the same time.

May 2, 1977

Foumi is always complaining about how hard she works. I admit that I don't work as hard as she does. I worry hard.

May 3, 1977

Noah's leg coordination is even worse than that of his arms. Almost nil.

May 4, 1977

Karl has announced that he is abandoning the drums. He did so in a way obviously meant to make his guilt-prone father feel guilty. It worked. I feel guilty. But we had no choice.

On our walk last night Karl and I discussed the tastes of various candies when we were children. I reached back into my Brooklyn boyhood memory bank to withdraw sense memories of *Hooten's chocolates* and *frozen twists* and *Necco wafers*. Karl recalled the candy tastes of his childhood—all the way back to Croton five years ago. Food is a recurring topic on our walks and I guess it can't be helped. After all, we don't have that many common topics. I think of bringing up sex, but then I wonder about how much he actually knows.

Noah and I did not get along too well when I tried to get him to exercise. I made the mistake of hitting him once. And then he kept coming into me, his hand jabbing forth as if to ward off blows. I wasn't going to be fool enough to hit him again. But he wasn't going to be fool enough to let me forget that I had hit him.

I drove Karl to school, theoretically because of the threat of rain. But actually because I think he is jealous that I drive Noah to school each day. But for that matter Noah should be jealous that I take a much longer walk with Karl each night than I ever take with him. I am stumped when Karl asks me who my favorite general is. Or what my favorite color is. Or, of course, my favorite food. I just love to walk with him, to listen to him talk, to realize that he is twelve and a half years old, and to marvel at how fast and continually he grows.

The high point of my day continues to be my after-dinner walk with Karl. Last night we discussed school menus, comparing his with what mine were like. I told him how my high school cafeteria under some federal program used to sell milk for just a penny but that the local candy stores offered small egg creams for three cents, forcing me to make a difficult choice.

Karl soon proceeded to confront me with another dilemma. He asked, If I could make one person whom I knew die just by saying so, who would I name? I was sorely tempted to name several candidates but I made believe there was no one upon whom I would wish such a fate. But he quickly came up with his sixth-grade teacher.

May 11, 1977

Noah sleeps late these days. In order to wake him I have to pull away his covers, open his curtains wide, and drag him to his feet. He then runs down the hallway into our room and leaps into our bed. Again, I pull him from the bed and he scampers into the living room and sits or lies there. Until finally he moves off into the kitchen.

May 13, 1977

Foumi has a running stomach, Noah is chewing up his shirts, Karl is getting into trouble at school. And I feel the possibilities in my literary life are definitely less than infinite.

May 15, 1977

I've come to my office this Sunday with Noah, who is sitting on my swivel chair, playing with a rubber band, and possibly wondering why I have brought him here. He rolls around on the chair and sits at the desk quietly. Now he rises, plays with the rubber band, regards me strangely as he shakes his head and returns to the swivel. So much for my play-by-play of his nonplay.

I tried to get him to do a little exercise yesterday, barking out commands to him. He refused to do anything. I had forgotten that just the threat of punishment alone does not work with him. He requires rewards. Just like any animal who is to be trained.

Now Noah is complaining in a singsong. He stands up and rocks back and forth beside the chair. I get up and hand him the rubber band again. He lies down on my couch and begins to twiddle with it.

May 16, 1977

Karl has been giving Foumi a hard time lately, refusing to cooperate with her in any way. But one of his friends who is adopted is making it even more difficult for his mother. He tells her he is not going to give her a Mother's Day gift, that he is saving instead to get one for his real mother when he finds her. If these kids are giving their mothers problems now, I can imagine what's in store for us fathers next.

May 17, 1977

We met with a committee of three women from the church and I'm sure we'll be able to make an orderly day-care transition. I am worried about the distance from our rooms to the bathrooms. But not that worried. I'm sure we can find a way to handle it.

May 18, 1977

My cholesterol is down to 253. Not that much of a descent after having made some effort to watch myself. Maybe I should talk to my doctor about possible medications.

Karl slept over at Erich's house. But then he had a headache yesterday and did not go to school. That always seems to happen after a weekend sleepover. So we will have to deny him sleepovers for the rest of the school year.

May 19, 1977

Noah is monumentally lazy. We have to prod him to do anything. Which makes him so hard to teach. Especially in the area of self-care. It is the most important thing he can learn and yet is the last thing anyone wants to teach him. I wish we could send him away for a year. Anywhere.

The doctor says I need not go on any medication. "Drugs" was the word he used. A drop from 301 to 253 in cholesterol, he pointed out, is a drop of 20 percent.

May 20, 1977

Foumi is terribly upset over Karl's report card. He's barely passing English and math. She thinks he's thick; I think he's immature. I also know teachers tend to give lower grades when the kid is bad in conduct. And Karl's conduct is bad. But Foumi claims that when she tries to tutor him she finds his thinking sloppy and his brain as sievelike as Noah's. I'm not inclined to worry just because of a report card. If Karl has learning problems they're still minuscule compared to Noah's. So what if he's incapable of becoming a nuclear scientist? I mean, Karl can always be trained to function at some trade or vocation. But Foumi is still alarmed. She wants me to do something. So I have confiscated Karl's toy soldiers for a while.

What bothers me a lot more than Karl's report card is the nest of mockingbirds outside our bedroom window, its occupants making noise all night long. The God that gave me Noah should at least spare me mockingbirds. All I need is for Noah to begin imitating them. Then it's really farewell to sleep.

May 21, 1977

I heard wisdom on a wake-up radio show this morning. "Treat every enemy as if someday he might be a friend. Regard every friend as a potential enemy." Which, come to think of it, is the modus operandi of the movie business.

May 23, 1977

I am disappointed in Karl. He lied to us yesterday, saying that he had practiced piano when he hadn't. The lie came to him too easily. Almost automatically. I also don't like the way he goes about doing his homework. In a most desultory way. Saying, "I'm lazy." As if that were a justifiable excuse.

May 24, 1977

I'm not the only one in the world who has problems with his kids. The seventeen-year-old son of one of my closest friends was arrested for robbing a small supermarket in suburban Connecticut. He was the driver, another kid was the "perpetrator." It was the second job they had pulled together. He got just three hundred dollars. The other kid, the perpetrator-promoter, netted over six thousand. I didn't know what to say to my friend. He hopes his son will get off because he is under eighteen. Fortunately, his son is a strong kid physically. He will have to become a stronger kid if he has to serve hard time. My friend's lawyer will try to delay the trial so that his son can build up a good record, showing positive signs of redemption by the time he has to go to court. But the legal process will be costly. I loaned my friend some money. Which is all I can do from here.

May 25, 1977

Foumi brought Reva Jones, our day-care teacher, over to our new site. She was delighted with the room, impressed by the church bricks. I hope our little cottage industry can have a good life there.

May 27, 1977

Karl showed me a fable he had written. He called it a "myth" but it was just a fable. And it wasn't bad. I should have encouraged him more than I did.

A friend came over to the house with her two-year-old son. I liked the way Karl played with the boy. And I loved the boy's pink-faced babyhood, oozing all the promise of future growth. Even Noah, for a short period, had such a babyhood. But now, next to the two-year-old, the ten-year-old Noah looked like a giant stuffed Teddy alongside a small, sophisticated electronic toy.

May 28, 1977

As I prepared his bath after a day on which I had given him scant attention, Noah gleefully shouted, "Daddy!" But then this morning when I lay down beside him on our bed and tried to embrace him, he kicked me hard. In the balls.

May 30, 1977

This holiday morning Noah woke me at six o'clock. He was up yodeling. I led him to the bathroom and then tried in vain to return to sleep.

Foumi is upset because day-care was a mess today. Only two children showed up. There should have been better communication with the parents. We should have conducted a preliminary survey to find out how many children would actually be coming.

How naïve we are. The state is reducing our vendoring fee, the sum of money it will reimburse us next year for each child in day-care. Foumi made the mistake of furnishing honest and accurate figures in our projected budget. I had told her to pad the budget. Instead, in this inflationary period, she pared it. I guess her desire to show some unappreciative bureaucrat what a good administrator she was has backfired. And Foumi reacted tearfully when she looked at the figure: "I will close down." "Do you think the state cares?" I told her and took her in my arms. My darling wife, she is not very bright in the pragmatic ways of the American—or State of California—world, and it will take me days of letter writing to try and get what they should have awarded us in the first place. The Sacramento slide rules never take into account honesty and we are always penalized for that.

This morning at breakfast Foumi and I had quite a go. I wanted silence, she wanted to talk day-care. I asked her politely to hold up on it until lunch. Unlike most couples we do lunch together. But she wouldn't stop. Just kept talking day-care. I told her to knock it off. Whereupon she resigned as head of day-care, announced from now on I would have to manage everything. She's like a dog who keeps coming at you. No wonder Noah is so feisty.

Noah weighs almost seventy-five pounds now, is fifty-five inches tall, and seems to be broad-bodied like a workingman. But a lazy workingman. Every time I try to get him to right my bed covers he just touches them. But when he gets up in the middle of the night or before us in the morning, he usually goes to the bathroom by himself. Which is a very good sign. He also has a teasing sense of humor. He seems to know sometimes how hard he is making us work in trying to communicate to him. But he still jumps and waves his arms when he is frustrated at his inability to communicate.

Karl runs hot and cold. One moment he seems very mature and

wise, and the next moment as foolish as a baby. Like Noah it is difficult for him to take a rebuke of any sort. Last night when he was dillydallying at washing the dishes I took one out of his hands and he all but broke down. Earlier, when we had been walking on the cliff he seemed in a state of euphoria as he told me he was now getting great marks in school. I would have been euphoric too if I could trust him enough to believe that.

June 6, 1977

More than one set of friends is having a bad run of it. But none of their problems compare to a Noah. And somehow we live with it. I'm sorry, but marriages breaking up and children going wayward and aging parents becoming senile leave me less moved than they should.

June 8, 1977

Karl is on the downhill side of school. He can smell vacation just one week away. Each night after school he is off somewhere on his skateboard. He delights in showing off to me his agility as he gets up a head of speed and then slinks and swerves down the street and out of sight.

Tomorrow is the last chance we get to use Katie Irving as a baby-sitter. Foumi and I will go to Santa Barbara for one of our mini-vacations and house-shopping quests. This time I am ready to buy. Our aim is clear: We want a place we can go to for weekends and vacations. We cannot go off to Hawaii or Paris or even Bakersfield. We have to take Noah with us and we need changes of environment both for him and for us. Otherwise, we will all grow up completely isolated—and insulated—in our house.

It would be nice if we could take the usual family kind of trips with Noah. But he is no fun on any trip. He does not like restaurants, he does not sleep nights in new places on unfamiliar beds. Traveling with him is like traveling with a crotchety old man completely set in his ways.

June 10, 1977

We went to Santa Barbara full of hope. We thought we would be able to pick up something. But we came back empty-handed. In just the past few months—since we were last there—prices have skyrocketed far out of our financial sight.

When I mentioned my disappointment to a friend he did not seem to sympathize very much. Why should he feel sorry for someone who cannot afford a vacation home? But then no one, except other parents, can begin to understand our situation. Certainly in the overall scheme of things the energy we devote to Noah must seem not only wasteful but worthless. But then what is truly worthwhile? Serving a Noah makes as much sense to me as serving a bitch goddess—or even a virginal goddess. It is a much less selfless obsession than that of most people I know. I am not worrying about a worldly career of success or failure. I am haunted by the fate of a human existence.

June 11, 1977

I spoke to Sacramento and we will be allowed to submit new figures. That should solve one particular day-care woe. But I don't know how to handle some of our parents. Yesterday I noticed one of the fathers greeting his son with great affection even though at that very moment the kid was misbehaving badly.

June 12, 1977

Noah's biological clock ticks as erratically as the brain that is supposed to regulate it. Not all of his teeth are in yet but he's already begun to sprout pubic hair.

June 13, 1977

We had a round robin of family fights yesterday. Karl seems to have lost his skateboard down some storm drain and I was annoyed with him for that. Foumi blamed me because Karl was watching too much television. And then I exploded at both of them.

June 14, 1977

Foumi is in a better mood today. And Karl should be when he returns home from school. After many phone calls I managed to have the city retrieve his skateboard from the storm drain. And I was able to pick it up at the L.A. Municipal Sewer office without too much bureaucratic difficulty. Not like the time I dropped my eyeglasses down the sewer on the corner of Houston and Sullivan Street in Greenwich Village. I was young and broke at the time and after much jousting with authorities I finally talked the Sanitation Department into retrieving them for me. Then I decided to sanitize them myself. I went home and dropped them into boiling water and watched the plastic frames shrivel up and die. Oh how Foumi and Karl love to hear me tell that story! Nothing like Pop's-a-fool to keep the family happy.

June 15, 1977

A report from the educational front:

This morning we took Noah to Area D headquarters for his annual classification interview with the Board of Education. On our arrival Noah was in a hair-pulling mood. Our hair. But when he realized he was in a school and not a doctor's office or a hospital, he settled down. He even sat quietly while the psychologist went through her ritual examination. Once more the Board of Education has decided that it does not have a place for him within its school system, so they will fund him in his private school again. They classified Noah as "mentally handicapped." I could just as easily have had him classified as "autistic." The difference is an authorization in the funding allowance. Up to eighteen dollars per day can be spent on the tuition for "M.H."; the elitist "autistics" can be funded up to thirty-five dollars per day. You takes your label and they pays the choice money.

Karl brought home his report card. B's in English and History; C's in Art and Physical Education; a D in Math; and his only A in Electricity. Both the history and math teachers wrote that he showed little effort; the art teacher commented that he was generally disruptive. Not a very good report card. Even Karl is upset with it. But oh that Noah could bring home a real report card!

June 17, 1977

I made a terrible mistake. Last night Foumi translate-read to us in English some of the novel she is writing in Japanese. I really think she has a good book there and told her so. But I was also critical of certain scenes. As I say, a great mistake. I should have realized that no matter how mature Foumi is in other respects she is still young when it comes to writing and therefore subject to all the insecurities of that calling—or curse. Because this morning she was lamenting, "Yesterday I thought I had a best-seller and today I'm not even sure I can get this book published."

I should keep my two cents out of the work of people who have little confidence in themselves. I am upset that I have upset her. But in her insecurity she asked for it. And insecurity, in writing as in anything else, she must learn, always costs.

June 19, 1977

Once more as summer begins I feel sorry for Karl. He has no great adventures to look forward to. As a family we will mostly stay put. Perhaps we might manage a small trip. But I wouldn't bet on it.

After a Father's Day dinner I walked down to the beach with my sons. Karl led the way—he knows all the cliffside trails—and Noah was happy. Noah is always so much happier when Karl is with us.

June 20, 1977

Noah was up at daylight, screaming. At breakfast he refused to drink his juice or milk, knocking them over. While Foumi was trying to dress him, he pulled her hair. And when I left the house she was crying, "I need an institution for myself. I'm dizzy all the time from the way he pulls my hair."

June 21, 1977

Today Noah is on a pinching rampage. It must be his teeth. Or because he's sleepy. Meanwhile, Karl is a joy. All his friends seem to be away so he needs our companionship—and our approval. He even cleaned his room without our asking.

June 22, 1977

The publishing scene in Japan disturbs Foumi. "They print such crap," she complains. She's reading the winner of their most important literary contest and finds it "academic bullshit." Perhaps she ought to try to get published in America first. But that means she would have to do her own translation, which I would then have to rewrite. And I'm not about to do that. Too much time, too much work, too many arguments. Poor Foumi. She has the misfortune of being an honest voice in a dishonest world. Rather than an echoing voice—a playback voice—which is what's always wanted.

June 23, 1977

Noah is still pinching and spitting, and very unhappy about something. And we have no idea what it is. Unless it's his teeth.

June 24, 1977

A letter came from the Writers Guild informing me that I have been nominated to serve on its board. I showed the letter to Foumi. "No way." She shook her head. "Not with a kid like ours." And she was right. I have always believed in writers and writing, in trade unionism and collective bargaining. But I can't spread my meager energies too thin.

June 25, 1977

We've set up Karl's summer so that it might be a productive one. He'll be taking typing at summer school in the morning, French conversation privately one afternoon a week; Foumi will drill him in math fundamentals, and he'll have his piano lesson and daily practice. We must make hay while his friends are away.

Noah is still pinching and spitting. It must be new teeth coming in. When he was a baby and we couldn't figure out what was wrong with him, it was an ear infection. Now it's usually the teeth.

June 27, 1977

Except for meals Noah has behaved well lately. At mealtimes he usually is unhappy about something on the menu. But then he calms down again when he gets his dessert fruit.

My friend whose son is in trouble back East phoned: "I was so proud when my son learned how to drive," he said. "I never dreamed he was going to wind up a wheelman on an armed robbery."

At dinner Karl asked me when Noah's birthday was. I told him that tomorrow Noah would be eleven. Karl said: "I'll have to buy him a present," and went into his room to count his money. I went into the bathroom and wept quietly. Noah's birthdays are the saddest days of my life.

3

July 1, 1977

To mark Noah's birthday I brought a carrot cake and apple juice to Noah's school. His teacher, Adele Mortin, says the birthday children love the fuss that's made over them. And I have to give him that.

July 2, 1977

Noah returned from school bearing some lovely cards and I'm sure he enjoyed the day. He did have a small tantrum after dinner but otherwise he's been fine. Karl's the problem. He is studying French but as always with things academic, he studies with little concentration and even less dedication.

July 5, 1977

Karl marched in the Fourth of July parade yesterday, his thick hair bouncing up and down on his head. I think he had a good time. I know I had a good time watching him. And then afterward, at a friend's picnic, Noah behaved admirably. So I had an even better time.

July 6, 1977

We're preparing our day-care move with little help from the parents and the potential loss of two children for the rest of the month. Perhaps next year we should close down during July.

Just as I used to gripe about having to go to Hebrew school, Karl is already making noises about his French lessons. But I think it's a good idea for him to learn to speak a foreign language. French can even be the key that gets him interested in learning Japanese.

A project that would have paid me a goodly sum has fallen through. But I'm not too upset; I was ambivalent about it anyway. Besides Noah always makes it easy for me not to want to be just rich. "Rich" can help, I've learned, but it can never solve.

We loaded the wagon with cartons of teaching materials and brought them over to the church. Then we took the kids to the new site so they could become used to it. When I began placing plastic blocks about the room Reva Jones, our teacher, who is black, asked me what I was doing. I said that I was trying to make the room a little colorful. Reva laughed: "Aren't I colorful enough?" Reva has a lively sense of humor and a quick tongue. I remember her reply when a woman argued against integration because her kid was afraid of black kids. "My son," Reva snapped back, "is afraid of black kids, too."

The morning was hectic. Loading and unloading, packing and unpacking, but we completed the move. Our day-care program now has a new home. I hope it works out for us. So much effort, so little return—like anything else that has to do with Noah.

Karl is a pain. We can't get him to do much work about the house, we have to force him to practice the piano, he won't review his French lessons, and he hasn't done any math since school's been out. But last night he picked up an old book, a paperback collection of war stories from *Saga*, a men's magazine

I wrote for twenty years ago. Later, he came over to me and said that he liked a piece I had written about Ernie Pyle better than anything else of mine that he'd ever read. "In fact," he added, "it was the best story in that whole book."

July 15, 1977

A family we knew in the East visited us yesterday. They had a brain-damaged daughter, an all but complete vegetable. Fortunately for them, the child died in Willowbrook at the age of six. They now have an adopted son who is normal.

July 17, 1977

The day-care center is working out well in its new location. I only wish one of its students could work out as well.

July 18, 1977

I took Noah to the doctor for his annual physical. It gets tougher each year. I have to use more physical strength to pin him down. And the doctor doesn't seem that glad to see him either. Who wants a patient that's so hard to handle? But Noah is healthy and looks it—especially in the summer as his long legs poke through his shorts.

July 19, 1977

I had forgotten to give Karl a note for his absence from summer school last week. So at breakfast I quickly wrote: "Please excuse Karl's absence on July 14. He was celebrating Bastille Day." Karl enjoyed my doing that but Foumi didn't think it was very funny. She says I'm teaching him to be disrespectful of institutional procedures. She's right, of course, but I don't think that's such a bad thing to be either.

July 22, 1977

Noah's summer school runs just one more week. Then we'll have to go full time at the day-care center. Which means the summer is already half over.

Foumi is upset with our male day-care aide. He always wants to leave early and is not following the curriculum. Foumi got tough with him. She had to as director. You cannot supervise workers and try to win a popularity contest. She has to do the dirty work while I have the luxury of playing good guy.

Karl's moods alternate dramatically. One evening he is a sheep dog as he walks alongside me on the bluff. The next morning he is an angry tiger, sulking as he boards his summer-school bus. He is a tough kid to judge. Both my kids are.

Karl has discovered summer at the beach with a vengeance. Every day after school he goes surfing on his Boogie, a styrofoam mini-surfboard. Noah has discovered how to clog up our toilet and he has also begun chewing through his pillows and sheets.

Foumi has described a writer's function in Hollywood perfectly: someone who is paid to realize someone else's dreams. The dream I will be realizing for the next few months will be an adaptation for TV of the novel *Lovey*. But since it involves the education of a special child it is a dream I can have a piece of.

Noah is still chewing up everything in sight. My blankets, my baseball cap, our sheets. The son of a bitch woke me at six this morning. Foumi says he's getting up early because he isn't getting enough exercise. I took him for a walk this evening. Tomorrow I will start arranging for a swimming pool for the day-care kids. In this hot weather we should get them swimming at least twice a week.

A friend of mine has an obstruction in his bile duct; so they will have to operate on him. A son of mine, Karl, has a summer cold; so I will have to tolerate him.

Karl returned to school after three days' illness. Just in time to enjoy the weekend. The kid times things right.

We've been giving in to Noah's tantrums too easily. We have to do something to get him to stop having tantrums. Karl still has a problem with his runny nose because of some sort of secondary infection. It's a shame. This is the best part of the summer for the beach.

Noah was tested yesterday by a psychologist from the L.A. Board of Education. She immediately found him untestable. And once more I sensed the sorry end of the script for Noah: the back ward of a state hospital.

I did well by our day-care kids, taking them swimming at the Rustic Canyon pool. Only Noah was difficult. He did not want to go in the water. The others seemed to love it. Four out of five is not bad.

At today's swim Noah was much better. He gave the water a chance before having a tantrum.

Last night Karl and I went to the Ram exhibition game. Boring. This afternoon I will take Noah for a long walk. It'll probably be more exciting than Chuck Knox football.

Noah slept well last night and was in a good mood this morning when I took him to day-care. Our new site, I noticed, is getting the comfortable look of familiar habitation.

Noah has a tantrum before dinner. I do not want to notice it. I want him to stop it on his own. I have to use a great deal of energy in order to ignore it. Because he is getting bigger. After all, he is eleven years old.

The summer languor is upon us. It happens every August. Suddenly time seems to stop still—or vanish into the vapors of the heat. Kids are dropping out of day-care, especially on weekends, and perhaps we should get away as a family ourselves. In fact, both Foumi and Karl keep talking about a trip. I'm the one who really does not want to leave the house. I do not like the forced confinement of a motel. I'm much more comfortable in our house than anywhere else. I guess I'm getting old.

We were down to two kids at day-care this morning. I took them swimming.

Karl is suddenly extra solicitous of Noah. Last night he suggested that we take Noah with us on our walk. Then he helped Noah go to the bathroom. And this morning he assisted him in dressing. Just when I give up on him in every other way he suddenly becomes a good brother.

He had better be. This morning when Noah was rolling on my bed I noticed that he has real down on his upper lip. Soon we'll have to shave him. Not only will he be difficult to manage but what if he becomes aesthetically distasteful to me? Then what do

I do? All that's tomorrow. But the nearer tomorrow gets the more it becomes Karl's domain.

August 22, 1977

My face is a blotch of scratches. I was watching the Ram exhibition game on TV, sprawled back on the yellow beanbag. Playfully Karl wanted to drop our cat T.G. on my chest. T.G. squirmed loose from his grip, seemed to somersault in midair— all this while I was sleepily watching the tube—and landed on my face. Immediately both the cat and I panicked and in the ensuing excitement my face got badly scratched. Fortunately, my eyes are fine and I'm not an actor but a writer.

August 23, 1977

Noah had a tantrum when I took him to day-care. He wanted to pass through the area of the church nursery school where normal kids play. So I took him up the back steps and he was happy. He does like day-care.

Karl is in a bit of a funk. Summer school's over and all his friends are away. Foumi still talks of our taking a family trip. But Karl has a secondary infection and Noah never gets any easier. He continues to eat all manner of sheets, blankets, and articles of clothing left about the house, chewing them all down until they're ready for the rag pile.

August 25, 1977

Life-style. I keep hearing about life-style. This morning I drove Noah to day-care and hustled Karl over to the Y so he could register for sleepaway camp. Next it was last-minute shopping with him for the necessary gear and supermarketing with Foumi. After lunch I dropped Karl off for his French lesson while Foumi and I went to the dentist. Then it was over to day-care to pick up Noah. Reva had bite marks on her arm—from Noah. He also had attacked Carlos, another of our children. Noah is definitely the worst of our day-care lot. He is also our "life-style." With an assist from Karl.

August 26, 1977

Last night Karl tried taking care of Noah while we went to the movies. When we came back he reported that Noah had pulled his hair. The closer Noah gets to puberty the more unmanageable he becomes.

August 27, 1977

As they waited to board the bus, I watched Karl line up with the kids who would be in his cabin at the Y camp. The others looked so much taller than Karl. But he was jabbering away the most. I guess his mouth evens out things for him.

August 28, 1977

Our house is so quiet with Karl away. I would really enjoy the quiet if it didn't make me more aware of Noah. How big and healthy he has become. He looks the way I thought Karl would look when he was a stocky baby. But now Karl has the lean look that I assumed Noah, who seemed to lack baby fat, would have. Kids certainly turn out different from what's expected. And Noah has turned out more different than most.

August 29, 1977

I read of a parent who claims to have cured his autistic son through love, by accepting the kid the way he was. But when I read closely I realized the kid wasn't too developmentally disabled—never had any toilet problems, for example; and that the autism diagnosis came from the parent himself. The number of miracle workers who are quick to generalize from a false specific is frightening. And the effect is cruel beyond words on other parents.

August 30, 1977

Since Karl has been away at camp there has been scarcely a toot of a tantrum from Noah. That doesn't mean his shirt chewing has abated or his memory span has suddenly increased. But it does mean I can enjoy him more.

September 1, 1977

We conducted a noble experiment and it worked. We drove to Santa Barbara and spent the night there. With Noah. He had a tantrum last night but a car ride assuaged him. And this morning after he became upset again, we headed back. But in between he ate a room-service dinner, a Foumi-cooked breakfast, and did not eat his own shirts. It's important for Noah to get out more. Perhaps we'll go away again next weekend when Karl returns. We haven't received any mail from him yet. I don't know whether that's a good sign or a bad sign.

September 2, 1977

Tomorrow, after his silent absence, Karl returns home; and last night Noah returned to shirt chewing. It might be because we ignore him at home. Or because he's bored. Or because we're bored. Anyway we have to start paying more attention to him in the house.

September 3, 1977

On his walk Noah and I had a little do. He wanted to take off his jacket. He was hot, I guess. I wouldn't let him. So we fought. I won. But I lost. I had to tug-pull him most of the way home. And then I finally let him take off his jacket.

Karl will be home by evening. Foumi thinks he hasn't written all week because he was afraid that he might be embarrassed by spelling errors. I think it was because he may have been having a bad time and did not want to upset us.

September 4, 1977

Karl is back. I picked him up yesterday afternoon at the Y. As usual he seems so much more than a week older. He is thin, he was tired. But last night we were all so happy to be together again in the house. Even Noah was gurgling. Karl talked a lot about camp and how much fun he had. Didn't we get his letter?

Foumi and I still feel we need another house. Not too far away. So that we can take family mini-vacations. It's important. But, at the same time, I know that Foumi and I will never agree on which house and in what area.

A sleepy day after Labor Day. I took Noah for a walk and Karl went to the beach with friends, and suddenly I am frightened. I had a vision of him drowning. Oh what fears I have for him! Irony is my enemy.

Karl's letter from camp came today. I complimented him on it. So now he's at the typewriter composing more letters to me. He's a smart kid. Also smart-ass. I just wish he'd put on some weight.

The older one gets, the fewer friends one has on a common level. It's not easy to find someone else with a brain-damaged child; a skinny, theoretically normal son; and a Japanese wife.

Foumi was angry with me this morning because I drove Karl to Newport Beach to spend a few days with a friend of his. Despite the fact that he left his room a mess.

I went into his room. It looks more like the room of a kindergarten student than of an eighth-grader. What distresses Foumi is the fact that he pals around with kids who are receiving the worst marks rather than the highest grades. She really worries about him.

And perhaps I shouldn't have driven him to Newport Beach this morning. I do tend to get too soft on him. But I did want him to have an additional vacation experience, something he could talk about, something he could claim was great fun, before going back to school.

Meanwhile, it is good that he is away because Noah is sick. The doctor says Noah has fluid in his ears and a tonsil condition, and prescribed antibiotics.

The death of Zero Mostel reached into my sleep. I awoke from a dream in which I was suffering a fatal heart attack myself. Mostel gave me four evenings of great pleasure in the theater. *Ulysses in Nighttown. Rhinoceros. A Funny Thing Happened on the Way to the Forum.* And, of course, *Fiddler on the Roof.* I also remember a wonderful performance he gave one afternoon in the Actors Studio in a Swiss play involving arsonists. He was as good a stage actor as I have seen. And there was his television performance in *Waiting for Godot* and his movie role in *The Producers.* Foumi too was taken by him. He was a joy we shared together. The last time we saw him was backstage at the Schubert when he was touring in the revival of *Fiddler* and Foumi asked him if she could touch his navel. "Sure," he said, "if you let me touch yours." He poked his finger playfully into her belly.

I picked Karl up in Newport Beach and tomorrow we will go on a brief vacation. I would like to take the family to Hawaii for a week. But then I project the trip in my mind's eye: We are seated on a plane. Noah begins to cry. I wonder if he wants to go to the bathroom. I take him to a claustrophobic toilet. He has a tantrum there. It continues as I bring him down the aisle back to his seat. He lies on the floor and a stewardess comes and leans over him. He reaches up and pulls her hair. It is indeed difficult to subdue him. I quickly forget about Hawaii.

But still we all deserve a change of air, an attempt to punctuate the end of summer. So tomorrow we'll be off to San Diego in the family station wagon.

Even the smallest journey is like an epic voyage when it comes to the Greenfelds. We made our annual mini-trek to San Diego. On Sunday morning we packed as if we were leaving for the Himalayas—we took food, we stocked medicine—and did not leave the house until after lunch. Intentionally. In this way we did not have to stop en route like a normal family. We reached the motel cabin with housekeeping facilities on Mission Bay after five, and Foumi cooked dinner. Karl and I went for an evening walk, Noah duly protested the new environment in his usual tantrum mode. We sat around and watched television. Foumi said she was having a rest because there was no phone.

On Monday Karl and I went over to Sea World, which Karl enjoyed but left me depressed; I always am when I realize all the childhood fun and pleasure that is denied to Noah. On Tuesday Karl and I swam and paddleboated but the only activity we could get Noah to participate in was a walk. And not too successfully.

Last night we returned home. A two-day vacation. But it's the best we can do. At least we got Noah out of the house. But as Noah gets older he becomes increasingly reluctant to try new things, to go to new places, to get near new people, to enter into new situations. It's as if he is now fully aware of his differences and insists upon remaining in the comforting cover of the camouflage offered only by familiar settings.

No sooner were we home than the phone rang. Trouble at day-care. Our male aide wouldn't be able to come in tomorrow. Foumi spent an hour on the phone trying to line up a substitute before giving up. And then she was greatly upset at the prospect of having to cancel day-care for tomorrow. She works so hard. With so little vacation.

September 15, 1977

Karl remains the reluctant student, extremely lazy, unwilling to work, quicker to offer an excuse than to execute a deed. In short, a real chip off the old block: me.

September 16, 1977

At the end of the year, Adele, Noah's teacher, will be leaving. And this may be Noah's last year at his present school too, the private school he first started to attend six and a half years ago. If only we could all stay still. Just as soon as we learn how to handle one phase of the Noah problem we have to move on to the next.

4

September 19, 1977

School starts tomorrow and I put together a new desk for Karl in the hope that it will help him turn over a new academic leaf. But I doubt it. He can't abide math. He's an awfully good reader though. I love to open the door to his room, expecting to find him asleep, and see him still awake, his head blurred into a book.

September 22, 1977

Yom Kippur. Karl won't go to school but he will take his private French lesson. And perhaps he'll be dropping French and take another subject in school instead. I have little faith that one can learn a foreign language in a public school. I'm not sure Karl can learn another language anywhere. Whenever we start to discuss the subject he gets very upset.

September 23, 1977

On the day-care front we're running out of children. We'll be down to three next month. We need four children to be able to make a go of it. Should I make a serious effort to recruit another kid and a few dedicated volunteers? Or should I just let it run down? I am ambivalent. I do not like to see Foumi so concerned about it. I know she can use all the time and the energy she expends on it to far better purpose. Either way it's a bad choice.

Karl lost his gym uniform. I will punish him by making him pay for its replacement out of his allowance.

September 25, 1977

I took our day-care kids swimming at the 100-meter Olympic-length indoor pool at the Y. Noah and Carlos were afraid of the water and Niko did not do much once he was in it. But I had a feeling of accomplishment.

September 26, 1977

During the night I awoke to hear Foumi in the bathroom, suffering from a bad stomach. So this morning I dressed Noah, prepared his breakfast, made his lunch, and drove him off to school. He's a hard detail to handle alone.

September 29, 1977

Karl is changing. I can't figure out what's happening. Last night I left a note on the breakfast table with three dollars for him to buy new gym shorts. This morning I found a thank-you. I'm still going to dock him though.

October 1, 1977

Foumi stayed up all night worrying about the day-care center, suddenly overwhelmed by all of its problems. There aren't enough kids, the teachers are leaving before they should, and there is the ongoing problem of transportation and all the phone calls Foumi has to make to the cab company. In addition, there is Noah. He is losing out. He is becoming worse.

Foumi always gets like this when she realizes anew that there is nothing we can do about Noah. If we start a school we are at the mercy of the teachers. If we start a residence we have to cater to the whims of the attendants and caretakers. And always there is the bureaucracy demanding that you enlarge, hire administrators and directors and psychologists and psychiatrists and consultants and behavior specialists until your budget gets so top-heavy that you forget the reason for your existence and become like any other institution. We have a problem whatever we do. But then

45

we always knew Noah was a no-win situation. It's just that to have that fact pounded home every day is no fun.

Karl didn't help any last night. I wanted to get Foumi out of the house for a breathing spell, just take a walk with her and have a quiet talk. "Watch Noah for a few minutes," I said to Karl. "How much will you pay me?" he replied.

October 2, 1977

This morning when Karl came to our bed he noticed a stain on the sheet and asked about it. Instead of telling him the truth about boys and puberty and men and semen I chickened out and blamed it on Noah. I said Noah chewed the sheet.

It also turns out Karl wasn't being that mercenary in asking for a Noah-sitting fee last night. He's just trying to make up the allowance money that he's been docked. And he is delighted with the stagecraft course he is taking in school. He likes working the light board and the sound table and putting up gels and all that theatrical technical stuff. Perhaps in that area he can find a home for his energies.

He is in the honors program and has a good English teacher, a decent history teacher, and an adequate science teacher. Only his math teacher is bad. Perhaps the fault with math in America lies not in the students but rather in the teachers. Good mathematicians do not wind up teachers. They go off to better-paying jobs in science and industry.

October 5, 1977

Now Reva is thinking of quitting and Foumi wants to get rid of our male aide. Foumi keeps harping about the problems of daycare from morning to night, claiming it's all my fault, that I got her into it in the first place. I'm sick of it. Hell, she has to take some responsibility for her own life. There are lots of things I can't get her to do no matter how hard I try. We should just close down.

October 7, 1977

Two writer friends of ours, a married couple, share a magazine column, writing on alternate months. Last month the husband told me he wanted to do a column about Noah and asked if it was all right. I said, Certainly. Today, while we were having lunch with them, they casually announced that they were donating the check for that column, over a thousand dollars, to our day-care center. What a windfall! And what a lovely act of friendship! We have been shafted by so many people, in day-care, in the movie business, that we were really moved by such a fine gesture. Thankfully, they didn't tell us what they were doing until dessert, otherwise we would have been slobbering into our soup. I am so pleased with their loyalty. I am so grateful for their action.

October 8, 1977

Karl came home from school with a split lip and a puffed cheek. Two kids had attacked him coming off the bus, calling him, among other things, "Squint Eyes." Foumi wanted to phone the school and report it. But Karl would have none of that. He said then he'd get beat up again. I don't like the situation. I don't like to see him intimidated. At the same time I know you have to respect the kid's wishes when trying to deal with problems in his kid's world.

Karl helped me take our three day-care kids swimming at the Y again. The last time Carlos refused to go into the water. This time he tried drinking up the pool. Noah complained about the pre-pool shower but did seem to enjoy the pool itself. Niko was fascinated more by the light rays about the pool than by the water itself.

October 9, 1977

A friend of ours in the field told us how to get more state funds for our day-care center: by simply changing its name and calling it "The Center for Recreational Therapy." Words, words. They'll do me in professionally. And personally.

October 12, 1977

A recent "60 Minutes" showed a segment about a residential school in the East where autistic kids helped train a racehorse. I thought there might be a possible place for Noah and a TV movie in it at the same time and asked my agent to look into it through the show-business door. He reported back to me that the school is run by someone who seemed just too show-biz wise. "We have a deal," he was told. "And we're into script already." So much for my parlay.

October 15, 1977

This morning Noah came to our bed carrying my watch, which I had left in his bathroom. Was he just idly playing with it? Returning it to its proper place? Or trying to tell me it was time to get up?

I did have a busy day ahead. Karl and I went to the Dodger-Yankee World Series game. I got lost going there, I ran a red light coming back, but we enjoyed the camaraderie of being part of a Series crowd together. I sometimes found myself reaching over reflexively and patting Karl's knee, remembering that my father had done the same to me at ball games, communicating the same kind of love. The love I have for anything that grows in my house. Including our cat. Including Noah.

I saw an old friend of mine, in from New York, at the game. His face was puffed up, he had the bloated look of dissipation, not jet lag. He seems to be drowning in the vice of his wife—drink. We inflict our vices upon each other in a marriage just as surely as we add our graces. I did not like seeing him like that. I wished there was something I could do.

October 16, 1977

Foumi spent the day interviewing kids for day-care. It seems that day-care has replaced Noah as the center of our lives.

October 17, 1977

Karl was sick, an upset stomach. Noah has a bad cough. And Reva's son broke his arm. So I had to pick up the kids and take charge of day-care.

October 18, 1977

I can wake up feeling all aglow, the happy residue of sleep on my eyelids, the promise of a great day abroad in every breath. But then getting Noah started, Karl going, listening to Foumi's worrying aloud, and it's all shot.

Noah was in a good mood for a few days but today he fell apart. A tantrum before breakfast. A tantrum at breakfast. A tantrum as I dropped him off at school.

Karl is over his upset stomach and ready for another soccer season. I bought him new soccer shoes and in his uniform he looks like a gaily colored French kid. He's still taking private French lessons. I hope he's learning something.

Last night at dinner Noah and I had a disagreement that ended, of course, in his having a tantrum. Foumi says it's because I challenge him. I don't think I challenge him. But I simply do not want him eating with his hands when there is a spoon in front of him. Nor do I want him reaching over and eating out of my plate. And he can be taught to eat properly. The fear of a tantrum on his part should not deter us from making the necessary corrections in his behavior.

Our malcontent male aide quit day-care in a blaze of acrimony, criticizing our peerless leader, Foumi; speaking as if we were a money-oriented organization churning out huge profits.

I guess it's all a matter of perspective. Because the raison d'être of our conglomerate woke us early this morning. How delicious it must be to sleep late of a weekend, to lie in luxuriant idleness until the double-digit o'clocks of the morning.

I tried to lift Noah off the floor. I couldn't. He was too heavy for me. Instead, I dumped him on his ass and he eyed me curiously, wondering what was happening to him.

I watched Karl play soccer yesterday. He's on a good team this year but he isn't very good. Why should he be any better as an athlete than his old man was? But he still does look terrific in his uniform. And his team won, which delighted him.

October 23, 1977

I spoke to some old friends, college friends from the days before I was myself, so to speak, and learned that one of them had a cancer of the tongue. Cancer of the tongue is like a promissory note. Surely more has to follow, more is due. What a thing to have to live with!

October 26, 1977

We took Noah to a class for Special Education teachers. So they could actually see someone with a severe learning disability and a behavioral problem. And Noah behaved like a positive angel, just roaming indifferently about the room. Foumi thinks it's because he knew he was the center of attention as we were discussing him and answering questions from the students.

October 27, 1977

An auditor came from the state and went over the day-care payroll records, which I keep. For a while it looked as if I had made a twelve-hundred-dollar error. But then it turned out he had made an error with his calculator. I felt pencil-stub smart.

October 28, 1977

Karl's Open School Night: I was pleasantly surprised. I really liked his science, history, and stagecraft teachers—all are men who seem to enjoy kids and know how to deal with them. And his math and English teachers, both women of Japanese descent, are certainly earnest. He should have a good year. It's the best I've felt about his educational prospects since he was in the third grade. Which means, if these things are cyclic, his next good year should be his freshman one at college.

Meanwhile, I delight in being able to kid with him. For example, he is learning the Bill of Rights now and we were talking about the Right to Bear Arms amendment. I said that was included because at Valley Forge it was too cold to bare legs. He really enjoys that kind of humor now and I am glad that I can furnish it. He knows I love to joke more than anything else; and so, I suspect, does he.

October 29, 1977

Everyone I know is on a weight-loss diet and I'm worrying about becoming too thin. It is frightening to be as skinny as I am. But because of my natural tendency to have a high cholesterol level I have cut down on meats, fats, fried foods, and sweets. I hope I'm healthy—not coming down with cancer. Because that's all our family needs.

October 31, 1977

On his walk Noah suddenly sat down on the lawn near the corner curb and refused to get up. I grabbed his hand and pull-towed him home as he protested every inch of the way. At home, when I urged him to go to the bathroom, he resisted, then finally complied. My reading had been right: He had to urinate but didn't know what to do about it.

Foumi keeps moaning that Noah, at eleven, is already too big for her to handle and that it is time to arrange some sort of residential placement for him. But at this point I don't know what I can possibly arrange.

Except a night out for her. So we went to the movies last night. I took along some spearmint gum and unwrapped it, enjoying the tart smell that always reminds me of the excitement I had as a boy, opening a baseball-player-card package on a lazy, endless hot summer afternoon when time spread out before me so expansively that I truly felt my life would last forever. As for the movie itself: Once more I realized the medium was designed to fill the group dark rather than to enlighten me personally.

November 1, 1977

A safe and sane Halloween. Karl went trick-or-treating with his friends and Noah enjoyed the chimes constantly sounding and costumed kids appearing at the door. I had put in a supply of potato chip packets and raisin boxes. The potato chips went over big but some raisins were strewn about my lawn this morning.

Sometimes I consider directing, joining the world of people who work together with electric energy at appointed times in prearranged places, the next logical step upward for me in the Hollywood scheme of things. Because in this temporal town that is where the transient power lies. But then I immediately wonder: Who will drive Noah to school each morning? Who will pick him up every afternoon from day-care? And I realize there is no way I can shake off Noah as my primary assignment.

Besides, directing, a minor art that calls for a major executive talent, would be a detour for me as a writer in the real scheme of things. So perhaps it is Noah, the deviant in my life, who somehow always steers me straight.

November 2, 1977

I bought Karl a soccer ball and each evening now he goes out and practices dribbling it around. But I still wouldn't give him a good scouting report. Not enough power in his kicks.

A friend of mine really knows how to deal with rejection. He was in Chicago and tried to make a dinner reservation at a posh restaurant. He was refused. The next day he booked every table in the joint for dinner using local celebrity names.

November 3, 1977

Day-care manages to stumble along. But since transportation is always such a problem maybe I should buy a van for it. Then it could roll along.

November 4, 1977

My memories are not as clear as they once were. Images that I summon up for recall seem vague and tend to blur. Am I decomposing? Is there a softening in the quality of my brain? Or is it the fact that I'm almost fifty?

November 5, 1977

Noah is back to all his old clutch, grab, pinch, and stick-his-hand-in-your-face tricks. Which makes him difficult to deal with.

But so is his brother. Karl made a map of the island in

Catch 22 to submit for extra credit in English. But when I told him that his markings on it were not all legible, he slammed it to the floor. I became furious. I did not like that destructive shit and was about to destroy him myself almost as if to prove how quickly destruction breeds destruction. It seems as if no one in this less than perfect family can take criticism.

November 7, 1977

I helped Karl with his book report; otherwise he would never have finished it. He's so lazy. Afraid to work. I worry when I see him imbued with the same lazy attitudes I had. Somehow I could get by in spite of them. I'm not so sure he can. Unless he develops some special talent.

November 8, 1977

I overheard Karl on the phone talking about his soccer team. He's so proud of their winning three in a row. I am too but I wish he were a better athlete.

November 9, 1977

An elderly couple lives across the street. Lately they both have been ill and the woman is now in the hospital. Yesterday I saw the man standing beside his iron picket fence with his Great Dane in tow, looking like the ghost of death himself. As I shepherded Noah into our car I called out good morning to him and asked about his wife. He weakly answered in a shrug. I was in a hurry and I did not have the grace to cross the street and carry on a polite conversation.

I should have. This morning there was the wailing of an ambulance. The old man had died during the night while his wife still lay ill in the hospital.

November 10, 1977

We saw Truffaut's new movie last night. A disappointment. If you keep going to the movies they're mostly disappointments. If you work in the movies, it's all disappointments.

I started the day by going to a Requiem Mass for our neighbor. While in church I could not help but recall my own misspent childhood in houses of Jewish worship. I remembered the boredom, the utter boredom, the eternal wait for services to end. I looked at the pews and recalled all the time my father had spent in helping to raise the funds to buy new benches for his synagogue. I wondered if that synagogue was still standing in East Flatbush or had become an Evangelical Baptist Church. I recalled myself vividly as a Jewish kid who wanted to be a writer, shy before the great altar of literature because I did not know all the gentile secrets of mass and liturgy, the exotic world of Christ and goyim. Now I have to concern myself with projects and deals and wonder if I am becoming a Hollywood hack.

Every three years the law requires that Noah receive an educational evaluation. Noah behaved quite well at the session yesterday. After all, he's getting to be an old-timer at it. He will be evaluated as "autistic." Since it's only for funding purposes and means he can stay in his present school, we won't argue the otherwise meaningless designation.

Noah's Open School Night. They ran through a typical daily schedule. It's not really very substantial. But Adele, Noah's teacher, is a fine person and that's the important thing. I'll always buy the person and not the program.

An autumn Saturday. A football chill in the air. Malden, Brooklyn, Ann Arbor, Japan, Croton-on-Hudson—an eternal Saturday, the day I love best. Karl plays soccer this afternoon. I will go and watch the last quarter. And then walk with Noah. But first a nap. And a dream or two.

November 21, 1977

I burned Noah's toast at breakfast and he responded with a tantrum. He should be able to suffer discomfort just a mite. God knows he inflicts enough.

But I hope he doesn't inflict too much this week. Grandma is coming from Japan and she may not be able to take it. After all she is in her seventies now. And this is also the week of Karl's thirteenth birthday. I need calm in order to consider what to get for him.

November 22, 1977

Noah woke us godawful early while it was still dark. I managed to creep back into the remnant of a dream. But not Foumi. She never can return to sleep once awakened.

November 23, 1977

Noah has a scratch on his nose. I don't know where he got it but it's there. I doubt if it will cure easily unless we can figure a way to keep his hands from constantly rubbing and scratching at it. He is also scratching and pinching and spitting at us again to show dissatisfaction.

Karl's report card: B's in English, Science, and History, and a C in Math. Not bad. But he can do better. And I think he would be if he were going to a private school. Perhaps I'm sending the wrong kid to the private school.

November 25, 1977

We Thanksgivinged at Karl's friend Erich's house. Noah behaved comparatively well. But he would not eat there. Nor would he eat the turkey we took home for him until we mixed it with some rice. This morning Foumi observed that Noah has the torso of an old man, love handles about his waist, rather than the build of a young boy. But why not, everything else about Noah is out of place, out of time, out of focus.

Focus: I asked a friend about his college-aged kids. And that's just the word he used. He said they couldn't seem to get "focused."

Tomorrow is Karl's birthday and I have agreed to get him a ten-speed bike if I can cross-collateralize it with his Christmas gift. He's willing to go along with that deal. But which ten speed? I'd best take him to the bike store. Meanwhile, today Grandma arrives from Japan. I do hope she's in good health. Two sickies about the house—Grandma and Noah—would be a little too much to take.

November 26, 1977

Karl happily picked out his ten-speed, 182 bucks of Nishiki, Grandma seems in good health, and Noah is suddenly very shy again, hiding behind his own shirt, whenever he sees Grandma. He does remember her, I'm sure, because he does not gallop off to hide in his room. Poor Noah, deprived of the reassurances that only memory can provide, he must live a life of constant fear, a new threat posed by almost every perception.

5

This morning I drove Grandma to a special reunion of old Japanese people and Noah to his daily reunion with special education. Noah wore short pants because it is a hot day and Grandma wore one of her dull brown dresses, which Karl refers to as her *"obāsan's* uniform"—*obāsan* being Japanese for "grandmother." Karl went for his own private French lesson himself. I'm not sure how much he's learning, but at least his teacher is pretty.

December 5, 1977

Foumi and Karl aren't feeling well. I do hope the flu bug is not descending upon us. So far I feel fine. And my cholesterol is now 214. Down from the 301 of last year. But I would still like to get it lower.

December 7, 1977

Many friends, I know, choose to forget the reality Foumi and I know firsthand. They like to think we somehow masochistically choose to have Noah at home out of whimsical or sentimental choice. They express concern about what keeping Noah at home does to Karl. But what would it be doing to Karl if he knew we allowed Noah to be put in a place where he would inevitably wind up even more disabled than he is now? Through a blinding.

Or a maiming. Or a simple pharmaceutical error. I hate the pervasive fucking liberal Freudian mentality almost as much as I deplore the Uncle Tom's Cabin conditions of most institutions.

December 8, 1977

Karl has a headache, Noah is having a tantrum, and Foumi is raging at everyone in sight. Not a good night to have a family. So I have slipped away to these pages. Otherwise, I would be a mess too. Anyway, this is my real writing. The rest is my alchemy.

December 12, 1977

Another argument about Noah. At dinner Noah had a tantrum. Foumi began to cater to his tantrum and I became even angrier with her. So we both shouted at each other, Karl looking on disgustedly and Noah wailing. I still insisted that Noah sit at the table. Even if I had to sit on him to make him sit. Which I did.

So this morning, even though Karl said he did not feel well, I still made him go to school. Figured if I was going to be tough on Noah I would be tough on him too. But Karl came home from school suffering nausea and really looking sick. It seems no matter what I do with either kid it's always wrong.

December 15, 1977

Karl stayed home from school for the third day running. And we've begun to wonder if the missing tooth on the left side of Noah's mouth might be permanent. His development is so uneven. And we have been warned that with kids like Noah everything is screwed up. If they learn slowly, for example, they age quickly.

December 16, 1977

Karl returned to school just in time to begin the two-week vacation period. Vacation for whom? Not for us, with him and Noah around the house.

Karl put up a Christmas tree, decorated it, and has proceeded to promote Christmas intensively. Noah and I blithely ignore his campaign, taking long walks together, Noah outfitted in a jogging sweatsuit, which makes him look spiffy indeed.

December 24, 1977

Sometimes Noah reminds me of a city cat, too long pent up in an apartment, wary of leaving it and venturing outside into the hallways of the world. And it is true that we are loath to take him to restaurants, to invite him to partake in family social activities— or in social activities with other families. Nostra culpa.

December 25, 1977

Karl is happy enough with his Christmas present from me. I had told him that because of our deal on the ten-speed I would have to give him a gift under ten dollars. So I gave him $9.99 in cash. But with his bike it averages out to quite a present. Grandma gave him thirty bucks in cash. And there were other gifts from Foumi and Noah. So as the kid who promoted Christmas he'll end up hardly deprived.

December 26, 1977

Karl was a prince today, helping out at day-care. As he shepherded Noah out the door this morning, both wearing the same jogging jackets as protection against a slight drizzle, I heard him gently say, "Come on, Noah. Don't be afraid of the rain."

In the evening, though, he was his ever-bitching self, moaning because he had missed the Dallas football game. I'll take him to see *Star Wars* tonight to make up for it.

December 29, 1977

I brought Karl to UCLA for an EEG. He has long been complaining of headaches and our pediatrician suggested the EEG as the next logical step. Especially in view of Noah and our family history. We passed through a maze of corridors in order to find the right place. And as I watched the passing gurneys and wheel-chairs and doctors and nurses and lab attendants and cleaning women crowding the labyrinthine corridors it seemed all chaos and confusion and I wondered how a large hospital could possibly manage to keep everything straight. I also remembered the time we had taken Noah to the hospital in White Plains for an EEG and how the nun there had found it impossible to administer the test. But Karl was a snap, he cooperated completely, and we have only to await the results. If the hospital doesn't screw up, I will really be impressed with modern bureaucracy.

December 30, 1977

Noah still sticks his fingers in my face and pinches at my chin. And he's become fat, Buddha fat, with a potbelly. No wonder I don't spend as much time with him as I used to.

Karl continues to grow and increase his cash flow. Last night we experienced the traditional parental pangs of waiting up for him as he baby-sat for Niko, one of our day-care kids. He came home after midnight, a proud wage earner, dreaming of future financial scores. He was also very proud of the fact that he could "handle" a special child. Why not? He's had some experience.

This morning I mentioned to Foumi that perhaps we should set ourselves the goal of trying to keep Noah home until he was eighteen, the age an ordinary child leaves home to go to college, to join the army, to start finding his way in the world. Noah's world will be a difficult place. The dormitories of institutions are designed for the convenience of the wardens, not the wardees. The prototype is the jail or the penal colony and the social conditions are as primitive as the jungle itself. No one has privacy, no one has space, and, worst of all for Noah, no one has patience. So let's try to keep Noah, I said, until he's eighteen. Foumi sighed and shrugged as if my suggestion were academic: "How big will he be?"

Foumi had lunched with Katie and Murray, two of our former day-care aides. Katie now works as a teacher at a state residence for the deaf in Maryland and Murray is interning at a private hospital in the San Fernando Valley. They both, Foumi tells me, did not want to dwell on conditions at these places. Especially nights, when the staffing is minimal.

An old friend with a broken marriage came by with his daughter whom I remember as a baby Noah's age. Now she is a womanly preteenager. Another baby grown.

January 1, 1978

I got off on the wrong foot—or hand—with Noah at our New Year's dinner. When he began to stab the air with his fork I asked him to leave the table. When he didn't, I slapped him.

I feel bad when I treat Noah badly. And I usually treat him badly when I feel bad to begin with. As a free-lance writer it has never been easy for me to enjoy a usual holiday because I have always rationalized that the ordinary days when I could not get any work done were my self-declared holidays. So I felt bad because I had spent the day not accomplishing anything in preparation for tomorrow, on which I will accomplish even less. I had taken Noah for a walk in the morning and then watched the AFC Championship football game. I had taken Noah for a ride in the afternoon and then watched the NFL game. No wonder I was so frustrated by evening. And I made poor Noah pay for the fact that my depressions were my holidays.

January 3, 1978

With Michigan playing here, Karl and I went to the Rose Bowl again. We got there easily and returned without any trouble. The only trouble was that Michigan lost again. Karl had a good time, packed away a memory or two I'm sure, and the last few minutes when Michigan seemed to be surging back were exciting. If they have to come to the Rose Bowl next year I do wish they'd win.

January 4, 1978

With the new year has come the realization that soon I will be fifty. Five-oh. Fifty. Count it. And I have begun to hear the ticking of the clock again. It is the same ticking I heard all through my teens and early twenties but then somehow it got muffled during my thirties and early forties. And now I hear it again.

Only now the question that preoccupies me has changed from: "What am I going to do with my life?" to "What have I done with my life?"

January 5, 1978

Day-care woes again. We're losing a fine aide at the end of the month and have to find a replacement. Hiring good people, we have learned, is not easy.

January 6, 1978

Our pediatrician called and said that Karl's EEG showed an anomaly that pops up on about 10 percent of the EEGs he reads. Something about one or two areas becoming slightly aberrant when overburdened. But nothing we need get too concerned about. I think he wasn't telling me everything because he heard Foumi pick up on the extension. I'll go by his office tomorrow.

This morning Noah's school was called off. No teacher. So we made some phone calls and hastily set up an extended day-care.

January 7, 1978

The sun is out, the rain has stopped, and I saw—or heard—a rainbow. I went to see our pediatrician, full of worry about Karl's EEG. But he assured me again that it was perfectly normal, that there really was nothing to worry about. But can I help it if I'm paranoid about my sons' brains?

January 8, 1978

Karl finally wrote a thank-you note to some friends who never forget to give him and Noah Christmas gifts. The prodding was mine but the words were all his:

Thank you for all the presents you've given to Noah and me. I'm sure if my brother was normal he would want to thank you too.

Love,
Karl and Noah

Noah's principal form of communication remains the tantrum. With it he tells us the rice is too hot, the milk glass is empty, the eggs need salt. It must be as hard on him as it is on us.

Foumi is feeling dizzy, perhaps coming down with a cold; I have a headache; Karl is frustrated by math. Only Noah, by and large neglected on his evening perambulations about the house, seems healthy and happy.

Last night Karl had history homework. No problem. He went right through it. But he still fights a losing battle with math.

Right now he wants to talk only about the Super Bowl. Which bores me. But at least he gets some reading done as he pores over the sports pages each day. And I watched him incredulously this afternoon when he came home from school and gobbled up four slices of toast and drained three glasses of orange juice. Yet he's still so skinny, his growing body just angling upward.

Radio and television are full with news of the passing of Hubert Humphrey. I had almost forgotten how much I had opposed him in 1968 because of his Johnsonian position on Vietnam and I still do not forgive him for it. I am not sorry that I did not vote for him: the politics of reality. Yet it is hard to view death without sentimentality, and he was an energetic politician. But I do wish they would stop saying that he died with courage. I don't think one ever has that choice anyway. The problem is always to live with courage.

Noah is going through one of his impossible-to-resist, easy-to-love periods. He likes to parade in my new hat, a tan corduroy fedora. He doesn't mind being cooped up in the house during the rain. He stands at the window for hours watching the raindrops falling. Just like our cat.

January 16, 1978

A letter in the *L.A. Times* about the antiquated conditions in the wards at Camarillo State Hospital made me ask myself again how long I can keep Noah home. One thing certain: no early retirement for this weary Jew.

January 17, 1978

Noah has become physically beautiful again. His aesthetic appeal to me—perhaps just like his own perceptions—fades in and out. Sometimes he seems to me a grotesque, an awkward beast, a monster manqué. But this morning, bouncing in the backseat of the car as I drove him to school, and again this evening, lolling luxuriantly as I gave him his bath, he was definitely beautiful to me. Has my notion of beauty become completely perverted? Or does it all depend upon how I view his essential immutability?

Karl grows. In orderly progression. Now he is my confidant. I tell him a problem and listen to his suggestions. I give him a script to read and respect his judgments. I am interested in what he has to say about any number of topics. I foresee that he will be smart, have a good sense of humor, and be attractive to girls.

January 18, 1978

Last night: I don't feel well. A winter cold. I lie down in bed and begin to watch television: Alan Arkin in an earnest drama about a mental institution. I hear a sharp scream from Foumi and I am reminded that I live in my own mental institution. I get out of bed and run down the hallway. She is confronting a bare-assed Noah. With toilet paper in her hand she is obviously trying to wipe him after a shit. But he is on the floor of his room, his ass almost touching the carpet, some shit still oozing out of it. I lift-force him back into the bathroom. We completely undress him and make him sit on the toilet again. Foumi snaps on the overhead electric heater. We give Noah time to complete his bowel movement. But nothing more is forthcoming. We get the naked Noah to rise from the seat, but he will not bend so that he can be wiped. Point-blank refuses. I become upset and lose my cool. I slap him.

This irritates Foumi more than Noah. She is right, of course. But suddenly I realize the overhead heater is beating down on my balding head. I turn it off. Foumi turns it back on. Says Noah will catch cold. Ridiculous, I say, the bathroom is warm enough. I become angry. She becomes angrier. A lulu of a row. She would rather argue about the heater than get the job with Noah done. I tell her she is pathologically stubborn, forever intransigent, always insisting that she is one hundred percent right. She says she has to be stubborn because I am so neurotic, that I am always looking for an argument, for a reason to leave her. Perhaps I am. I am getting bored with my life. Or rather with the problems in my life.

Lunch today: A woman director asks me a big question: Would I still be married to Foumi if we did not have Noah? I do not know the answer. Nor does it matter.

January 20, 1978

I went to the funeral service today of an editor's son, a twenty-five-year-old TV reporter who died in a crash in Seattle. Afterward some friends and I talked about the special pathos of those nonsensical nonsequential tragedies that occur whenever kids die out of order. But I did not bring up the pathos of the families of special kids who cannot live in any order. I could not sleep much last night. I heard Noah stirring and continually debated with myself about whether to go down and check his covers. I didn't. Instead, on the few occasions when I lapsed into sleep, I dreamed of a Noah I was beating up, feeling guilty all the time as I did so.

January 21, 1978

I went to the doctor. I thought I was losing weight. Somewhere in the back of my mind I had decided I was coming down with cancer. But the doctor gave me the Fairbanks cure. He put me on the Fairbanks scale and weighed me. I've gained a pound and a half since my last visit. So much for my cancer. I guess I just have a cold. But no cure for that either.

January 22, 1978

Karl is feeling bad because his soccer team not only was scored upon but lost for the first time. So ends some dream of glory. But tonight he'll watch the Pro Bowl and forget all about it.

Noah is restless. He has been eating erratically. Like me I think he has a cold. Unlike me he does not know that the discomfort will eventually end.

January 26, 1978

Noah was angry with me this morning. Because I was ignoring him, not paying any attention to him. I had lingered in bed throughout breakfast, so when I went to say good-bye to him he abruptly reached up and pulled my hair.

January 28, 1978

Noah was making noise toward dawn, awakening me. I got out of bed and led him to the bathroom. Then still half asleep I returned to bed, figuring I would rest there while waiting for him to do his business. Instead, I drifted back to sleep, still hearing Noah's sounds as they mingled with my dreams, but chose very consciously to ignore them. In the morning I found Noah was sitting on his bed, his p.j. pants still down. The toilet bowl was full of shit. He's a good boy, God I love him.

January 30, 1978

My muscles still ache after two days of playing basketball with Karl. And he completed an athletic weekend with a win for his soccer team. He brought home the team picture, too. He looks sensational in it.

Noah has a rage of tantrums—which in my lexicon is a plural classifier like "a pride of lions"—at almost every meal. I assume he is more aware both of his wants and of his inability to communicate those wants at the same time. Doubly frustrating.

February 1, 1978

Shot baskets with Karl again. He gets frustrated too easily. But he has ambition. Not enough height though. He told me gleefully, though en passant as he tried to dribble by me, he's getting a C in math. He shouldn't be that happy about it.

Pinched Noah this morning. He was pinching me. And he was really surprised when I pinched him back.

February 3, 1978

Last night I was slightly appalled at Noah's growing girth as I gave him his bath. So today at his school I noted that according to the scrawls on the blackboard measuring chart in the classroom Noah presently is 4 feet, 4¾ inches tall and weighs in at eighty-four pounds. How tall was I at eleven and a half and how much did I weigh? I suspect a lot less than that.

February 4, 1978

A friend of ours is in the hospital, suffering from some inexplicable loss of memory. The doctors think there is a fever, a viral fever, which they can neither seem to locate nor do much about. Her husband has asked us as "brain experts" to look in on her tomorrow. God knows we aren't experts but we were certainly planning to visit her anyway.

February 5, 1978

Yesterday: Noah had a loose stomach. I woke up just in time to find him wandering into the living room, the shit dripping down his ass onto the back of his legs. I retraced the path to the bathroom with him in tow, and then picked up the trail that had led him there: his shit-stained underwear and pajamas. The bathroom floor was spattered with brown droplets, the toilet seat all brown, and the bowl was filled with his watery feces. I cleaned him, dressed him in fresh pajamas, put him back in bed, and mopped the bathroom. Then I tried to go back to sleep myself but within a half hour Karl was up, stirring about, and soon we were all up and about, shortchanged the well-earned indolence of a Saturday.

We kept Noah home from day-care. But I drove Karl to his soccer game and left him there. Later he reported that his team had won and that he had contributed three assists.

Today: We went to the hospital to visit our friend. A visit that left us in tears. At first she did not recognize us. Later, when we returned to her room, she knew us. She was hyperactive and her eyes seemed glazed over. She has had, we learned, four seizures in the past two days and her memory only functions in flashes. She has no idea of where she is for any extended period. My heart breaks for her and her husband and their daughter. But still she has so much more going for her than Noah. She can talk, she can think—even though she cannot seem to do both in complete concert—and while they still probe and test trying to find out what is wrong, there is still hope. Oh, how I hope she recovers. It's far better to lose a leg or a limb than part of one's brain and its functions.

February 7, 1978

Foumi and I visited the L.A. City Special Education school nearest our home. We found the ratios good: a teacher, an aide, and a graduate student in each classroom. But even though there were only two kids present out of an enrollment of six in the "autistic" class, the teacher seemed too woefully inexperienced to handle them. In the multiple-handicapped class, where the kids all had speech, the teacher seemed a lot better, more self-assured. As usual, when we visited such a school we saw many kids that we knew from previous schools and programs. None of them seemed to be doing better. Perhaps we would have been disappointed if we expected something but we've long grown accustomed to expect nothing from public education.

American classrooms, Foumi pointed out to me as we were leaving, are just not conducive to study. Not in Special Education anyway. The teachers are too busy advertising on walls in almost billboard fashion, with all their learning-aid posters and samples of students' alleged work, what they actually may not be accomplishing in the kids' heads. The big schoolyards too, every inch covered with concrete, are not geared for these kids. Why can't they have islands of grass and soft surfaces on which to run and stumble and safely fall?

When I happened to report our morning impressions to an editor friend she asked: "What is the solution for Noahs? Can't anything be done?" I said that first we had to get rid of the old medical and educational institutional models, which were society's reflexive response to special problems, and instead base our response upon the human needs of the kids and their families. For example, the Noahs of the world should be in residential settings that simulate the family; and in educational environments that are geared to stimulate the kids. But go try to explain this to the bureaucratic mentality that believes that greater numbers of any kind make for a greater good.

February 8, 1978

The sky after yesterday's rain was unusually clear, the light almost artificially crystalline, we could see Catalina, and Karl got a good report card: C in math but A in history. He is so much like me. History was my subject, humor my forte. And like me he is not the greatest athlete but loves to play sports. And now in the eighth grade he is beginning to need glasses just as I did. But unlike me he will never go bald. Not with his Indian thick head of hair.

Noah is sick again. Another loose stomach leaving a trail. But our fault. Foumi and I had been watching TV together. One of us should have kept tabs on Noah.

February 10, 1978

Noah doesn't seem to have any fever but we kept him home from school today just to play it safe. And I'm supposed to begin working on a sequel to the movie *Oh, God!* But I doubt if I can make it as funny as the Warner Brothers contract. Under Assigned Material is listed: "The Concept of God."

February 11, 1978

I lay awake in bed this morning thinking: The one mistake I have not made in my life is to try to do too many things other than writing. The biggest mistake I have made in my life has been in trying to do too many things within writing. I have written novels, nonfiction books, essays, reviews, plays, movie and television scripts. In writing for the dramatic mediums, too much of my writing has wound up as waste writing. As I near fifty I would like to devote as little of my energy to scripts as possible. But now to serve the devil I start to work on an *Oh, God!* sequel.

Noah sick remains the saddest thing I know. Yesterday he just lay there in bed sweetly, his eyes pleading for relief.

February 13, 1978

Noah sick remains the cruelest thing I know. Now he has a fever and it has turned him bellicose. He pinches, he scratches, he pulls hair, he is like a monster beset. Foumi somehow can handle it. But I can't. I finally slapped the poor thing. Which was absolutely wrong. He only became more violent in response.

February 14, 1978

Karl went off to Santa Monica with his friend Erich on a great adventure. They will ride the bus there and even get a transfer. When I was their age I would roam New York City far and wide for a nickel.

February 15, 1978

Karl, who returned safely from the wilds of Santa Monica, last night told me he had read the play *Of Mice and Men*. When I began to question him about it in detail he informed me that he had "skipped all the italics." Which explained why he did not know that George had murdered Lennie. And when I pointed out to him that such intelligence was revealed in the italicized stage directions, he became flustered and announced that he would no longer read any plays.

February 17, 1978

Noah's illness upsets us. The fever is gone but he still has no energy. Now he just wants to sleep. When I tried to wake him this morning he just turned over. But not before giving me a list-less pinch as if just for the record.

February 18, 1978

Kids, normal or special, always get better on Saturdays when there is no school. After days of pinching me each morning when

I went in to wake him, today Noah awoke gleefully, came to the kitchen, ate a hearty breakfast, cheerfully allowed himself to be dressed, and went off to our day-care center, giving Foumi her first day off in two weeks.

I emptied the house so she could enjoy her respite. I drove Grandma into Santa Monica to meet a friend. I took Karl to his soccer team's playoff game. They lost, which ended their season. After the game, to help assuage the defeat I took Karl to a hobby shop, where he bought a model ship, and then to the Apple Pan, a diner whose hamburgers he loves.

February 19, 1978

While dressing Noah this morning I pressed his left hand against my right one. It's almost as big.

And now Foumi is nervous. And so am I. Karl is going on a long bike ride with a friend. And Karl isn't that skilled a bike rider. On the one hand we have to let him do things by himself. On the other hand we can't let him do dangerous things either. No end to parental quandaries.

After I finish the *Oh, God!* sequel I will give the tab key a rest. No more movies or television for a while. Because I know I have three options at this point in my life: write a novel, direct a picture, or leave my wife.

February 20, 1978

Just like a normal kid after the weekend Noah became sick again. His flu is not over. Last night he had a loose stomach again. Still, he seemed in a good mood. But we did keep him home from school. This afternoon I took him to day-care, though. If only to give Foumi a rest.

February 21, 1978

Karl is now a veteran of the Santa Monica bus system. Yesterday he made his maiden trip to the hobby shop there with a friend. His bus traveling is going to wind up costing me a lot more than the bus fare.

February 23, 1978

Noah is demonstrating every day that he wants a Coke, which we gave him while he was sick and are now trying to wean him away from. What he does is tip over the contents of whatever beverage we serve him. He and I do not see eye to eye on the issue. Poor kid, he just can't figure me out. One minute I'm lovey dovey. The next minute I'm cuffing him with a fast left. The kid has guts, though. He fights back.

And as he is rebelling more, he is also increasingly trying to help himself—to dress himself and to feed himself. As if he doesn't want to be a baby any more than we want him to be one.

February 24, 1978

Yesterday—as every Thursday—I picked up Karl after his French lesson. He had to sit in the backseat next to Noah, who was returning from day-care. Whenever we came to a red light an impatient Noah scratched and pinched at him. I told Karl to endure the discomfort patiently. But it was as hard for him to take as the delay was for Noah. As the trip was for me.

This morning, I spoke to Adele, Noah's teacher, about Noah's increased pinching and scratching since he's been ill. She thinks that he simply does not want to return to a routine again. That he was happy just lying around. And she doesn't know what to do about it either.

February 27, 1978

I wasted too much time today discussing a project I don't want to do: something about an all-girl band in the forties. It's what I call a "whim" picture. Someone in power gets a whim to do a picture based on a fleeting image and a writer is hired to sweat it into a mural.

But I did celebrate my birthday. Fifty. An old man. My gifts: a handmade wooden plaque with "50" emblazoned on it from my old army buddy David Vowell; underwear from Foumi and Karl; a bottle of cognac from Grandma. And a mysterious smile or two from Noah.

March 2, 1978

Noah has a big scratch on his nose. It came from either a zipper on a sofa cushion or the carpeting in our bedroom, which he rubs against sometimes when he is having a tantrum. I put some Mentholatum on it and hope it will heal quickly.

March 3, 1978

A friend of mine, a really fine book reviewer, casually dropped a line over the phone that I must remember: "The first thing that goes in a writer," he said, "is the truth. After that, all he has left is his reflexes."

March 4, 1978

Karl and I drove through the rain to the Forum to watch the Lakers play Philadelphia. It was a good game, the Lakers winning by one point, Dr. J putting on a marvelous show even though he didn't play that much, Norm Nixon reminding me of Walt Frazier of the Knicks' golden years. Karl had pizza and a burrito and nibbled peanuts and drank soda and had a grand time. And so did I, basking paternally. Except for the fact that Noah was constantly in my thoughts. I would never enjoy the most simple activity with both of my sons in the normal way. I can never get over that fact. The dreams of a father, no matter how sick the child, do not die easily.

6

March 5, 1978

Noah is in a sweet mood, Karl is of good cheer, and Foumi is delighted because she has finished a piece that she was writing. So all is going well with my family. The rain has even stopped and it is a lovely day. But still my heart beats, "More!" I will want more until I die and perhaps even die because I want more. But what is it that I want more of now? Just more Noah.

March 6, 1978

My agent tells me his father advised him when he started his career in show business to: "Look gentile but be Jewish; look gay but be straight; and always have a positive cash flow." Not quite Polonius. But neither is this town, for all its rotten state, Denmark.

March 7, 1978

Noah's scratch on the nose is healing. At the same time the zits and blackheads of adolescence are beginning to break through his baby skin. And his grip really has become strong. Last night when he grabbed my hand it was hard for me to unclench his. The kid can exert pressure in more ways than one.

Last night he was very irritable, scratching and attacking us, evidently trying to tell us something. We knew he had not had a bowel movement in four days. So we gave him a suppository.

Finally, at eleven, we put him to bed. At twelve o'clock I heard stirring. I went down and found a trail of dung, as if dropped by a dray horse, on the way to the bathroom. Foumi joined me to clean both him—and it—up. And when we returned to bed, Foumi was again talking of institutionalizing him.

March 8, 1978

Noah is more of a pain in every way. Not only his midnight droppings. I simply derive little joy from him lately. And the day-care center is becoming more of a problem than a solution. I do not look forward to an evening of filling out tax forms any more than I relish helping Foumi cut Noah's hair.

March 9, 1978

Another terrible Thursday. First I pick up Niko and Noah at day-care and then Karl at his French lesson. I sit Niko next to me, and Karl and Noah have to sit together in the back. But Noah does not want to share the backseat with anyone. Yesterday he went on a rampage, attacking Karl, all but trying to gouge out Karl's eye. Karl was beside himself in terror and anger. In the confusion I yelled at Karl as much as I did at Noah. When we got home I apologized to Karl, but it was too late. Karl ran to his room and slammed the door.

March 11, 1978

The day went by in a whirlwind of trivia. Dressing Noah. Taking Karl to a friend's. An hour doing day-care bookkeeping. A meeting at MGM. A drive to the dentist to see if the tooth that fell out of Noah's mouth this morning was, indeed, a baby tooth (it wasn't). A visit to the IRS to check on day-care's FICA status (we need not pay Social Security). A conference at the house with some tree surgeons (the eucalyptus need topping). And then a problem at day-care with one of the kids. Finally, in the evening, I was able to relax, throwing a football around with Karl. It hurt my arm.

Karl did make my day, though. He left the football behind in my car and when I asked him why, he brightly replied: "In case someone happens to stop you and threatens, 'Your football or your life.'"

I woke up this morning feeling so good, a Sunday ripe with pleasant possibilities. But then Noah attacked Foumi at breakfast. We think it's his teeth again. But even if it's his teeth we don't know what to do.

And this afternoon, poor Noah, someone got his teeth into him. I was taking Noah for a walk when the skies began to darken and it turned cold. So I altered my usual route, shortening it, by turning down Northfield, with Noah tailing behind me. Suddenly two dogs leaped out of a driveway and rushed toward Noah. Noah, as always afraid of dogs, turned away. Then one of the dogs, a large shepherd, nipped him in the ass. I didn't see the wound at first; Noah's pants didn't appear to be torn. But when I pulled down his pants I could see that his skin had been broken. I took down the name and address of the apologetic owner who had charged out of his house just a moment too late to check his dog. He assured me that his dog did not have rabies. Still, I rushed Noah home and put some antibiotics on the wound. I called our doctor and checked the status of Noah's tetanus immunity (he's okay there). And then I phoned the Health Department. They'll investigate the dog and quarantine it. All we need now is for Noah to have to undergo rabies shots. As if he isn't mad dog enough as it is.

March 13, 1978

I talked to our brain-diseased friend in the hospital. She seemed so much better, looser, able to talk. But her husband informed me that he is still dismayed at her slow rate of improvement. "Better slow than no," I told him.

March 14, 1978

Karl showed me a letter that he was sending to *Time* magazine:

In your Special Report on Socialism you have a chart giving West Germany a political freedom rating of 100. I question that be-

cause in West Germany one does not have the political freedom to be a National Socialist. In West Germany National Socialism is illegal.

Karl Greenfeld, Grade 8

P.S. I am not a Nazi.

Smart-ass kid. But then *Time* is a smart-ass magazine.

March 17, 1978

Noah's been awful lately. Every night he has a tantrum when he returns home from day-care. He pinches and bites whoever is sitting next to him in the car. Last night I even slapped him. He knows I am not very happy with him these days and that makes him even unhappier. The Golem. My Golem. But I don't think I can take much more of him.

March 20, 1978

Another bad weekend with Noah. Constantly pinching and biting. Very unhappy. But last night while I was brushing his teeth a tooth finally came out. There are still two more to come. And I hope that's what has been bothering him.

Because I can understand how he must feel when he has a loose tooth. As if he is literally falling apart. And that has to be scary. Any normal child can be reassured that it's just his tooth and that nothing else about him is loose or coming out. But not Noah.

So, angered by our inability to keep him from falling apart, he throws a fit. Karl's friend Erich, who was sleeping over, was caught in the eye of Noah's tantrum. But he wasn't the least bit fazed by Noah's conduct. Erich's used to it by now.

March 21, 1978

Noah is still quick to bite and to pinch-grab and to nail-dig. We live in a constant state of unease. Almost every meal and almost any request is occasion for him to have a tantrum. And he seems to be saving his worst behavior for Foumi and me. We know his teeth are bothering him but perhaps he is also trying to tell us that it is time for him to leave home.

What would happen if Foumi became sick tomorrow? Or if I suddenly fell ill? I guess we would try to get Noah into a state hospital such as Camarillo on an emergency basis. Or seek to hire someone to stay with him. But who? I just don't know what we would do. I don't want to think about it either.

Foumi has finished her book, an account of life in America from her Oriental point of view. She's excited about it and keeps telling me how terrific it is. I know it could be a great success in Japan. But first, of course, she has to find a publisher. Even if she can't, I'm still very proud of her.

Maybe Noah caught my psychic warning. Except for a small tantrum this morning, he seems over his vile mood.

What do I want for Noah? I want a residence. I want a humane situation, small, life-sized, without a massive bureaucracy hovering over it. I want people caring for him who are dedicated rather than money motivated. I don't know where one can find such people these days; the church once provided nuns and zealots. A caste system supplies the necessary people: Imagine Noah in India, a Brahmin, with all those bowing sweepers to attend him. I guess my big mistake this karma was to have Noah in twentieth-century America.

What a Sunday! Foumi always picks on Sunday. Noah awoke in an incredibly good mood. But then Foumi decided that since he has not had a bowel movement in five days we had to do something about it. I argued against it. But she stuck a suppository up his ass. He proceeded to go berserk in his discomfort, scratching until his nose was red with blood, and pinching at us. All day I stayed about the house waiting for his shit to come. But none came. Foumi then decided to give him a Fleet's enema. Again, it did not seem to take. He scratched and pinched and abused himself until he was bleeding profusely from the bridge of his nose. But then he did drop some shitty water in the children's latrine and finally let loose with a barrage in our bathroom. So it was shit-cleaning time and mutual incrimination time again and another weekend gone. Except Karl and I threw the football around. And played some Ping-Pong. He beat me in Ping-Pong, which made his day.

March 27, 1978

I think one of the problems with Noah now is that he's beginning to sense his own strength. And he wants to test it out on us. Which is asking us to pay a pretty steep price for his growing awareness.

Another parent we know, a widow, is having a different problem with her beautiful but bizarre daughter. On the one hand officialdom kept telling the lady that she couldn't handle her. On the other hand, the institution where she finally placed her is now telling the poor lady that they can't handle her either. What is the solution?

March 28, 1978

Some capillaries have burst in Noah's eye, the result of his scratching at it. And he continues to pinch and dig his fingernails into everybody at any opportunity. Karl thinks it's because Noah is suffering the pain of molars breaking through the gums. He underwent that experience just a short while ago. Whatever the cause, we are close to the breaking point with Noah. It is no fun to have him pull hair right out of your scalp and then put it in his mouth and swallow it.

So last night I called the Operant Conditioning Center (not the real name) in the desert and arranged for us to visit the place. The Administrative President, or titular head of it, has an autistic son. The woman who I think actually runs it is the Executive Visiting Adviser. She runs a similar place in the Midwest and has always struck me as a bit strange because of her infantile sense of humor. But at least she seems to have a dedication, even if it is only a philosophical one. She's a strict Skinnerian who carries operant conditioning to its nth degree, and evidently that sometimes gets her into a lot of trouble.

I guess this is my season for examining controversial treatments. Today I visited a homeopathic doctor. Not for Noah but for myself. She looked deeply into my eyes with an optometrist's instrument and told me that my high cholesterol level was the result of an uncertain sugar regulator within my system. So for two weeks she instructed me not to drink or eat sweets "in order to clear my system and see what happens." I don't mind eschewing sweets but no alcohol at all will not be easy. I do like my wine at dinner.

March 29, 1978

We drove out to the desert to visit the Operant Conditioning Center. It is located in a large stucco tract house that has been divided into both residential and schoolroom areas. It also has a huge three-car garage which could be utilized for other purposes and a very large backyard. As usual I was more impressed by the real estate than Foumi was.

They seemed to have an abundance of student aides working one on one with their five residents. Mostly they were rewarding the kids with juice squirts and feeding them their breakfasts in big bite sizes in response to their performance of assigned tasks. At the pace they were going, feeding seemed to be an all-day activity. It was almost lunchtime already.

The Executive Visiting Adviser was cold to us. The Administrative President was warm. He said that though each kid represented $35,000 a year in funding from the state he still wound up with an annual deficit. Payroll accounted for over 75 percent of his budget. He had a staff of eleven, five of whom were on duty during the teaching day, two in the evening until bedtime, and then one all night. The state wanted him to skimp on food, he said, to spend no more than a dollar per day per kid, and he refused to do that. He admitted privately to us that he realized that behavior modification was no cure but at least it made it possible for the kids to live outside of an institution even if they could no longer live in their own homes.

As a program, it certainly seemed to me something worth considering for Noah. But it turns out Foumi was also looking at it as a model for opening a school and residential facility of our own in West Los Angeles. Buying or leasing a house and all that. Given our limited day-care experience, I am wary of getting involved in the crazy-kid business in any but a retail manner. Let others go wholesale. I want Noah taken care of, but not at the price of having to take care of four more like him.

Everyone deals with Noah better than I do. When he scratches me, picking on the tender cuticles and pressing down hard on them with his own fingernails, I excite easily and overreact. Foumi, on the other hand, stays calm and so can manage him better.

At OCC they told us the kids stop having tantrums because of contracts made with them. The kid is informed, for example, that if he is quiet for thirty seconds he will be rewarded. I suggested we try that with Noah. Foumi laughed: "Noah has no concept of time." And she began to disparage OCC. Foumi is the utter perfectionist who finds the fault in every system. She looks for perfection in the sky while birds shit down on us. That is at the center of our every hassle. And the more we argue, the more we shout at each other; and the more Noah suffers. No one wins, we all lose.

My hands are full of scratches, my ears are full of laments; the scratches are from Noah, the laments from Foumi. Each morning with Noah is a chore. It is difficult to awaken him, he rebels at eating breakfast, he has a tantrum when it comes to dressing him. Getting him off to school is the hardest part of the day.

Except for his return home from school. Then he usually attacks by pressing his fingernails into anyone in sight. At dinner he hurls his milk to the floor and after two bites of food he galumphs off into the living room. We try to ignore him. We try not to ignore him. We do not know what to do. So we continually argue.

I view the school and residence at OCC as a possible short-term solution; Foumi looks at it as a nirvana that definitely falls far short. Which is like the essential difference between us. While I am afraid that I might not be able to live through today, Foumi fears that she might not live to be one hundred.

April 1, 1978

I continually worry about what to do about Noah. As if I really have a choice. Which I don't. There are very few parents who wouldn't kill for their normal kids, so what's so special about having to live for your abnormal one? Noah just can't manage for himself. He needs twenty-four-hour care. And if what we are doing doesn't seem to make any sense then perhaps infanticide or euthanasia does. But most people just do not want to think about the plight of brain-damaged children. It's an inferno too close to home.

And Foumi had to lecture her staff at day-care this afternoon. They seem to have become sloppy, rushing off from work, not cleaning up or putting away teaching materials properly, that sort of thing.

April 2, 1978

Grandma has gone to San Diego for the weekend with a friend. Foumi, Karl, and I put in a new bathroom rug this morning and then Karl went off to Santa Monica to check out some new army models. Noah seems calm and contented. When we walked this morning he chirped happily beside me. He had no tantrum at breakfast or lunch and Foumi was able to tutor-teach him this afternoon without incident. Whatever has been bothering him seems to have passed. Again I must remind myself not to raise my voice or forcibly impose my will upon him when I am angry with him, but instead to treat him just the way I treat Karl. Because if Noah cannot quite understand the logic of reason, he can always hear the hysteria of emotion.

April 3, 1978

I have been having second thoughts about OCC. On their behavior modification extremism: If a kid is mutilating himself, then anything that can stop that mutilation is justified. But their complete emphasis on left-brain activities does not leave me with much enthusiasm. We've learned through long experience in Noah's case that an M & M's reward for saying "Mmm" is not his road to speech. I am also wary of all the record keeping that seems to occupy them so. I just can't trust people who seem more interested in extrapolative scientific results than in intrinsic human processes.

April 4, 1978

The less I bark at him the better Noah behaves. I'm letting him do things in his own sweet slow time. Perhaps that is the only way to handle him? Why must I always spoil his joy by attacking whatever it is that shapes his sense of fun?

April 5, 1978

A therapist told me yesterday that kids like Noah become impossible in adolescence, can't be taught anything, and that one's hands are full just in keeping them from going through self-destructive behaviors.

Noah will be twelve in three months. The difficult years are yet to be. Grow old along with me. But who will be growing old along with whom?

Karl's adolescence doesn't seem to be a particularly shining bright spot either. At least in terms of education. He gets to do no writing in his English class. His drama and stagecraft classes are completely verbal too. I guess I made a mistake. I should have ruled out public education and sent him to a private school. I should have realized that what is bad for one kid is even worse for the other, that where Special Education fails so too must normal education.

April 6, 1978

Karl is in trouble in school. His drama teacher asked the class to do some envelope stuffing for the PTA. Karl saw no point in doing it, said there was a service committee for kids who liked to do that sort of thing. The teacher asked him about his school spirit. Karl replied that school spirit was just petty nationalism.

Karl seemed mature and intelligent, quite beyond his thirteen years, as he told me what had happened. But then a moment later he revealed his true age. Maybe he would have more school spirit, he suggested, if his school had a football team.

When I asked Noah to make his pre-bed urination he obligingly defecated too, his first bowel movement in five days. He and I, indeed at the moment, are enjoying an era of good feeling. I'm feeling better because he's feeling better. Or vice versa. One of us is the tail and the other is the dog, and I'm not sure which is which.

I came across a good quote from Gertrude Stein: "Some of us may become major figures but we're all minor writers." It certainly describes our current literary scene.

Noah walks behind me on the cliff, pulling up weeds and testing them with his mouth. An acquaintance has described me to a friend as a "hero." I turn around and look at Noah. If I am a hero I am the most reluctant hero in history.

As Americans we like to think *pecunia vincit omnia*, money conquers everything. But the governmental expenditure of money alone is never a solution. It wasn't in Vietnam and it isn't in terms of the developmentally disabled. The medical establishment and the care-providing bureaucracy are full of South Vietnamese Colonels. Very little money ever trickles down to its destination. The administration of the money eats up most of the money that is to be administered.

At dinner Noah threw his refilled milk glass to the floor. This really angered Foumi and she chastised him. Noah went into a tantrum. I quietly told Foumi that one glass of milk was enough, that she need not force him to eat so much. This provoked her into a tantrum of her own: If I knew so well how to take care of Noah, then from now on I should prepare all of his meals and feed him. I maintained my calm, so her mood passed. But poor Noah. As a result of his tantrum he has another scratch on the bridge of his nose. Perhaps the day is soon coming when he will require extreme behavior modification as a kind of preventive first aid. I could not just stand by and watch him inflict serious injury to himself.

April 12, 1978

Karl asked me when I first decided I wanted to become a writer. I told him that it was when I was about his age. He then asked when I first was printed in *The New York Times*. It was when I was fourteen years old, and I told him how it came about:

Our high school journalism teacher kept urging us to break into the public prints and promised extra credit for doing so. He suggested the Letters to the Editor columns as providing the best opportunities. I remember my friend Charlie Sullivan was the first one in our class to have a letter printed. The *Brooklyn Eagle*, at the time, had an Old Timers Page featuring nostalgic reminiscences. Charlie wrote a letter to it wondering about a group of fictitious characters he created who used to hang around an equally fictitious bar. The *Eagle* ran the letter and Charlie got his extra credit. So I wrote a letter. In deadly earnest. To the Sports Section of *The New York Times*, which in those days carried its Letters to the Sports Editor on Saturdays.

I can still remember opening the pages of *The New York Times* on that moist December morning when I stopped by our apartment in the midst of my job, delivering milk and bagels and rolls for the corner grocery. Oh how elated I was! I don't think a Nobel Prize–winner has ever felt better. I took the paper with me and pushed my cart through the street, pausing every few moments to unfold it and reread my deathless prose. Oh the joy of seeing yourself in print for the first time in a public journal! Ever since then I've been periodically in need of a media fix.

"I think the Heisman Memorial Trophy Committee erred in its selection of Frank Sinkwich of Georgia as the recipient of its vaunted award," the letter began. And I then went on to sing the praises ecstatically—and statistically—of Paul Governali of Columbia. I didn't know any more about Governali than about Sinkwich, never having seen either play, but at least Governali was a local product. In fact, I thought about that letter again recently when I noted in the local sports pages that Paul Governali had died in San Diego.

Talk about letter writers, Foumi is an inveterate one. Shortly after we opened our day-care center she had me edit the following letter she sent to Ralph Nader in Washington:

Dear Mr. Nader:

In Los Angeles we opened a day-care center for developmentally disabled children.

A State of California regulation requires day-care workers to get x-rayed every year. I know by now that X rays every year are hazardous. I have had an inoculation of BCG in Japan so that I already have an immunity to tuberculosis. I feel they are cultivating on me some kind of cancer unnecessarily.

Here in this country they are not aware of BCG inoculation so it is very difficult for them to understand my position.

Please let me know what I should do.

Yours very truly,
Foumiko Greenfeld

Foumi showed Karl a carbon of her letter. And a few days later Karl handed her this letter as if it had just come in the mail:

Dear Mrs. Greenfeld:

You wrote me about X rays. I would like to point out that X rays are harmful. I have proved that by testing turtles. Out of ten turtles tested, five formed a rock group, two went to the suburbs, and three stopped watching color TV.

Also I believe you wrote me about BCG. I also tested some turtles with that. Within twenty minutes they were all dead.

Sincerely,
Ralph Nader

P.S. Please don't write me anymore.

April 13, 1978

I have been ignoring Karl's normal education while concentrating on Noah's lack of Special Education. So I went to Karl's school and met with his counselor. I told her that I was distressed. Karl has no real English class and his drama class is but an acting class, so he is not getting any written work in English. Which is ridiculous. He is in honors classes in which he is not learning any fundamentals. Was the purpose of the honors program egalitarian, I asked. Setting him back so that other kids could easily catch up to him?

She quickly agreed that Karl was not being taught much in the way of fundamentals and suggested that I put Karl into a private school for gifted children. "If Karl were my son," she said, "I would do that."

But Karl still insists that he doesn't want to go to a private school. And his English teacher agrees with him—or, at least, doesn't want to lose him. She called to tell me how much Karl was getting out of her class. So not knowing what to do I'll probably do nothing, knowing at the same time that whenever I listen to Karl about education I make a mistake. His education. My mistake.

I also went to see the homeopath this morning. She gave me some sort of medicine and when I mentioned Noah expressed an interest in treating him. The lady strikes me as a little bit of a witch. But if she's an efficacious witch, why not give her a shot? At least she's a doctor who knows that doctors know nothing. Which is a beginning.

April 14, 1978

After driving Noah to school this morning I went over to the Beverly Hills Hotel to have breakfast with two old friends from Brooklyn. One is now a magazine publisher and the other is a TV cable system executive. We laughed a lot but there was also some serious talk about tax shelters and stock options and all that. I felt out of place, out of time. The publisher should have had his guitar and the cable executive should have had a book under his arm and we should have been in a Brooklyn candy store or luncheonette, all young and slim and very hairy, rather than in the Polo Lounge. Old images die hard.

April 15, 1978

Last night we went to the Playboy Mansion for one of the dullest parties I've ever been to. I even wonder why I went. Except, I guess, we're all voyeurs at heart. To compare Hefner to a Gatsby is a cliché. But it is the only way one can possibly make him seem interesting. The place, from the little I could tell at night aside from a Japanese garden and grotto, attempts to look like a British lord's manor. But the effect was like that of an inept American trying to simulate a British accent.

Before we went I agreed to pay Karl his usual Noah-baby-sitting fee. Which is one dollar. Except when we visit friends who live out past Malibu. In that case it's a two-dollar evening. I told Karl that those friends were planning to move to Brentwood soon and hence would also become a one-dollar evening. "No," Karl insisted. "Once a two-dollar evening, always a two-dollar evening. It's like being Jewish." He's been a good kid lately, often spending evenings at school doing volunteer work on the stage crew. I just wish we did not have to ride him so hard about math.

April 16, 1978

A photographer came to take some pictures of Noah. Who is a most difficult subject. The sight of an insistent camera drives him into a tantrum. So Noah was giving the photographer, a tall young blonde, the usual hard time. We didn't realize how young the photographer was until Foumi told her about Noah's molar problems. "Yes," she said, "I remember I had the same problems, the pains in my gums, a few years ago." She finally did get what she thought would be some good pictures.

April 17, 1978

As Karl, Foumi, and I were watching "Holocaust" on TV last night, Foumi wept. She weeps at anything to do with the war. But I have to admit that I was often close to tears myself. During one commercial break I went to Noah's room to tuck in my own personal holocaust. When I leaned over to kiss him good night, he ground his teeth, rolled his eyes, and pulled my hair. Again it struck me: He is simply a madman. Each day with him is a gift. But each day without him could be an even greater gift.

7

April 18, 1978

We watched another episode of "Holocaust." But I'm beginning to get bored with it. I am happy though that most Americans seem to be watching it too. But I just hope they're not watching it for the sheer enjoyment of seeing Jews die.

A Japanese publisher's representative in New York called and told Foumi how much he likes the book she's been working on, and that he was sending it off to Japan. It would be more than a little ironic if my painter wife had a literary success in Japan, it would be wonderful.

I've been asked to go to New York myself for some meetings because of the TV movie, "Lovey." I don't have to go contractually and Foumi says I shouldn't go but I guess I will.

April 22, 1978

As I walked in the door last night upon my return from New York Karl began to talk to me about a problem he's having in school over saluting the flag. Foumi, meanwhile, was calling Noah out of his room. He came into the living room in his sleeper, shyly smiling. I asked him to kiss me and he bobbed his head toward me, his raw red nose scabbing from a self-inflicted wound. And when I hugged Foumi, I realized again we need to be away from each other in order to truly appreciate each other.

April 23, 1978

About going to New York Foumi was right. She's always right. I should not have gone. I did not enjoy the meetings with the producer, with the director, or with the network. I don't know who was stroked or who was had or what was accomplished. The network wanted to be sure that even a new arrival from Mars could understand the story. The director was more interested in developing a subplot than in servicing the main story. The producer just wanted everybody to be happy. But I was happy with the script the way it was, before I went to New York.

April 25, 1978

While I was in New York, Karl decided not to salute the flag in his homeroom. This upset his teacher, who's trying to make a federal case out of it. She wants Karl out of her homeroom, claiming she has put up with his abominable behavior long enough but now it's gone too far—even though just last week she gave him a good report in conduct. The counselor and dean both don't know what to do. Foumi went up to see them yesterday and pointed out that her generation in Japan had been taught to salute their flag, the Rising Sun, blindly. Until the Americans came and ordered them not to do so.

The best thing for the authorities to do, of course, is just to ignore Karl. The kid is somehow trying to assert his individuality; he is half Asian and he was born in Japan. But instead they're busy trying to add counts and indictments to Karl's rap sheet. It now seems he once snapped his notebook shut too loudly in Science and there is that protest he made against envelope stuffing in Drama. So the authorities are upset. But they weren't very upset, Foumi recalls, when he was robbed in school on one occasion and beaten up on another. They seem to be overly concerned about the wrong things.

April 26, 1978

I called the L.A. Board of Education, the local area superintendent, and the principal of Karl's school. They all agreed that under the law Karl does not have to salute the flag and that he can remain seated during the salute if he so chooses. Today he will meet with his homeroom teacher and his adviser to work it out. I told him not to let the adults browbeat him in any way, to say he wants to talk it over with his parents in case they try to railroad him into a decision he does not want to make.

Karl told me not to worry, that he has his own "lawyer," a kid in the class who has been writing "To Whom It May Concern" letters to the teacher, defending Karl's rights. It's a shame the authorities can't enjoy the fact that the kids are trying to practice democracy, that Karl in fact is behaving, if idiosyncratically, also quite idealistically. And his "crime" is minuscule compared to the crimes of racial slurs and drug dealing and assaulted kids that happen every day in that school. I remember when I was his age. I was often found guilty of committing such heinous offenses as "talking in the corridors." How can I get mad at Karl?

April 27, 1978

Karl had me geared for a showdown with his teacher but it never came off. Karl wasn't in his homeroom during the flag salute and he clear forgot about his lunchtime appointment with his counselor and teacher.

April 28, 1978

Karl remained in his seat during the flag salute and the teacher didn't say a word. I guess this particular educational mini-crisis has passed. But we might have one pending with Noah. Adele, his teacher, is still planning to leave his school.

April 29, 1978

We decided to send Karl to a private math school in West L.A. run by the Japanese for their nationals here. He has to learn fundamentals somewhere. But when I took him there it looked like chaos in action. Looking at all those Japanese kids, bent over with their stubby pencils, reminded me of the first time I had walked into a Hebrew-school class. Except for Japanese faces, of course.

We agreed to let the people from the "Today" show visit for an hour today. I figured it would help the cause of brain damage or autism or whatever you want to call it. So I asked Karl to wait around a few minutes during that time. No, he said. He did not want to be on television. To be on television, he felt, you have to earn it. You have to do something special. And all he had done was have a brain-damaged brother. That wasn't his idea of earning something.

I explained to him the importance of people like us talking openly about our problem with Noah. I pointed out that the only way to deal with any problem is by being honest and unashamed of it. And that by publicizing the problem we could help the public better understand the plight of the developmentally disabled and their families. Karl did not argue with me but said he still didn't want any publicity. However, I noticed that Jack Perkins of NBC did somehow manage to waylay him for a quick interview.

May 2, 1978

The director of Noah's school visited a special school run by a young behavior modification teacher we once knew. "Our classes here," she reported, "are like university seminars compared to his place."

May 3, 1978

The state licensing people came to inspect our day-care program and were visibly impressed with what we were doing. Which has Foumi thinking again of opening our own special school. But I just don't want to get into education, which I know is a full-time responsibility. Or should be. And having a writing career and dealing with Noah are enough full-time responsibilities for me at the moment. If Foumi could manage a school on her own it would be one thing, but I know that sooner or later my minimal participation would be required. And even that would be too much.

The segment about Noah was on the "Today" show this morning. And last night Karl was in a quandary. He asked me what I would do in his place: stay home this morning and watch, or go to school. I said it was up to him. He decided to stay home, claiming he was very tired and it would give him a chance to catch up on his sleep. Karl's appearance on television, which he scrutinized, was very good. He all but stole the show from the star, who slept through it.

But this evening Noah will have another chance to catch himself. The network called and said it would be repeated on the "NBC Nightly News." Noah celebrated the intelligence by having four slices of toast at breakfast. Lately he's been eating prodigious amounts of food. He had three bowls of rice at dinner last night.

Karl is apprehensive about his appearance before the camera on the "Nightly News." "It's not like the 'Today' show," he mumbled to me last night. "Kids are in school when that's on. But they watch the 'Nightly News.'"

Thankfully they are spared watching Foumi put Noah to bed. Last night he suddenly attacked her, biting her arm and then butting his head against her teeth. It was the first time he'd done that.

Karl loves to talk about spots and gels and cables and all manner of backstage technical stuff. I'm delighted to see him so involved in his stagecraft class.

When I walked into the house at seven o'clock last night Foumi was on the twin edges of hysteria and despair. Noah had attacked her again, pulling her hair and biting her. I've been putting off Noah's future for too long. We have to find a residence for him immediately. My solution last night, of carefully handling him for the rest of the evening, is no solution at all.

May 10, 1978

Noah seems in a good mood today. And so is Karl. I bought Karl a wet suit and he's already gone off to the beach to surf. I went to the homeopath, who insists I should still stay off sugar, even the least little bit, that my body can't handle it. I did not tell her that I still chew gum and implored her to allow me a little liquor once in a while. "No," she shook her head, "it's bad for you." I acted upset by her pronouncement. As if I'm really going to listen to her anyway.

May 13, 1978

Karl went surfing again yesterday but for some reason was moping about the house today. I should have been the moper. Last night I became impatient with Noah and slapped him. Which only heated him up and did neither of us any good. How can I expect him to control himself when I can't control myself?

May 14, 1978

Grandma leaves for England at the end of this week, which means I will have to pick up some of her slack. At breakfast, for example, she's been helping to serve Noah. And she has come in very handy as a live-in baby-sitter. She'll be gone two months and, of course, we'll manage. But I do wish Foumi and I could go away for a vacation ourselves. Anywhere. Anyplace.

May 15, 1978

A stuck-with-Noah Sunday: Since Foumi wasn't feeling well, he was all mine. In the morning we went for a walk and he had a terrible tantrum: After spotting a dog he lay down on a lawn, rolled on it, and pulled up clumps of grass and stuck them in his mouth. I managed to get him to his feet and walk on home.

In the afternoon I took him for a ride and then for another walk. This time he seemed happy enough. But when we returned home he had another tantrum. He refused to eat his dinner and, continually clutching at me, dug his fingernails deep into my cuticles. I know the best way to handle him at such times is to ignore him. But damnit, sometimes I just can't help it and I yell. Which goads him further.

Karl had a much better day, bike riding in Venice and the Marina, which he described as "so fun." In fact it was so fun that he forgot to set his alarm this morning and woke up too late to catch the school bus. So I had to drive him to school.

May 16, 1978

Each day I come to my office, type this page or so, and then shuffle on to other papers. But the problem of Noah always remains and now seems larger than ever. The fact of the matter is that soon I will no longer be able to control him physically. So I have been thinking of going East to look over some of the residential possibilities there for Noah. There is the place that raises horses, there are the Camphill sites that I've heard only good things about. But even if I could get Noah into one of those places, how would I get him there? I'll be damned if it's possible to manage Noah on a plane anymore. Unless I drugged him. Or got a private plane. Or else got a lot of help during the drive cross-country, the nightmare stays in motels. But then, how would we get him back for holidays? Unless we were to move back East ourselves. Questions. Questions. And no answers in the back of the book either.

May 17, 1978

A letter came from a woman in Colorado offering me the best advice I've yet received: "Fight as hard as you can and then give up." Which is my current plan. She also goes on to point out that "institution is a bad buzz word." True. One day I may yet love that word. It will represent surcease, it will mean freedom.

And, indeed, I recently read a piece in the Columbia alumni magazine about deinstitutionalization itself not being the answer. Just closing the doors and kicking old people and the mentally retarded and the mentally ill back into the communities is no solution. The communities do not want them, never have. Most people do not enjoy having their flawed pasts, freak presents, or bleak futures around. That's why they put them in institutional

95

gulags in the first place. Sometimes I think it all boils down to this: The way we treat—or mistreat—our Noahs is the way we will treat—or maltreat—ourselves in the future. If we live long enough we will get what we mete out because what is senility but brain dysfunction?

Some of us have to bear too much, though. Foumi was on the phone with a Japanese woman in Palos Verdes who has a child like Noah who is nineteen. Bad enough. But worse: The woman also has cancer. And still worse: She has a helpless mother, senile, incontinent, and in diapers, living with her. The only thing the woman seems to have going for her is her Palos Verdes address. Which means she must have some money. But I'm sure there are cases like hers in the ghetto too. Job is not the only hard-luck story—just the first one to get a lot of ink.

May 18, 1978

California hot. A smudge of brown lies over the ocean. I began to walk to my office this morning but the heat was just too much and I turned back and got my car.

At a dinner party last night we saw our friend who had been hospitalized with the brain virus that caused her memory to play tricks. She seemed much better. But she's still not quite all there yet. Her husband told me he has to force her to make a very conscious effort to remember anything; otherwise she immediately forgets it.

I often wonder how much memory Noah has and how it functions. He remembers favorite foods, certain people, and all dogs. I guess it's some sort of discretionary memory that isn't reliable, like a distant radio signal that at one moment comes in and the next moment fades away completely.

May 19, 1978

We had bagels this morning and Noah, after devouring two, wanted a third. We turned down his request. Immediately, he began to pinch himself. I think he thinks he's hurting me. And he is. I can't stand seeing him abuse himself.

Foumi and I have been toying with the idea of living in Japan again. We're not sure how we'd manage the transport of Noah there or how to make Karl want to live there—he's such an

American kid. Whenever we discuss a possible move with him he mounts arguments against it. Last night, for example, he cited the fact that it would be difficult for Noah to learn a second language.

But Foumi fielded that one, suggesting that the stimulation of a new language might provoke him into speaking in either language. She recalled a Japanese friend's spastic daughter who had never spoken a word until she was five years old and then spoke for the first time as her parents prepared to leave for America to spend a year in Iowa. "I don't want to go," she said clearly. She did go and now understands both English and Japanese and can think most intelligently even though she still must lie on the floor, helpless physically.

May 21, 1978

I was on television, a local channel, being interviewed about my special son, when I suddenly realized it was a lot easier to spend an evening dealing with a media Noah than with the real one.

May 22, 1978

On Sunday Karl called from a beach club in Santa Monica notorious for its anti-Semitism. He was there with a school friend. "It's nice here, Dad," he reported. "You should join."

May 23, 1978

I'm in a good mood, enjoying Noah, who is reacting accordingly, all sweetness and charm. It is almost as if since he does not have enough brains to generate his own attitudes he is completely a creature of reaction.

May 26, 1978

We were talking about Karl's plans for this summer. After all, he'll be thirteen and a half. The summer I was thirteen and a half was the summer after Pearl Harbor. I remember I wanted to work, I had completed my third term at Townsend Harris High School. I had had to take the subway into Manhattan every day to get there and felt that I was certainly mature enough to do a job and earn some money. But the law at that time required that one be fourteen in order to get working papers. So I spent one month with my family in the Catskills in a cottage cluster, a *kochalayn* that had a communal kitchen, my father coming up on the weekends, my best friend at the resort being the hard-drinking handyman who would tell me wonderful stories about his life as a sailor at sea.

I don't remember how I spent the other month except I do have a memory of myself lying in bed until late into the day in our sweltering Brooklyn apartment, reading. Already I knew that I wanted to be a writer. But the more I read, the more I also knew I had nothing to say as a writer. Not yet anyway. So I would close the book and dream of a life of adventure that I could later report. Like Jack London. Like the hard-drinking handyman. Until my mother would finally shame me into getting out of bed.

May 27, 1978

Last night I was awakened by the sound of Noah in our bathroom. I went there and waited patiently for him to complete his bowel movement. I caught him as he rose from the toilet and gently urged him to bend over so that I might wipe him. Instead, he dashed into his bedroom, bouncing onto his bed. I was furious with him and he knew it. With a pained but innocent expression on his face he followed me into the children's bathroom next to his room and meekly allowed me to wipe him. When we returned to his bedroom I inspected the sheets on his bed. Miraculously, there was not even a hint of a stain upon them. A lucky night.

But a difficult day. With Karl. He says he does not want to go to the Japanese math school anymore, claims that he cannot do any work there because of the noise. I told him that if nothing else, it is important for him to learn under pressure. But still he did not want to go back. Until I applied some more pressure.

May 28, 1978

I took Karl, after his pestering insistence, to see—rather hear— the show *Beatlemania*. I had to sit with my fingers in my ears throughout the whole performance. But Karl says he liked it. Especially technically.

A try at a picnic with some friends yesterday in Will Rogers State Park. They brought their baby girl, we brought Noah. Who seemed obscenely large next to her. Noah ate prodigiously but also behaved badly, having a tantrum whenever he felt he was being ignored. And he was ignored when Karl and I played football with my friend and his son. And I must say Karl treated my friend's son, who is much younger than he, as a kid brother, acting deferentially toward him by allowing him to catch whatever passes were thrown his way.

Karl and I had an argument. On a moral point. But perhaps I carried it too far. What happened was this: As we were walking along the cliff street, I was throwing tennis-ball grounders to him and he was fielding them and throwing back to me as if I were a first baseman. But then twice in a row he made obviously wild throws. "No more," I said, and would not throw him another grounder. "I promise," he said, "I won't make any more crazy throws." I threw him another grounder. He made another "crazy throw," this time losing the ball. I was angry with him because he had not kept his word. He said that the last "crazy throw" had been an accident. No, I insisted, he had done it purposefully.

And so we walked along, on either side of the street with some thirty feet between us—like the scene in *The Bicycle Thief*—with Karl sulking and me angry as I bawled him out. I explained to him that that little incident meant I could no longer trust him, that his word was worthless to me. Then silently we returned home.

When we walked into the house Karl asked Foumi if she had put away the record she had been listening to. No, she said, she hadn't. "But you said you would," said Karl. "I forgot," Foumi shrugged. "See," Karl turned to me. "She gave me her word and she didn't keep it." How can I teach that kid anything?

June 1, 1978

Noah has gone to bed late the past two nights and risen before 5:00 A.M. This morning I had to chase him back to bed three times so I could get my last dregs of sleep. Foumi couldn't. So she got up and made his lunch, prepared his breakfast, did the wash, while I didn't trundle out of bed until after eight.

When Karl awoke he complained that he was not feeling well. Foumi thinks that's because he tries to spend as much time during the school week at play as he does during the weekend. The kid so likes to play. But then so did I. He is so much like me when I was his age. I could have played my life away—and perhaps I have.

June 2, 1978

Last night Foumi packed, saying she was ready to leave, and I would have been happy to see her go. I was in the bathroom help-watching Noah take forever to undress so I could give him his bath. She came in and handed me a bill that had come in the mail that morning. I immediately exploded. Which was wrong. But she should have had more sense than to hand me a bill in the bathroom when I was about to give Noah his bath. It wasn't the time or the place. And when she wouldn't admit that she had made a mistake in doing so, I called her crazy. Then down came the suitcase and out came the drawers. I told her I shouldn't have exploded, implored her to stay, but she kept packing.

"Let her go," Karl advised. But I knew I could not let her go. And the only way to do that was to walk out first. Which I threatened to do. We raced for the door. She went out the front door. I went out the back door. We met at the car and fought for the door handle.

Then we both laughed and returned to the house.

It's not good, I know, for Karl to sit on the sidelines and watch us fight. But it just might teach him how to be political. Not the least of my many failings is that I'm not a very political person. I have always tried to live my own life according to my own style. I've never liked to think about the best way to achieve pragmatic results. Which is a fine ideal for me but leaves my family in a miserable reality. For example, if I had gone along with the self-serving hyperactive parents from the Valley a few years ago I would now have a residential placement for Noah. But I just could not play ball with those people. They planned to stage a local telethon annually to raise money for a group residence to which the children of the leaders—and I was one of them—would be guaranteed priority admittance rather than those most in need. It didn't strike me as morally right then. It still doesn't. But I still don't have a placement for Noah either.

June 6, 1978

Noah continues to eat shirts, blankets, bedding, and now he's taken to tearing away the wallpaper in our bedroom. But it is my stomach that hurts. I have a constant bloated feeling. I hope it's nothing, that I'm just suffering the effects of a cold I don't even remember catching.

June 9, 1978

One of the all-time terrible days in every way. I did not work. Just showered and lounged about the house all morning. Then I went to a reunion lunch with my Seventh Army buddies. Time wasted. Now that I don't drink I clearly heard all the old stories over again. Stopped by at my agent's. Called Foumi. She was furious. With Noah, with Karl, with me, with the world. Noah had a loose stomach and she was on her way over to day-care to pick him up. She had caught Karl lying to her about doing his math assignments—he was way behind. And it was all my fault that she never had any free time.

I picked up Karl at his French lesson and was appropriately angry with him, keeping up the mad until I got home. And at dinner I let loose something I never should have said. I was chewing him out for lying to us about doing his math when it just suddenly slipped out. "Sometimes you make me glad Noah is the way he is." I looked across the table and Foumi was crying.

Foumi is so frustrated these days. She just spent two days lining up an extended extra day-care program. What happened was this: The director of Noah's school had called Foumi to say that Adele, Noah's teacher, was sick and since she could not find a suitable substitute, the director was canceling the class. Both Carlos and Bobby, the other members of Noah's class, also attend our day-care. The director, in effect, passed the problem on to

101

Foumi. And even though Noah was sick on Wednesday, Foumi arranged a program for the other boys.

Foumi is so good. But last night she was complaining how everybody takes advantage of her. "Including you." She is tired, worn out, feels constantly hemmed in. She needs to get away by herself if only for an afternoon. But she will not go anywhere by herself. How can she have freedom if she is afraid to have independence?

This morning I called the State Office of Special Education to find out about the certification process necessary to start a school. I know we can have a good school if Foumi is the director. But I'm also not very keen on being involved in a school. We have enough problems.

What to do about Karl, for example, and his tendency to lie? It is, indeed—to sound old-fashioned about it—a defect in his character. He claims he lies only when he fears he'll be punished anyway if he tells the truth and so it's a calculated risk. Not bad thinking in terms of the real world. But our family is not the real world and he must learn to abide by its moral code.

One of these days I would like to write a novel about all the lying and cheating and chicanery in the movie business. I know that if I let that subject just pass right by me, then I have no right morally to lecture Karl. But the shape and the form still elude me and I guess only when I discover that will I be impelled to start work on it. I am someone who never does anything until he has to anyway.

Foumi, on the other hand, expends a great deal of energy anticipating every possible crisis. Whenever a crisis materializes she is, of course, prepared. But for the wrong crisis. Because most crises do not materialize in the shape or manner anticipated anyway. So according to my point of view, most of her energy is misspent or wasted.

Karl is like me, as is Noah, essentially lazy. I want to have a good time, to enjoy myself, to be unburdened and without cares, to have the gift of each day in which to play—my writing. It is sometimes necessary for me to be alone for long periods; it is even more important for me over the long haul to have a constant buffer about me against random loneliness.

Foumi is still on a tear. This morning I did the laundry, the dishes, and cleaned our room, while Karl vacuumed the living room and the den. How much work Foumi actually does around the house! Yet she was still railing at me. This time it was about how I never helped her career as a painter or a writer. How could I have? I could have taken her paintings from gallery to gallery, she says. Did she take my work from publisher to publisher, from producer to producer, I argue. But this is *your* country, she says. I can't help that, I counter. Then let's go live in Japan, she says. We did, I reply, but we came back. And so it goes on, wave after wave of frustration, washing over both of us.

8

I screwed up again. Foumi was working with Noah at his sorting exercises when he tore out of his room. I had just taken in the laundry and as he was about to pass me, I loaded his arms with it. He immediately did an about-face, running back into his room, dropping laundry as he ran. Foumi decided to make a situational adjustment to her teaching by telling Noah to put the laundry into the proper drawers. I screwed up by becoming impatient while he hemmed and hawed, and finally cuffed him on the neck. Then while Foumi was reminding me that I should not punish Noah just because his brain could not problem-solve and I, in turn, was reminding her that she was the one who had given his brain the particular problem to solve, Noah, increasingly frustrated and angry, ended up scratching and pinching himself. It's always as much a no-win situation with Foumi as it is with Noah. I was wrong. I am guilty. I shouldn't have gotten involved with them. Damn the laundry!

Karl has been home all weekend, grounded because of his math lie, and I must say, it's been nice having him around the house. He reads books, he indulges in adult conversation. That's because he has nothing else to do. All his friends are at the beach. He's so bored he's actually lovable. He even offered me a stick of gum. Spearmint.

So I drowsed away this Sunday afternoon with guilt on my mind and spearmint gum in my mouth. The taste of my youth. The gum that baseball-player cards came with before bubble gum became the rage. That tart, sticky taste that reaches all the way back into the throat. My madeleine cakes that remind me of summer in Malden when I was a boy and an afternoon could last forever.

June 12, 1978

Since Karl's been grounded he's been an admirable fellow, doing all his homework. Last night I enjoyed listening to him and Foumi work on his math while I read a collection of John O'Hara's letters. What struck me particularly was a letter of advice to his younger brother who also wanted to become a writer. O'Hara urged him to write every day, even if only in a journal, reminding him that we remember Samuel Pepys but not who was king at the time.

Which sends me to these pages. But what else to record? That both Noah and a mockingbird were up all last night, Noah's song disturbing me while the mockingbird's kept Foumi awake? That this morning Foumi and I spoke for the nth time of starting a residential school or simply finding a place run by others even if we have to return to the East? That this afternoon, after cutting my hair short, my barber told me I now look more "presentable"? His word. But also the word my mother always used to use.

June 14, 1978

Noah had a toilet accident in school. Which could be a sign that he's coming down with a summer cold. That's all we need. Because the way others with a cold sneeze, Noah shits.

June 15, 1978

I picked up my menace and Niko at day-care and then Karl at his French lesson. At the long light at the Pacific Coast Highway, Noah suddenly turned on Karl and attacked him, biting his hands and pulling his hair, while burrowing into him with his own body. Karl was a helpless mess of tears and shouts, his excitement only serving to further upset Noah. "Next time," cried Karl as he finally extracted himself, "I'll take the bus!"

I had been thinking of buying a new car. Oh how I would like to get a cozy fun-to-drive sports car, a Mazda RX-7, for example.

But I guess I'll have to settle for another station wagon, even bigger than the compact one I have now, because of Noah. He requires a lot of room, he likes to be given a wide berth. Whoosh! There goes my sports car.

Because of Proposition 13 we have to worry about the future of our day-care center. I read in the paper this morning that the Assembly Ways and Means Committee has voted to reduce the state mental health program from $82 million to just $12 million. Which means, in all likelihood, we'd fall into that $70 million cut. After all, crazy kids who have no speech can't be expected to cry out too loudly in protest.

June 18, 1978

I fathered away Sunday morning, waking earlier than Foumi and preparing breakfast for both of the kids. Then I took Noah for a short walk, but he vigorously balked at the idea, pinching and complaining every step of the way. Karl, sullenly moping about the house, was no great joy either.

June 19, 1978

I was furious yesterday. The shooting script for "Lovey" arrived and the best scene is gone. It is almost as if they're trying to make it into the story of an unmarried Special Education teacher now. I was still steaming even after I showed the revised script to Foumi and she said it wasn't so bad, that the ending was still effective and that the whole script still made the point that education was necessary for special kids. So why fight it? It's only television. Show business. There is no way for a writer to get involved in theater, film, or television and not find himself in show business. I should consider my rage vented, save my energy, and move on to my next project. Any writing requiring the frequent use of the tab key, I keep telling myself, is not really writing.

Karl, too, came home from school upset. It seems he did not get his school yearbook because he was "talking" in class. He also discovered that he would not be in stagecraft next year, which bothered him a great deal. He said it did not matter but tears escaped his eyes. Evidently, the stagecraft teacher had signed the permission slip, admitting him to stagecraft for next year, and then decided to withdraw the permission. I told Karl to ask him for an explanation.

Only Noah saved the day—if not the night—for us as family. Last night was a full moon and he barely slept. But this morning he was in a good mood and after he returned from day-care he was still cheerful. At least he hadn't received any disquieting news during the day that he knows about.

June 20, 1978

A depressing day for Foumi. A Japanese publisher turned down her novel. It's hard enough to live in a foreign land. It's even harder when your own land seems to reject you. My heart went out to Foumi. So I stayed around the house, did the shopping, helped cook dinner, and picked up Noah at day-care.

June 21, 1978

I spoke with Karl's stagecraft teacher over the phone. He told me he had decided that he did not want Karl in stagecraft because he "fooled around" too much. (Sometime, I fear, in the future of our republic, a child will be executed after being found guilty of the heinous crimes of "talking in class" and "fooling around." Which is why I'm against capital punishment.)

I agreed with him that Karl often acted immaturely and his behavior evidenced it. But I also told him how much Karl liked stagecraft and that school would loom as a bleak experience for him without it. The teacher then said he might have a spot for Karl in his class for the spring semester of next year. But I am not in the movie business for nothing. I wanted something up front. I asked for the first ten weeks of the fall semester with Karl on probation during that period. But oh no, the teacher said, he had tried that with a kid this year and it hadn't worked out. Then I said that I had an idea: I would monitor Karl's behavior this summer and if it struck me as too immature I would let the teacher know. He agreed to that, and I got Karl back into the class.

Once more I've bailed out the kid. It's almost a habit. I worry about him though. Because in the future I won't always be around to do it.

I bought Noah a new pair of pajamas yesterday. He looked sensational in them when he went to bed last night. This morning he still looked well in them—except for the collar, which he had completely chewed away. But by the time Noah had finished breakfast, the pajamas looked as if he had been wearing them for a hundred years.

June 23, 1978
This morning I managed to get over to Karl's school and look at what is called his Cumulative—or Permanent—Record. There is nothing bad on his junior high school record other than his grades. His counselor, as she pored over the record with me, remarked that with his intelligence he certainly should be doing better than C work.

The comments of his grade-school teachers were all good—except for his sixth-grade teacher, who if I remember correctly was his candidate for wishful death. The man evidently reciprocated Karl's feelings in part but not in degree. He wrote: "Disruptive behavior, hostile, not working up to his capacity." Karl's other teachers all seemed to have liked him.

The message about Karl is always the same. And now that he will be entering the ninth grade it is more pertinent than ever: He can do well if he applies himself.

On the educational front I also finally spoke to the state official in charge of licensing private schools. The chief stumbling block, if we were to launch one, would be in getting the proper staffing. We would require a teacher with a Severely Handicapped credential to be on our payroll even before we had a payroll, so to speak. I'm not as anxious to start a school as Foumi is, because of the paperwork. And then if you hire someone to handle the paperwork and someone else just because they have the proper credential, before you know it you wind up running a mini-institution. So you're back to square—or circle—one.

A crew from "60 Minutes" has left us, having shot over six hours of film which they'll edit down to fourteen minutes. I did not do well in the interview with Dan Rather yesterday. Karl told me so and I sensed it myself. Foumi felt she had not done well either. We were both perhaps a little too intense to make the points we wanted to make.

Karl, the reluctant scene stealer, perhaps came off best in his interview. He was very media cool and I'm sure they'll use every foot of him. I'll also have to buy fireworks for a Fourth of July shoot-off as a payoff for his cooperation.

But the surprise about the whole experience is that it seems to have been good for Noah; he thrived under the attention. He was stimulated by the presence of new elements in the house. It reminded me that somehow we should all get away together.

Noah was screaming and pulling my hair as I tried to dress him. He was trying to tell me that the cat was in his room. But I did not see the cat hiding under a chair until he finally let go of my hair. I then put the cat out and immediately became angry with Karl. He had observed the whole scene but had not bothered to identify the cat as the cause of Noah's discomfort. Karl whelped back that no one had asked him to. And it was back to live action at the Greenfelds this morning.

I must say, in immediate retrospect, I have great respect for the professionalism with which "60 Minutes" operated. That they succeeded in getting us to cooperate with them in the first place surprises even me.

What happened was this: A few months ago, Imre Horvath, who identified himself as one of their segment producers, called. He was very cool and laid-back, saying he had heard of Noah and was interested in possibly visiting us. No way, Foumi said.

Imre called again a few days later saying he was still interested. And kept checking in with us every week or so. Gradually, we felt we knew him. And one day, when he had me on one extension and Foumi on the other, earnestly explaining our family situation and all the special problems engendered by a Noah, he suddenly interjected that what we had just done in effect was all that "60 Minutes" would want us to do.

And a few weeks later he appeared at our doorstep. He was in town, he was on his way back from Seattle where he had been shooting a fire department, and he thought he would just stop by and say hello. A big disheveled Hungarian with a fiery red Solzhenitsyn beard who had studied to be a medievalist but somehow wound up first a film editor and then a segment producer, he collapsed in our kitchen complaining of a terrible earache and began to explain his job. He was one of some dozen and a half segment producers. That many were necessary to produce the 120 to 140 segments that comprised a "60 Minutes" season. Since each segment took at least six weeks to prepare, if a producer could get eight completed, he was doing well. And one of the reasons he had dropped in was to see how we were, au naturel, without the lens. We reminded him that we had not agreed to anything but he discounted that, saying he had also come because he wanted to establish a comfortable and trusting relationship with us. And because of his quick intelligence and fine sense of humor it wasn't difficult for him to do so. He visited our day-care center, had a Sunday brunch with us, and we laughed a lot together.

In fact, when he called us after his return to New York and said his ear was no longer troubling him, it was as if a sick relative had called in with the news that he was better. We really felt warmly toward him. But not warmly enough to grant him the five days of shooting he requested. We told him we'd give him four, a long weekend beginning with Friday and ending with Monday, preferably at the end of this month. We also limited the time that could be spent at our day-care center. We didn't want him to interfere with our other kids in any way. Imre assured us that he would be coming on tiptoes with a specially selected crew of three, the cameraman, assistant cameraman, and sound man. They would understand that we went barefoot about our house, that we would not tolerate smoking, and above all that we did not want to upset Noah unduly. If he did appear to be upset at any time, all bets were off. Imre agreed.

Meanwhile it turned out it was Karl who was most upset during the days before their coming. "Why do I have to be on '60 Minutes'? Just because I have a brain-damaged brother?" he said, repeating his old argument. "You should do something good to earn the right to be on television." But this time I had an answer ready for him. "Not necessarily," I pointed out, "look at Nixon."

Last Friday morning at nine o'clock two Lincoln Continentals drove up to our house. First, Imre entered the house and asked us how we wanted the crew introduced into the situation. We said, one at a time. So at fifteen-minute intervals they came into the house: Greg, the cameraman; Jim, the sound man; and Vic, the assistant. They proceeded to film Noah and me walking out our doorway. Then Greg got in alongside Noah and Jim lay in the back of my station wagon as I picked up Niko and drove the kids to the day-care center. There they filmed the arrival of the other kids and some of their first activities. I drove to my office while they returned to the house to film the rest of Foumi's morning, her straightening out things and working away at her own book. At noon I picked up Foumi and we went to lunch in Westwood with the lady friend of a writer friend in from Connecticut.

In the afternoon they filmed me walking to my office, making an entry into this journal, and then trying to work on my movie assignment. Afterward, since I had to shop at the local supermarket, they decided to shoot me there. While they were setting up, a man came up to them and said: "You ought to film the price of peaches, that's a disgrace." A lady in passing observed, "Good! Someone's finally doing an exposé of this market." If the camera is a drain it is also certainly a lure.

And a drug, too, as numbing as it can be exhilarating. By the time they filmed us at dinner in the evening I had completely forgotten that I was wired with a mike on my chest and a small FM transmitter in my back pocket. I had been wired, in fact, since early morning.

The Saturday shooting schedule consisted of another visit to the day-care center in the morning. Then they—and we—were off until they returned in the late afternoon to film dinner. (Karl tried to play the spoiler. He constantly referred to the camera's presence while I tried to avoid any confrontation with him by repeating the old standby: "We'll talk about it later.") After dinner, with the crew still around, Foumi gave Noah his bath, we cut his nails and put him to bed, and then the family relaxed, sprawling before the TV set to watch W. C. Fields. I don't know about Foumi and Karl, but I was immensely tired even though I had done little all day.

On Sunday they focused on Foumi's paintings, which adorn our walls, my walking with Noah, and Karl biking off to visit a friend. When he returned with his friend, Warren, they also filmed them as they played with firecrackers in our backyard, and Foumi as she put Noah through his sorting exercises.

What Foumi does is this: She has drawn pictures of various flowers, birds, and animals on little cards. And then she asks Noah to sort them according to color or category. She also has him sort various sizes of screws and different objects according to shape or color. He is lazy but he does have the ability to execute these tasks with an amazing and casual quickness. But usually he dallies, often he protests vehemently. However, with the "60 Minutes" crew around he behaved beautifully. It was as if he's always wanted a four-man crew to record his skills.

On Monday Dan Rather would arrive. Naturally, the crew preceded him to set up. I played a joke on them, greeting them in a woman's wig that Foumi once had bought so Noah would have hair other than hers to pull at. And we decided I would play the same camp joke on the straitlaced Rather. When the bell rang announcing Rather's arrival I swished to the door, still wearing the wig, and opened it. Immediately, his mouth dropped. But I couldn't keep the joke going very long—nor did I want to. I removed the wig and shook his hand in solemn welcome. Still the expression on his face had been priceless.

For two hours Rather interviewed us. Now I knew that on television one has to be very cool and low-key. But it was hard not to be myself, sitting on my chair, in my own living room, after an hour of chatting, notwithstanding the glare of the camera lighting. So I just talked too much and too excitedly. I am sure that I did not come off well.

In fact, it was only when we did the "reversals," Greg shooting over my shoulder at Rather while he rapidly repeated the questions he had already asked us, that I realized exactly what I should have answered.

Karl, though, did much better. Rather relaxed with him, sitting on the carpet beside him, and set up an easy camaraderie. Karl was simple and honest. When Rather asked him what his feelings about Noah were, Karl admitted they were "mixed." Karl further stated his disinclination to appear before the camera but he knew "it was good for other families with kids like Noah."

After Karl's interview, the crew took one last shot of Rather,

Noah, and me walking along the cliff. As Noah pranced ahead, Rather and I talked of books and things, and, of course, Noah. Rather struck me as a straight guy, who may lack the fine cutting edge of a sense of humor, but instead does ooze a kind of American old-boy-down-home honesty. His concern for Noah seemed genuine.

He also earned my sympathy—or, at least, empathy. Until last weekend I had never before realized what an energy drain the lens was. When Rather told me he received 3,500 fan letters a week, I was surprised. But I soon understood the reason: Many of my neighbors were out and waving to him as he prepared to leave.

One of the questions Rather had asked me was if I ever had the urge to just go, to walk out of the family. That evening I did. It was time to call it a wrap. We had taken down the addresses of each member of the crew and said good-bye to them, like classmates scattering at the end of a spring semester. I was standing outside our door talking to Rather as the crew went back into the house to say good-bye to Foumi. I turned to Rather and told him this was one of those times I wanted to take off. He shook his head knowingly. Soon they were all in the cars, a three-car Lincoln Continental convoy all loaded down with equipment, while I waved after them, calling out, "Take me along!"

I walked back into our house and sat down to a late dinner with Foumi and Karl. I squirmed in my seat for a moment. I felt comfortable—yet strange—without a transmitter in my back pocket. I missed the camera, the heightened sense of being it induced. But I missed even more the warmth of four additional helpful presences in our house.

So did Noah. Without the photo flood bulbs glowing from our lamps, the house must have looked dim to him as he walked about from room to room, looking for the presences that were now missing. I think the experience has been good for him: the constant sense of purposive activity, the constant stimulation provided by new people. I only hope the TV report also proves helpful for other families such as ours.

June 29, 1978

Karl and I went to Culver City for his "60 Minutes" cooperation payoff. But the firework stands were not yet open. We'll have to go another day. Karl was disappointed and showed it. And I was disappointed in the way he showed it. As if it were my fault.

Now that the "60 Minutes" invasion is over I realize how well we all behaved before the camera. If there were fights they were sotto voce and almost refined. We helped each other not only in caring for Noah but in performing our other chores. We weren't automatically bad mannered to each other. Perhaps one of the reasons the lens so tired us is that we were so energetically monitoring our usual rotten conduct toward each other.

I still regret how badly I came off. Usually when I'm in a TV studio for an interview I'm very much aware of the time—all those clocks before me—and the fact that there are a very few minutes. I make my answers short and pithy. I am aware of what my attitude should be: Cool. Laid back. Quiet. Restrained. My voice well modulated. I do not pick my nose or scratch my balls. But Monday, within the confines of my own living room—even if I was wearing their mike and looking into their cameras, it was still my chair in my living room in my house—I became a blustery, loud, assertive, talkative nose picker and ball scratcher. I did not have that edge of control so necessary for the tube. I know I'm not an actor but that's still no excuse for me to come across as a fool on national television. Fortunately, my family—including Noah—redeemed me.

This morning Karl had asked me if he could have dinner at his friend Erich's house because it was Erich's birthday. Which reminded me. In two days Noah will be twelve years old.

I often wonder what would have happened if we had had another child after Noah? In what way would our attitude toward Noah have differed? I now think that it might have been good for us in the long run. It would have made it possible for us to give Noah up—and give up on Noah—a lot more easily and a lot sooner. But then I realize such conjecture is all academic. We just couldn't have handled another baby and Noah at the same time. Still, I would like to have had another baby. Someday, all too soon, Karl will be leaving us. And I don't want to be left with just Noah.

June 30, 1978

It's a week ago today since we first faced the cameras of "60 Minutes" and I still wake up at night recalling everything I should have said about the so-called autistic condition, all the insightful comments I could have made about the state of Special Education, all the cogent attacks I could have levied against the psychogenic establishment—in short, that I should have acted like a politician saying whatever I wanted to say instead of responding to the actual questions. But I'm not a politician, so that was that.

Tomorrow is Noah's birthday. We could have had him celebrate it in school this morning. Instead we will celebrate it at the day-care center tomorrow. I'll bring a carrot cake and apple juice. Twelve years old. And he looks it too—except for his brain.

July 1, 1978

Last night a girl who is a friend—and just a friend—called and I spent a long time on the phone with her. When I finally hung up, Foumi was furious with me. In fact, she was so jealous and angry, that she went to sleep in the den. After eighteen years of marriage I can't always understand her but I do know she is a green-eyed tigress when it comes to jealousy. I'm possessive too. So I'm fortunate that she does nothing to set me off and drive me crazy. I simply must abide her jealousies over my time and my involvement. They're worth the fact that I'll never have to play Othello.

July 2, 1978

Noah's bad behaviors are returning. He fights when we try to brush his teeth and he has been having tantrums whenever he is unhappy. There must be a way to teach him an easier—and more acceptable—means of communication. But then I've already said that a thousand times.

Still I enjoyed yesterday, just lounging around the house with the family this holiday weekend, without any foreign intruders. The only time I left the house was to go shopping with Karl for his fireworks. And it was worth doing. Call it bribery, call it payoff, but he's been a joy ever since.

July 5, 1978

I ended the holiday with a runny nose, Foumi has a cold, and Noah isn't feeling too well either, scratching and pinching, so we kept him home from summer school this morning. But Karl enjoyed a safe Fourth, blowing up his thank-you fireworks at his friend Erich's house where he slept over after enjoying their picnic yesterday. Poor Noah. Because of his ailments he could not go to the picnic. So he missed the child joys of Fourth-of-July hot dogs and watermelon and corn on the cob. Not me, though. I put in a brief appearance and managed to eat my seasonal share.

July 6, 1978

I'm the one who's really sick today but I took Noah to school anyway. Then I went to a department store and bought a color TV set, a small-screen Sony. Foumi has been against color television because of the radiation danger. But I've decided that it's time we succumbed to the technological future—or present. Besides, Noah might be more apt to watch color than black and white. Which he is largely indifferent to. I picked a small screen because I thought it would give a clearer picture. I also wanted a set that would be light enough to move from room to room.

July 7, 1978

Last night we watched our new color television. Karl complained that the picture was too small. Foumi decided the set was too heavy. Noah didn't look at the screen at all.

July 8, 1978

We're all sick. I have a cold, Karl is in bed, and Foumi, complaining of dizziness, is among the walking moaning. Only Noah seems healthy. And happy. Another tooth fell out yesterday. I hope that explains all the pinching and screaming he's been doing all week.

One thing worth his screaming about is the fact that his school does not have swimming this year. The pool pump broke, and the penny-watching director is not about to fix it.

Foumi worries that Karl will waste the summer. But what's wrong with wasting the summer—especially when you're a Tom Sawyer–Huck Finn thirteen and a half. Perhaps Karl can discover something worthwhile that he really wants to do for himself. I notice he has begun to do some writing on his own. But

Foumi's still concerned about his seeming aimlessness. I'm not. I am a laissez-faire person and, I assume, so is he.

Right now, for example, I should be working on my movie assignment. After all, I have to finish it by the end of this month. Or next month. Or by the end of some month anyway. But I'm playing around with some notes for a novel instead.

July 9, 1978

We spent the day in developmental disability. Our friend, Jessie Furukawa, a Special Education consultant with the state, was in town. She visited our day-care center and afterward we had lunch with her. Jessie wisely observed that Noah should be taught in smaller time spans. She also encouraged us to start a school.

There certainly is a need. A humane need. Jessie told us that OCC uses such aversives as pinching kids beneath their nails and putting others out in the hot sun on a scorching day. She also mentioned that at another behaviorist-run school upstate about which we had previously heard only good reports, drugs were used as medications; and that as an aversive some kids were forced to stay in bed all weekend long. We had been considering those schools as eventual possibilities for Noah.

A new possibility has also presented itself. In the mail was a letter from an Israeli psychic healer announcing his presence in Los Angeles. Perhaps I ought to give him a shot. What do I have to lose? Except my time, my money, and my sanity.

July 10, 1978

I woke up this morning thinking of two and a half novels I might write. I had been reading *Scott and Ernest* by Matthew Bruccoli before falling asleep. Fitzgerald only wrote two and a half good novels: *Gatsby*, *Tender*, and *The Last Tycoon*. Hemingway also only wrote two and a half good novels: *The Sun Also Rises*, *A Farewell to Arms*, and *To Have and Have Not*. I am fifty years old. Certainly, I can write two novels before I die. And I'm sure I have another half of a novel in me. It's something to dream about.

Meanwhile, since the first publisher in Japan to see her work has passed on it, Foumi's dream of literary success has been temporarily shot down. So I must encourage her, remind her that one turndown is nothing in the life of any worthwhile work.

At Noah's school there is a little girl, a beautiful black girl, who can't be more than nine or ten. Her name is La Tanya and she is there just for the summer. Whenever La Tanya calls out "Noah!" he comes to her and touches her hand. It is lovely to see. Adele, Noah's teacher, says it is the first time he has related to another child. It takes a girl, a beautiful girl with a beautiful name, every time.

9

Foumi, still upset over the rejection of her novel, is now making woman's lib noises, accusing me of not cooking, not cleaning, not helping about the house. Then how come she was able to finish her book? I shout back. And then we both shout at Karl.

I was at him this morning because he has the pink-eyed symptoms of conjunctivitis as a result of his long, tough hair falling into his eyes. I urge him to have it cut shorter, but oh how I wish I had hair like that. Noah also has long hair, but his is much thinner, the way mine once was. The rest of Noah is getting fatter. I've told Foumi to stop allowing him three-bowls-of-rice dinners. Otherwise, we'll have a tantrum Buddha on our hands.

July 14, 1978

This morning Karl came with me when I took Noah to school. Together we watched La Tanya pull Noah about in a wagon, Noah accepting her livery services most contentedly. I think we should try to recruit La Tanya for our day-care center. Kids can help cure each other as surely as addicts and alcoholics do.

July 15, 1978

Foumi has hired a credentialed teacher to work at our day-care center full time in August. Which means we can further explore the possibility of opening a school in the fall.

July 16, 1978

Foumi's arthritis is bothering her: It's even hard for her to lift her arm above her head. And I suddenly have the nightmare vision of Foumi suffering from some great infirmity and my having to deal with both her and Noah. There simply is no room for another tragedy on my agenda.

July 17, 1978

In the morning when I enter Noah's room and pull back the curtains and he stretches out sleepily, yawns, and looks up at me with half-opened eyes, and it is as if he has the power of speech but is still not wakeful enough to use it, I long to hug and kiss him because he seems so refreshingly normal. But then when I say, "Good morning!" and he does not reply, I wake up to reality again and together we start another day.

July 18, 1978

I'd really been feeling sorry for Karl this family vacationless summer. But last night he came into our room while I lay in bed reading and announced, "Today was the most fun at the beach ever." He then showed me some of the miniature painting he has been doing on his Dungeons and Dragons medieval figures, some kind of craze that has been occupying him lately. "You may yet wind up a Jewish painter," I told him. "What's that?" he asked. "A starving artist?" I'm really afraid that Karl might wind up a writer just like me. Perhaps just because of me. Writing is not the kind of profession one wishes on an offspring.

My other offspring has the pot of a man of forty rather than the flat-ribbed stomach of a boy of twelve. But then we've been told that once children like Noah begin to age, they age quickly, going from forever babies into premature old men. Which is one way of avoiding the pangs of adolesence.

July 20, 1978

Noah has a stomach cold of sorts. He's pinching a lot and just can't seem to go to the bathroom lately, and it's not for a lack of trying.

Karl is staying up until midnight, reading, talking, listening to music, watching television. Last night Foumi and I entertained him with tales of our ocean trip to Japan in 1962. He loved it, sitting around the living room with us after midnight, an almost-adult talking with his parents as an equal.

July 21, 1978

Driving Noah to school this morning I studied him in profile seated beside me. He had that psychopathic mean, angry look, the look I cannot stand, the look that bodes badly for his future.

At school this morning he went straight to La Tanya and sat down in a wagon until she began to pull him around. Noah really likes her. His first girlfriend. Adele said he'll do anything La Tanya tells him to do. I wish La Tanya would tell Noah to start talking. But that's beyond even her.

I've been thinking again of looking into the Institute for Human Development, the Philadelphia-based group that champions patterning. The theory behind patterning is that enforced creeping and crawling on hands and knees activates the brain cells responsible for normal neurological development. Teams of volunteers are required for the effort. But I really don't want people trooping through my life, running my house as if it were a church social. Also, at this point Noah is simply too big for patterning. Communication rather than movement is his problem, and I still wonder exactly how much he can understand and not understand verbally. All I know is he is afflicted with an absence of will and with terminal laziness.

July 22, 1978

Karl sits around the house reading a great deal, Noah is in a finger-pinching mood, Foumi complains that she is tired, and Grandma writes that she'll be returning in ten days. I am not sure I look forward to that. She takes up space, the use of the den becomes restricted when she is here, and even Noah needs that area to walk and bounce around in. What am I saying? That little old lady will always be welcome. As long as she does not speak English. Across the language gulf we can be completely indifferent to each other.

July 23, 1978

Last night a young friend of ours, a TV director, just thirty, was over for dinner. Afterward he played D and D with Karl. That is some sort of game that evokes a magical world of imaginary lands teeming with medieval fancies. As I watched them play together I realized the advantages of having a young father. Which Karl does not have. I am simply too old to play too many games with him. But at thirty our young friend is closer to Karl's age than he is to mine.

July 24, 1978

At his school this morning Noah seemed to be in such a good mood. Then he suddenly blew, pulling hair, taking off his shoes, banging his head against the grass, even attacking La Tanya. No matter how we slice it the future looks grim for him.

And the present isn't treating Foumi too kindly. She complains that her "brain is tired," she has arthritic pains, and she cannot sleep well. She needs a vacation. But then we all do.

Karl in particular has had a busy summer educationally: Math from the Japanese place we send him to. French from his private lessons. History through his own reading. And English from the weekly writing assignments he had to turn in to me.

July 25, 1978

Helmet day at the Greenfelds: Karl has been lobbying for a new skateboard. I agreed that I would advance him the money—on the condition that he would wear a helmet when skateboarding. He rebelled against the idea. He was even further upset when I added that I would expect him also to wear the helmet when he was riding his bike. That did it. He exploded at lunch. And was on the verge of tears for the rest of the day. But I can't help it if I'm head shy. Who wants to chance having another brain-injured son in the house?

July 26, 1978

The great helmet controversy rages on obscuring all else. But I have agreed to look at skateboard magazines and read about the efficacy of helmets. I'm sure they have to help.

Unexpectedly, a first cousin of mine, who is just a few years older than I, dropped by. He was in from the East helping his daughter get settled in a new job in San Bernardino County. I hadn't seen him for years. He looked good even though he is just over a prostate operation. Which he told me is a family disease. It seems my maternal grandfather died of a prostate cancer. Tell me the disease and I'll immediately contract the symptoms. Last night I had to get up to piss three times.

July 27, 1978

I awoke at seven. Noah was up earlier but when he began to bang on the piano I got out of bed, served him breakfast, and prepared his lunch. But then somehow it was all as if I had started my day at eight o'clock anyway. I didn't accomplish a mite more. Which only proved to me again that one should always linger in bed as long as possible.

There is a sitter service, theoretically set up to help parents of special children and bankrolled for that reason by the state. We thought we might use it. But the service gave us a difficult time when we asked to interview any potential sitter. Another rip-off of the developmentally disabled.

So Karl took care of Noah last night, earning a few brownie points. Noah himself helped clear the table after dinner. As usual, the sponge, which he hates to use, has disappeared. I have a hunch he threw it away.

July 28, 1978

At school this morning La Tanya again pulled Noah about in a wagon. I tried to see if it was possible for Noah to switch roles and pull her instead. But no deal. He would have none of it.

And today when I tried to end a jocular punch in a love tap, Karl really let me have it. I know he is still annoyed because of the helmet controversy. But he is also always moody and sensitive and shy when it comes to any gesture on my part that might be construed as affection. I can understand. I was like that with my father. But I still forget.

Foumi still talks of starting a school, establishing a group residence. And I guess all that's down the line. But meanwhile I live my Peter Pan dream, enjoying the Noah who will never grow up. I mentioned the whole business of living without a future to a friend. "But you have to have hope," he said. I'm not so sure. I think you have to have guts.

I advanced Karl the money for a skateboard; he will pay it back to me gradually. But Foumi didn't like the idea. She thought he should have had to save up for it himself. But why defer the enjoyment? I want him to enjoy himself. Even if it means he knows his old man is a soft touch. I also bought him a helmet and gloves. But perhaps I should have made him pay for them too.

Karl believes everything evens out in the end—the ultimate solace of an unhappy youth. I'm sure Karl thinks that because of Noah. Still, it would be nice if things did even out for him. Because he does have a refreshing sense of humor. In the wake of the "60 Minutes" experience he and his friend Erich were discussing what would happen if a feature movie were to be made about our family. They decided that Noah would be changed into an eighteen-year-old majoring in geology, Foumi would be black and played by Diana Ross, and Karl would be a Vietnam vet who came back a paraplegic. "What about me?" I asked. "As for you," said Karl, "you'd be cut out of it."

Noah is not feeling well, clutching and pinching and having many tantrums. I suppose he has some sort of summer cold.

Karl, too, is unhappy. Because of my helmet edict. I read in today's paper that the director of the National Safety Council recommended helmets for skateboarders. So there it was, no two ways about it. Skateboarding is dangerous, and wearing a helmet will remind him of that.

But Karl says he would rather not skateboard than have to wear a helmet. I suspect that's because he's so concerned about what his peers might think. Well, if he's going to be that self-conscious, then he doesn't deserve to skateboard. He has to learn to rise above peer pressures in order to become an individual anyway.

August 2, 1978

I had lunch with a producer. He had a "concept." Nothing else. I have reached the age where I might as well work on my own "concepts." Why should I go dime-a-dancing down other people's streets? As Foumi says, this is the town where everyone wants someone else to work on implementing their own dreams. I'm old enough to noodle on my own dreams, thank you. The blank paper I stare at should be my own.

August 3, 1978

Karl and I drove to the airport to meet Grandma. Age shrinks a person, I know, but still how slight she seemed. Even smaller than when she left. But then according to her passport she'll soon be seventy-four.

Her grandson is twelve and still has growing pains. Or something. Noah's been having several tantrums a day. Foumi thinks it might be his teeth. I've given up thinking what it might be. I just know it isn't increasing my chances of having an old age at all.

August 4, 1978

Noah was up until one o'clock crying. The teeth? A sore throat? A congested nose? I gave him some congestion medicine and it seemed to work. He finally slept.

At breakfast Grandma was helpful. Soon Noah will be bigger than she is. Soon Noah will be bigger than all of us.

Having Noah has enabled me to cut off people. What I mean is this: I know that my relationship with Noah is terminal, one day I will have to send him away and then play the game with myself that he is dead. I have done that in recent years with friends who have betrayed me, with old lovers who have disappointed me.

Did I always have that tendency or do I do it now just for practice? Or has my whole life been a splendid preparation not for a writing career but for being Noah's father?

Do I still have guilt about Noah? Of course. I have guilt about Karl, too. Guilt and responsibility for both my children. In fact, guilt is responsibility that one does not always want to accept. But Noah wailing on and on into the last two nights—how long can I accept that?

I shall continue to search for treatments and cures. But I don't want any treatment that philosophically says: "Come and we'll show you what to do and you go home and do it; and then if it doesn't work, of course, it's all your fault—not ours." No thank you. If you have a treatment you have to do it. It is unfair to place the entire burden back on the parent. No parent, no family can gut it through alone. We need help.

For example, we were looking forward to a mini-vacation the week after next. We lined up a baby-sitter whom we like and trust. But she just called Foumi and said she couldn't make it. There goes our respite.

August 5, 1978

As I summarily refused to listen to any more helmet complaints last night, Karl said: "I can tell you haven't written all day because you're so irritable." The kid knows just where to get me.

Later, I began to think: What if Karl were to die suddenly because of some accident not involving a skateboard at all? How would I feel? I guess I would regret that I denied him the pleasure of skateboarding without a helmet. The kid does not need an advocate when dealing with schizophrenic me. But I still won't change the rule.

August 6, 1978

The Spastic Children's Foundation, where Noah stayed a few years ago, has said they would take him again for a week of respite. From experience we know they may not be the best place but at this point they're our only game in town. We need the vacation.

It was still dark this morning when I heard Noah give out with his new sound. It's no longer a high-pitched keening scream; now it's almost an animal roar. Deep from the throat. I think it's the roar of puberty.

I really noticed his increase in size when I took him swimming yesterday. I wasn't sure I could use the pool of a friend I usually take him to, so I called another friend. "Sure," he said, "anytime." "Okay," I black-joked but also really meant it, "one of these days I'll drown Noah in your pool." If I were to do Noah in, I have finally decided, it would be in a pool. I would take him out to the middle of the pool. In his life jacket or with a tube. Then I would take the life jacket or tube away from him. And split. And not look back. If I could.

I seem to have everything planned but the getaway.

The teacher with the Special Education credential whom Foumi hired just sits there. She's a big, fat oaf who does nothing. We'll have to get rid of her.

We'll also have to get away ourselves. Karl, of course, now says that he does not want to go anywhere. But Foumi has reminded me that Karl never wants to go anywhere. How can kids be so conservative and contrary at the same time?

Since the problem of Noah has been at the center of my life I have known fewer depressions. Is that because my life has become increasingly insulated, more heavily anchored down, with fewer options and even fewer choices? And does that leave me with a fuller—or less fulfilled—life?

My feelings about sending Noah off next week are so confused. Already I'm full of guilt. Why shouldn't we be able to take him with us? Just put him in the car and take him with us? Because then we wouldn't be getting away from him. Then there'd be no chance of our having any vacation at all. But doesn't he deserve a vacation, too?

August 13, 1978

Not one of the world's great Sundays. Took Noah swimming. Washed his hair. Tried to cut it. Noah went out of control and I hated him. I reacted too quickly when he grabbed at me and pinched. A mistake. Best to ignore him. But I couldn't. Perhaps he really is better off without me. Or perhaps he is as nervous as I am about his going into Spastic's tomorrow.

August 14, 1978

Noah recognized the Spastic Children's Foundation building immediately. And when we led him to the day room he squinted toward the television set and then found himself a couch over which to drape himself. Again I went through the Keon experience. That was the first time I took Noah, barely four years old, to a special school and realized that he fit into such an environment, that his place was among the handicapped and the grotesque. But still I always shiver the same shudder anew. This time Noah was in a world of wheelchairs and gurneys and walkers and crutches and canes and all manner of twisted legs and bent arms and constantly nodding heads. Not an easy sight for me to take no matter how inured I've become.

We left him there and went for the intake interview. Which was painless enough. We were greeted by the senior social worker as if we were old friends. Then she passed us on to a new and very sympathetic social worker for the paperwork. We warned her about Noah. She was sure they could handle him. She then went on to tell us that she herself had had a young son who suffered from violent seizures before dying a year ago. But, she smiled and sighed, she was fortunate that she did have another five-year-old son who was an abstract painting genius. She said she felt that the Lord had given her the afflicted son because He knew she was strong enough to deal with him. Foumi and I, of course, do not have God. Only faith in each other.

When we left the building neither Foumi nor I said good-bye to

Noah. We figured it would be better that way. For him. But not for us. We were both in tears when we got into the car for the ride home.

Later I called the Spastic Children's Foundation. Louise, the ward nurse, told me Noah was doing fine. "Trying to map the place out." She said he remembered being there before and was quiet. But we remembered his being there before too and were slightly disquieted.

August 21, 1978

Our trip began last Tuesday after we learned that Noah had spent a good first night away from home. So with Grandma staying behind to guard the nonexistent family jewels, we taxied to the airport, flew to San Francisco, and rented a car. Then we drove over to Sausalito.

On Wednesday we drove north through Marin County to Jenner. There we spent an afternoon and night at the windy Timber Cove Inn, where there was nothing to do and it was good to do nothing. The inn is situated on a strip of land that juts out into the ocean and the constant sea breeze reminds you that only boats belong in such a geography. But they served a very good dinner. So good that I had heartburn and thought during the night that I might be having a heart attack. (I have been having chest pains lately and should check them out.)

Thursday we continued driving in a leisurely way up the California coast through Sea Ranch to Mendocino. We stopped at the Heritage House, which was quiet and serene and very much like a deluxe version of the MacDowell Colony in New Hampshire where Foumi and I first met eighteen summers ago. Karl, of course, was bored. Mendocino seemed too mendacious—in a tourist sense—for me, too much of a stage set. I had planned on calling a writer there I knew who has an epileptic son. But I didn't because I did not want to think about Noah while we were away. I mean every time I thought of Noah it was with guilt. It was probably the same way with Foumi and Karl too. Because we rarely mentioned him.

On Saturday night in Eureka we did see a terrible movie, a really bad Pink Panther. But sitting in that movie house, with the local crowd that was so obviously enjoying it, I realized I was too old to ever write a really commercial movie. The audience consisted of people so young they could still munch from their over-brimming popcorn buckets with uncrowned teeth.

We flew home yesterday, Sunday, rented a car at the airport and drove over to the Spastic Children's Foundation to pick up Noah.

He was in almost the same position we had left him, sitting in his pajamas on a chair in the day room in front of the TV set obviously oblivious to what was blaring on it. Every once in a while he would casually turn toward the screen for a second, not so much to watch it but as if to see if it was still there. He himself looked like nothing less than some war refugee or death-camp survivor. And he seemed so much older, taller, thinner than just a short week ago.

Noah stood up when he saw me and then retreated to the back of the room, where he reached for a boy's nose and then touched a girl's hair. The girl kept coming after him, writhing in her crippled way. Noah did not seem to want to leave the room and for a moment I had the strong impulse to leave him there.

We had to urge Noah into the ward, where he lay down on his bed as if we had been asking him to go to sleep. Finally, slowly, we dressed him as the ward aide explained the reason he was in his pajamas: he had just been bathed and so it would have been silly to dress him again. Foumi wasn't so sure. She also wondered if he had been medicated.

In the car he was quiet as we drove home. But at the first familiar sights of the Pacific Coast Highway he began to chirp. And when Grandma opened the front door of our house he ran to the love seat in the living room and bounced happily upon it. And at dinner he kept wanting more and more milk. It was good to be home. It was better having Noah with us.

August 22, 1978

Noah was calm last night, just chewing his shirt, but still celebrating his homecoming. I tried to take him for a walk after dinner. He put one foot out the door and then ran back into the house. The house across the street is being remodeled and perhaps that upset him. Otherwise, he was quiet. He probed me with the flat of his hand when I bathed him, but I kept my temper. I have to keep calm with Noah. Not provoke him. He never means badly. I must treat him—as I must treat Karl—as a creature his age, his tantrums and crying notwithstanding.

Karl has let me know that he should not have gone on our vacation and I have let him know that we should not have taken him. But he also knows how to joke with me using the psychogenic vocabulary: "I am hostile to you because you are not loving enough," he said. "You make me feel aggressive."

August 23, 1978

Noah remains in a good mood. Hasn't had a single tantrum yet. I think he's afraid of being sent back to the Spastic Children's Foundation. Or perhaps, with my new resolve, I'm less apt to excite him. He wants me to listen to him, I've decided, and I'm trying to.

August 24, 1978

Noah: Had his first tantrum since returning. But he does seem to have matured inordinately, or my perception of him has altered inordinately in the six days we were separated. He looks to me now more like someone on loan from an institution; he still has that stereotypical look of dazed acceptance, of energyless limbo, which he is just beginning to lose. And his hair still smells of institutions, that mix of old people and soap—or just old soap. His tantrums, his rages, I'm beginning to feel, are his life, his activities, every bit as much as the finger exercises I perform on this machine are mine.

Karl: With his long hair, he still has his good looks. But if his hair were cut short, I wonder. Perhaps one day his good looks may desert him. Never having had good looks, I can't identify with the problem.

Foumi: Her novel has been rejected again. Her chances for publication diminish. I think I will have to take care of Noah by myself and send her back to Japan for a few weeks so she can give it her best shot, peddling personally. God knows, it's so hard for any unknown to get published anywhere. If getting her book published first in English would help, then I could go over any rough translation she does and, if necessary, give it a rewrite.

America: I don't think any of our presidents can withstand the extended glare of the media spotlight anymore. Carter now looks as vulnerable as Johnson did in his second term. And there isn't even a Vietnam. Just a general disappointment in his smiling nothingness.

Noah is sick this morning, Karl irritable, and Foumi still under the weather because of her book. I gave Noah some children's cold medicine and made him drink a lot of water and juice. And while Foumi and Karl have been general pains in the neck, Noah just lies on our couch quietly, like some wounded animal who has suddenly been struck down but still manages to retain his essential dignity.

My friend sweated out a hard year waiting for the final sentence to come down on his son. And now he is in a state of shock. Somehow he had thought that his son would beat the rap for participating in an armed robbery. But the kid, now eighteen, will have to serve hard time, a year in the state reformatory. Paternity, as I have learned, is a losing proposition.

Foumi felt bad too, but she reacted with black humor: "I wish somebody would take our son off our hands for a year."

I once told a neurotic friend I did not have time for his childish problems because I had a son who would never grow up. "Then you should feel all the more sympathy toward me," he replied. "My father also has a son who will never grow up: me."

Parents and kids. Kids and parents. What else is there? Except for parents and parents. And kids and kids.

Noah was up in the middle of the night, screaming and crying. I brought him to the bathroom to urinate but he couldn't. I gave him a cup of water but he would not drink it. I cleaned his nostrils but he was still beside himself. Finally, I put on earplugs and went back to sleep fitfully. This morning Noah had a very hard bowel movement.

At breakfast Karl was telling me a joke while I read in the

newspaper about Charles Boyer's death, at his own hand as they say. His own son too had committed suicide—at the age of twenty-one. I looked over to Karl as he was delivering the punch line, his eyes shining in anticipation of my pleasure. For a quick moment I wondered what it would do to my life if Karl were to suddenly die out of turn. Then I tried to laugh at his joke without shivering.

August 29, 1978

Noah had his worst tantrum since returning home from the Spastic Children's Foundation. It was at dinner last night. He had either wanted more rice or more salad or more juice—I just don't know which—when he suddenly left the table and ran to our room, slapping himself and screaming. I did not worry. Usually he is careful not to do any great injury to himself. But soon I heard loud bouncing sounds. He was throwing the books in my nightstand bookcase all over the room. And then he began to rub his face hard into the rough carpet piling and strike his hands hard against the sides of his head. When he finally subsided— some thirty minutes later—the bridge of his nose was raw, the skin all friction-burnt away.

Noah is now twelve. In no time he will be sixteen, seventeen, the same age my friend's son was when he served as the wheelman on an armed robbery. And just as I have told my friend not to let his son's conviction and imprisonment seem a symbol of his own life, so too I must not allow the fate of Noah to become the meaning of my life. Every parent, of the normal and the abnormal, can give only so many years to an offspring. Eventually, even Noah has to be on his own. I cannot continually be responsible for him. The day will soon come when I simply must pass him on. Out of my life. Karl will leave my life and so too must Noah. There has to be some sort of statute of limitations on paternity and parenthood.

And then when Noah is finally gone, what will I be left with? My abiding love for Foumi. And my need to write. Hell, there can be a lot of meaning in my old life yet.

10

August 30, 1978

This morning we took Noah to Area D for his annual L.A. Unified School District classification. He was assigned to his current private school for the coming year. But we'll be free to look into any of the public school facilities if we choose.

The state hospitals might accept Noah but then he'd be put in a back ward and given nothing to do. Noah needs both educational and medical care at the same time, a hard parlay to root in.

August 31, 1978

All day Noah was constantly pinching and obviously unhappy. During dinner, there was one outburst after another, until he ran off to our room and rubbed his already skinned nose into the rug, scraping it back and forth. Finally, as we somehow managed to sit down to our dinners, it became quiet. Suspiciously so. I went to check and saw a trail of shit leading from our bedroom to our bathroom to the children's bathroom, big globs of it, and standing at the door to the children's bathroom was a naked, shit-smeared Noah. While Noah dug his fingers sharply into us, Foumi and I cleaned him. Then we spent a half hour applying ourselves to the shit-stained carpets. Noah had another tantrum before we gave him his bath and got him into bed, ourselves too exhausted even to finish dinner. The only solace of the evening lay in the fact that Karl was spared it: He was sleeping over at his friend Erich's house.

This morning we kept Noah home from school. Foumi is worried about his stomach. I'm worried about his fate—and ours. Through all this I've been trying to work. Yesterday I did a paltry page and a half of script. I doubt if I can do as much today.

September 2, 1978

What Noah needs now is perhaps some good old-fashioned behaviorist one-on-one. Because he simply is not shaping up. At least not with us. My hands are scarred with the pressings of his nails, the pinching of his thumbs.

Summer's end. I have had no summer.

September 3, 1978

We had lunch with a former aide who worked at our day-care center last fall. Now he's working at an institution for the emotionally disturbed in New Jersey. And he's disillusioned. The kids are thoroughly zonked out on Mellaril and Thorazine to make it easier for the staff. He lives with these kids in a dorm, spends the most time with them, and makes just a marginal salary. The professionals who spend the least time with them make the most and have the biggest say. George is angry because his textbooks and college courses never prepared him for the reality of working in the field. The reality, of course, is mostly failure. But failure does not sell. Truth is a very difficult commodity to unload. No one ever wants to hear it. Even I constantly push hope to myself, when hope, in this case, is essentially a lie. Perhaps the biggest illusion facing us is the illusion that we know beans about human behavior. We only know how to create new vocabularies about human behavior. We have no idea about what makes the brain tick. And our feigning knowledge instead of acknowledging our ignorance is destructive.

September 4, 1978

Karl does know how to break me up. We were watching the Jerry Lewis Muscular Dystrophy telethon when a bar owner called in, challenging all other bar owners to match his pledge. Karl then began: "I'm a Palestine terrorist. I'm hijacking a plane for muscular dystrophy. I challenge all my fellow terrorists to hijack a plane for Jerry's kids." And when a fellow writer friend called me this morning Karl handed me the phone, saying: "John's challenging all other writers to give to MD."

September 5, 1978

Noah lately has been irritable, insomniacal, and generally more irascible. Which always causes tension between Foumi and me because we each have our theories: It's his teeth. He has a cold. He has a sore throat. He's letting us know he didn't like Spastic's. It finally seems to me that living with Noah is like living in the midst of a never-ending insoluble mystery story, one in which clues forever keep dropping but inevitably lead nowhere.

September 6, 1978

At day-care yesterday Noah was in a chipper mood and jumped over the rope. Everyone was quite pleased with him. But it is something he was able to do years ago.

September 11, 1978

Noah continues to smile and be happy. So I'm happy and smiling. This morning when I entered the living room he hummed "Da dee" to me in greeting. And last night Foumi thinks she heard him say, "I want to go *nene* [to sleep]" in his high-pitched whine.

September 12, 1978

Karl returns to school today, Noah tomorrow. But then he's late at everything.

September 17, 1978

Noah is back to a tantrum every night. Most nights I treat him tenderly. Last night I was tough. I slapped him with a ruler. It worked. This morning, though, he was up early, raring to pinch.

I asked our doctor to write a Mellaril prescription for Noah. I don't plan to use it. But it wouldn't hurt having it around the house, as security. Noah had two tantrums last night. One before dinner because he was hungry. One after dinner because he had not received his dessert quickly enough.

I wrote a note for Karl. To get him into Typing. At least that course can help him in the long run. If only to become a company clerk if he ever has to go into the army.

September 20, 1978

Something happened the other night when Foumi and I went to the movies that gives me pause. In the cashier's window was this sign:

> General Admission $4.00
> Senior Citizens 3.50
> Children Under 11 . . . . 1.50

When the cashier asked me, "How many?" with a wise-guy impulse for some reason I said, "Two Senior Citizens." "How old are you?" she asked. "If it's any cheaper," I replied, "I'm under eleven." She pressed out two Senior Citizen tickets.

In the theater lobby Foumi elbowed me hard in the ribs. "Don't worry," I said, "the usher at the door will stop us." But the ticket taker blithely tore the tickets, handed me the stubs, and waved us in.

As we took our seats Foumi gave me a rib-cracking poke. "Never do that again!" she warned. I told her it was all because of her graying hair. She said it was my balding head. Neither of us paid much attention to the movie.

September 21, 1978

Last night we gave Noah Mellaril, just 10 milligrams, for the first time. And he did quiet down. I think he's been having tantrums because of the weather, the hot, dry Santa Anas blowing in from the desert.

Foumi is tired and despondent. We need help for the day-care center and can't seem to get any. We have just one more week in which to find another person. Otherwise we'll have to close down in October. I should pick up some of the slack, pitch in more. But I just can't work there these days. I'm really not very enamored of Noah lately. He greets me with a pinch of my arms or a clutch of my shirt, he averages two tantrums an evening, and wakes me with another one during the night.

They're making it difficult for me to get Karl into typing class. But I can deal with the school system a lot better than he can. As a parent I sometimes think I am taking advantage of Karl by imposing my will upon him. I mean, after all, he is no match for me. But the school system really bullies kids.

September 22, 1978

Nature is beginning to take its abnormal course. This morning I wrote to the Camphill school, a Rudolf Steiner facility in Pennsylvania, to find out about the possibilities of placing Noah there. Now is the time to think of sending him away. He simply isn't happy at home—or at school—anymore. He has a tantrum upon arriving home from school each day; he has a tantrum after dinner; and with a little bit of bad luck has another tantrum before sleep. Last night we even gave him Mellaril. We thought he had swallowed it and when he seemed to calm down Foumi even marveled at its efficacy. But this morning we found the little pill on the floor beside his bed.

I have been on the phone all morning to college employment offices seeking student help for our day-care center, and to Sacramento seeking state financial help for our day-care center. As matters stand now, the State of California is being impossible. Perhaps we should close down. The pressure is too much for Foumi. And I just don't have the time to shoulder my share of the burden. I have to make a living.

Unreconstructed Freudians are like religious zealots. They see everything in terms of their own vocabulary. And the vocabulary becomes an explanation unto itself. I've just finished reading a book about a feral child that kept me in a constant rage: A social worker gives love to that child, thus reawakening it, and they both live happily ever after. So I reread Annie Sullivan. She says in so many words, "Obedience before love." All our present-day would-be miracle workers also forget that Helen Keller was able to learn four or five words in Annie's very first day of teaching. Innate ability—rather than love—is the basic precondition of learning. Love is caring enough to teach obedience.

September 25, 1978

We've had a hot weekend, over 100 degrees, but we've been spared the heat of family squabbles. Foumi went to San Francisco with Grandma, Karl and I relaxed before the TV set watching football and baseball, Noah paraded about the house freely. I think the weekend was good for Foumi and Grandma, they both seemed to have enjoyed it. I know the boys and I enjoyed it without them.

September 26, 1978

I went home at noon bearing deli sandwiches, and lunch went well. But after lunch when Foumi decided to change Noah's pants he had a tantrum and bit her. I managed to quiet him down and left him in his room. But then Foumi went in there to ask him if he wanted some dessert. I exploded, saying we had gotten along better without her. She argued back: I was destroying her confidence. And now I have the disquieting hunch that either of us alone can handle Noah better than both of us together. Because Noah senses how easily we tend to fight over him. And so like a normal child tends to know how to divide and conquer.

An autistic girl we know, a child more developed than Noah, was left yesterday in the charge of her grandfather. She was roller-skating within a fenced-in yard. While her grandfather inadvertently catnapped she opened the gate and disappeared. When her mother returned home she frantically called the police and learned that her daughter was in the Emergency Room at the hospital.

What had happened was this: She had been hit by a car at a busy intersection. And when the police had asked the child her name she had told them: "I'm Virginia, I'm autistic." Fortunately, she's also all right. She'll be able to go to school tomorrow.

This morning I planned to take Noah swimming. Except my wagon has sprung another leak and the air conditioning is on the blink. Now I'm wondering whether to pour any more money into a moribund car. Foumi has the sense to know when a car or a machine is wearing out. I don't. I cling to one, repairing it endlessly. Should I have it fixed? Or begin to figure out a way to manage a new car? And, in that case, which car? A sporty model to my taste or a roomy one for my growing family? So a writer spends his day, pondering important questions, trying to arrive at crucial decisions.

Because of the continuing heat Foumi arranged for a full day at our day-care center. And once more I marvel at her efficiency. But I dream of days like yesterday when I can go swimming with Karl and Noah and not worry about not working. How I love to spend an afternoon with my sons in a swimming pool. Karl dives right in but it takes a long time to coax Noah in his life preserver to take his first tentative steps into the pool. Once he's finally in, he delights as Karl or I push him around.

In reading about Annie Sullivan again, I am reminded that Helen Keller had a prodigy's brain. Noah, on the other hand, may simply be retarded, with no great intelligence struggling to be set free. Which neither diminishes his agony nor ours but might make a difference when it comes to the best possible treatments.

Annie Sullivan, by the way, uses a great phrase to describe the downhill slide of life, the fiftyzheimer's disease: "dying detail by detail."

Last night Karl had a homework assignment: an expository essay on the virtues of television. I looked at it. He began with a run-on sentence, he misspelled "which" as "wich," and his thinking was lazy and illogical. I was angry at his ineptitude and let him know it. Noah, meanwhile, like our cat, was just quietly lying on the floor, the coolest place in the house. I was not angry with him.

"Eighteen years!" This morning I turned to Foumi and said: "A fucking eighteen years!" "Eighteen fucking years," she corrected me, and we both laughed.

I can still clearly remember the day. We were in our new apartment in Brooklyn Heights but our bed had not yet arrived. It was the day before Yom Kippur and I had the license. I thought we could just mosey over to Borough Hall in Brooklyn and get married there. But no, they insisted on our having an appointment. So I thought we'd postpone our wedding to another day. But a friend told us that was bad luck and drove us across the bridge to City Hall in Manhattan, where an incantational marriage ceremony was performed by a civil-service clerk.

Afterward we taxied uptown for a drink and some wedding cake with friends. Then we returned to our apartment, where we spent our wedding night in a sleeping bag on a parquet floor, harder than any Spanish earth. But we were young and there were many better-mattressed nights to come.

How swiftly the years have passed. I should go out and buy Foumi some sort of a present. But then we aren't very good at buying each other presents. Because the present we want most is the gift of time to do our work.

Last night I slapped Noah around. I wanted to brush his teeth and he wouldn't let me. I have to realize, as Annie Sullivan pointed out, that simple obedience is a form of blindness, or mindlessness, too. I must control myself, I must honor his feelings.

Poor Noah. He has to weather my tantrums. Last night was not his fault. I was in a strange mood. Almost calm and dreamlike, yet a half note away. I wanted to reach that note and he would not let me. I did not want a hard time from him and he gave me one. So I really batted him around. He held up his hands to defend himself and clutched and pinched at me and I slapped him across the face and on the ass. Just because he wouldn't let me brush his teeth. Big deal. Forgive me, Noah. I know not what I do. You deserve far, far better than me.

An awful day: In the morning I needlessly watched football on television. Which infuriated Foumi. In the afternoon Karl showed me a composition he was working on. I tore it apart, destroying his confidence. Which made me feel terrible. In the evening I went off to a cocktail party in the Hollywood Hills full of young film types. Which I did not enjoy at all. And when I returned home Foumi complained to me that day-care was driving her crazy; Karl was hangdog at his desk, rewriting the crummy paper; and Noah didn't seem that happy either.

But what is really upsetting me this Rosh Hashanah day—beyond day-care and Karl's inability to compose a decent paper and Noah in general—as I sit here at my true pew of worship, is the fact that I have yet to write anything at all today.

October 4, 1978

Foumi had to run day-care herself because Reva broke a bone on Sunday.

October 5, 1978

I must go East and check out the Camphill residential school in Pennsylvania and Benhaven in Connecticut and see if I can get Noah into one of those places. He is old enough—and big enough—to send away now.

October 6, 1978

Last night was Open School Night at Karl's junior high. Since it's his senior year this was our third visit there, but I still didn't know my way around. However, I did notice that the Boys' Rooms, as in my day, still have doorless stalls. I made some discreet inquiries. The girls do have doors on their stalls. Sex discrimination.

Karl has a good English teacher, a fine printing teacher, and the same terrific history teacher he had last year. Only his math teacher is a bore. I felt good about Karl's prospects for the coming year. Until we returned home and talked with him. So far his life had been a "bummer," he said, because of Noah. Our family too was a "bummer," he declared, and went off to bed.

I went to the Dodger-Yankee World Series game, enjoying it immensely from a fine seat in the auxiliary press box, and afterward had dinner and drinks with some old friends in from the East. So I didn't get home until after 2:00 A.M., expecting a raging Foumi, but instead found her just immensely pleased to see me again. She talks a good game without me but oh how she misses me when I'm not around. And, I guess, vice versa. I really needed a boys' night out—and a warm welcome home.

This morning when I entered the living room I grunted a good morning to Noah, who was draped over the couch. And he grunted it right back, slurring his sounds but mimicking my own just the same. I tried to elicit a few more verbal responses from him, repeating, "How are you, Noah?" a few times. And just, "Noah." But that was it, he had said his once-a-year word.

Noah woke up at 7:30 this morning to have a bowel movement. As usual he divided his bowel movement between two johns. He started in ours and ended in the children's. I wonder why he does that? Does he start in ours, then feel he's made a mistake by doing so, and decide to rectify it by finishing up in his john? Or he is like a dog somehow leaving messages?

Karl is already in trouble in math. Twice he has been kicked out of class by the teacher and sent to something called "Opportunity," which is obviously a euphemism for some sort of punishment. I know I should be angry with Karl but I have set aside this afternoon for watching the Series with him and I don't want anything to spoil it.

Last night Foumi and I went to a local movie house in Brentwood. As I edged toward the box office window Foumi said: "I don't care what you do but I'm not a Senior Citizen."

"Don't worry," I said, "I won't pull that again." But when I saw there was a difference of two dollars in price—which isn't a lot of money but is another barrel of popcorn—I reneged and said "Senior Citizen."

"How old are you?" asked the teenage cashier.

"How old do you have to be to be a Senior Citizen?"

"Over sixty-two."

"Well?" I Jack Bennied.

The girl studied me and then pointed at Foumi, "Her too?"

"No," I quickly replied, "just me."

Foumi still wasn't exactly thrilled with my performance. But these teenage kids selling tickets just can't judge age anyway. And I like the idea of lying forward now just as I used to lie backward and try to get in for children's prices when I was long past twelve. Lying forward also means I can derive some of the benefits of longevity even if I don't attain it. In fact, I have been thinking a good deal about death lately—not with fear as I had in my youth but more with genuine annoyance. I just don't have room for it in my plans at the moment.

October 17, 1978

I went to school yesterday to see Karl's math teacher. Karl has been talking too much in class, committing the venal crime of being "disruptive." I told the teacher I'd tell Karl to knock it off. Which I have.

I wish Foumi would knock off her worrying about day-care. We have a continuing personnel problem. Yesterday, for example, a newly hired aide didn't show up. I finally managed to get someone for today and tomorrow. Foumi takes it all too seriously. Responsibility does not mean one has to stay up half the night worrying about it.

October 18, 1978

Last night Karl and I took a walk and spoke of comedy. Karl tends to employ the same defenses I've always used, trying to make jokes to even out odd situations. But I tried to remind him of the universal truth that there are some people in this world, among them algebra teachers, who do not always appreciate jokers.

I sent off a reply to a letter from a friend who had visited us a few weeks ago. In passing, he observed that having a Noah was like Dalton Trumbo's remark about the blacklist: There were no villains.

I wrote back to him:

> *I disagree with you. I thought there were villains in the blacklist and I think there are villains when you have a Noah. Anyone who lies to you or plays politics with the problem is a villain. Anyone who in any way obscures the possible path toward the truth is a villain. In other words, all the usual values weigh more heavily rather than less so in accordance with the gravity of the problem itself. Indeed, the people I rage against most are the people who not only should know better but actually do know better. Christian compassion is not my native reaction. I am Old Testament Jewish and I do rage and I can hate and I never forget. There are villains and there are fools in the field, and I refuse to suffer them lightly.*
>
> *You also asked: "Why not an Anne Sullivan for Noah?" After you left I carefully reread not only* The Miracle Worker *but also Helen Keller's* The Story of My Life *and her biography of Anne Sullivan. The difference between Noah and Helen Keller, among other things, is that Helen Keller could be taught and wanted to be taught. In Anne Sullivan's first day with her Helen picked up a half-dozen words of finger language, in the first week almost one hundred words. The sense of individual meanings for individual words, which she was able to mimic with her fingers, came within six weeks, culminating in the famous "water" incident. So very early on it was evident that not only was Helen precocious but she could also provide Anne Sullivan with constant feedback, which is so important. Anyone working with Noah has to wait a long time for the slightest modicum of feedback.*

Yesterday I spoke with an actor who has a son with brain problems and is doing patterning for him. He says it's only six to eight five-minute periods a day. The theory behind patterning still appeals to me because it is derived out of working with stroke victims. But I still just can't see armies of volunteers parading through our house and I don't know how we could manage the mechanics of the necessary trips to the patterning gurus in Philadelphia.

October 22, 1978

I once almost slugged a social worker in Keon, Noah's first special school back in New York, who asked me: "Are you ready to give up your paternity?" But you know something? He asked the key question.

11

It's brushfire time, and they're getting close. One is threatening nearby Mandeville Canyon. The power is off at home and I'm in my office now waiting for the rice cooker to get done. Noah didn't sleep last night, keeping us awake. And I suspect he was up because of some second sense, like that which certain animals have before earthquakes and other natural disasters.

October 24, 1978

The fire burned through the chapparal and the sagebrush all the way down to the foot of the Presbyterian Conference Grounds on Sunset Boulevard. At nine o'clock last night I walked up to Sunset Boulevard and stood across the street and not only smelled the smoke but heard its crackle and felt the heat. On my way home I passed in front of Palisades High School, which was the area's Emergency Evacuation Center, and spoke to some people who lived up on El Medio over toward Las Pulgas, about three quarters of a mile away from us. They told me the fire had burned up to their doors. Later, at home, I heard on the radio that St. Matthew's Church had burned down.

Earlier in the evening I had Karl water down our roof. We also packed in case we would have to evacuate. Foumi took her paintings and a full complement of vitamins; Karl his Dungeons and Dragons and Hobbitt books; Grandma her medicines; myself a few pages. Noah was unusually quiet. It was as if he knew no matter how terrible a tantrum he'd have, it simply wouldn't be noticed. Which was true. Meanwhile, our senior citizen neighbors on either side of us were calmly chatting as they put out their garbage cans for Tuesday collection.

They were right. By morning the fire threat had passed.

October 25, 1978

Noah wanted his dinner last night. But the food was still too hot. He had a tantrum. I told him to go to his room. He raced back and forth between his room and the kitchen, screaming and galumphing. Finally, he ran into the kitchen, wailing as one word: "I-wanna-eat."

Foumi will be going to Japan, so we had to go to the Consulate downtown. Grandma came with us and we had a grand lunch in Little Tokyo. Grandma, at seventy-five, suddenly seems to have aged a great deal and I hope she doesn't become ill while Foumi is gone. I shudder to think about it. I shudder even more to think about what I would do if something were to happen to Foumi.

October 26, 1978

Noah's day: He's usually up before Karl's alarm goes off at 6:30. But we try our best to ignore his morning sounds. And sometimes he does actually sleep past Karl's awakening. We get up at 7:45, toilet, dress, and breakfast him; prepare his sack lunch; and get him ready to leave the house by 9:00, at which time either I or Niko's mother—with whom I carpool—drive him to school. His school runs from 9:30 to 2:30. He is then taxied over to our daycare center. I pick him up there at 5:15 and he's home at 5:30. Then he usually has a tantrum, dinner, and lounges around eating his shirts, our sheets, towels, anything he can get his mouth on. I give him his bath around 9:00 and he goes to bed about 10:30. It's a pretty full day for him and he doesn't get much reading done.

October 27, 1978

My boys are restless. Last night Noah was unhappy and he started scratching at his nose, hurting himself. Finally, I just couldn't stand watching him. I forced him into our tub. He became frightened, afraid I was going to give him a cold shower. And when I gave him a warm bath instead, he calmed down. But his nose is bloody red.

Karl's counselor called this morning. He has been kicked out of his English class and he's also having some trouble in P.E. He's a bright kid and they don't know what to do with him. Not that I know what to do with him either.

October 28, 1978

When we came home last night, Noah had just fallen asleep. But neither Grandma nor Karl had brushed his teeth. I woke him and dragged him to the bathroom and did his teeth. But the virtuous action boomeranged. Noah cried and howled and did not fall asleep until nearly two o'clock. So, of course, neither did we.

Foumi went up to school to see Karl's counselor. The counselor told Foumi that Karl was "rebellious and insubordinate" and she was concerned that Karl might have to be removed from the honors program because of his behavior and then would subsequently fall in with a "bad crowd." She said her own daughter had behaved similarly and soon evidenced a drug problem and was now in Iowa with her grandparents.

As for Karl's being "rebellious and insubordinate," I say we should be happy that Karl is acting out his rebelliousness in school rather than at home. I also think the school shouldn't overreact either. Instead of sending him to the principal's office they should just laugh at him. But Foumi does not take the matter as lightly as I do. I can't help it though. I can remember my own junior high school behavior and the small transgressions I committed that were regarded as ax murders.

Meanwhile, I am listening to the radio, Michigan beating Minnesota in football. And I'm feeling the chill of an Ann Arbor autumn breeze as I'm sitting deep in the end zone, savoring a victory, but at the same time looking forward to a hot chili supper back at our Co-op House.

October 29, 1978

I TV-footballed away a good deal of my Sunday. But in the morning I took a moody Noah for a car ride, driving up around

149

the area most ravaged by the fire. I noticed that though there was no discernible pattern in the way the fire burned, most of the burned-out houses had shake roofs—like ours. If I ever remodel our house I will certainly give it a slate roof.

After lunch I took Noah for a walk. He seemed in a better mood, too. Until a block south of Sunset he lay down on the grass and became actively unhappy. I force-tugged him all the way home.

Then I drove Karl to his friend's house, intending just to drop him off. But Karl's friend's father wanted to talk to me about a group he had joined which he described as "a civilized est, an est without jargon" that left him "feeling very good about himself." He said that he had been dissatisfied with his job, among other things, and now he was going to begin investigating the choices in his life. I wish I had a few choices in my life to investigate.

A nice thing happened today: Jim Comery, the sound man of the "60 Minutes" crew, called. They had heard about the fire and they were worried about us. I told him we were all fine, unscathed—or unbrushed—by the fire, and how touched I was by their concern. He said they'd done many stories over the years but there were few people they felt as close to as us. Strange—or not so strange—we feel the same way about them. And I think it is Foumi. She makes people love her. Alone I could never engender love. So it has to be Foumi.

Back East the leaves must be falling, the tingle of winter is in the air. Here, only the hint of Halloween, the decorations in the stores downtown, and the paintings on their windows. The most frightening thing, though, is Karl's continuing problem at school. The teachers seem more immature than he. But then if they were so mature, they wouldn't be content hanging around with students all their lives.

What always gets Karl into trouble is his mouth: In a discussion about vocations, for example, the teacher said, "After one was finished being a stewardess there wasn't much she could do." Karl, without being recognized, piped up from the back of the class: "She could always write 'The Diary of a Mad Stewardess.'"

Not the world's greatest punch line. But not the crime of the century either.

I'm really getting annoyed with Karl's school. Granted the kid is a wise-ass, but he is also a kid. And they're playing army games with him. Yesterday he came home with a slip calling for two days of Detention—in addition to the three days of "Opportunity," whatever that is, he had already served and the five laps of track he had run—all because he took out a volleyball he wasn't supposed to. P.E. teachers are not the brightest people in the world, but I will go meet the sucker tomorrow. Meanwhile, I am sick of the kid getting triple jeopardy. And if he has committed a bunch of misdemeanors, they still should not treat him like a felon.

In one week Foumi will be in Japan. Grandma will unburden me of most of the cooking and the laundry. Noah's former teacher, Alys Harris, will help with day-care. Still I wonder how well I will be able to manage without Foumi. It will be our longest separation since our marriage.

November 1, 1978

Karl certainly is behaving badly as he seeks to be the center of attention, taking on his teachers as individual challenges and smart-talking to them in his sullen way. I simply don't know what to do. And if he keeps getting into trouble I cannot help him. It would also be a mistake to do so. But his teachers take things too seriously. This morning I had to go to his school and see his P.E. teacher, who complained to me about how disruptive Karl is verbally. What the hell is there in P.E. to disrupt verbally?

November 2, 1978

At dinner Karl said he was depressed, that he was planning to run away from home, and that he had learned how to make a bomb so that he could blow up his algebra and homeroom teachers. And on and on he ranted. I think he did so to take the focus off all of his misdemeanors. But still it was disconcerting. I feel the school has created a problem, labeled it, and then handed it back to us. I can't let things go on this way.

We have to give him some escape valves. At the same time we

have to keep some sort of pressure on him. It makes me unhappy to see him so unhappy. And it's an irony I've always feared: Karl turning out to be the problem. We must grow with Karl, not just idle along as with Noah. Raising a normal child is even more exasperating than dealing with an abnormal child.

November 3, 1978

Yesterday a substitute English teacher asked Karl to hand in an essay a day earlier than due because, she said, he had been misbehaving. It's an unfair thing to do and I wrote her a note saying that I would not allow Karl to hand in the essay a day early because I thought it was inappropriate to confuse an academic assignment with a disciplinary one.

I've been hard on Karl lately but I won't let his teachers gang up on him for petty grievances. I spoke to one of his classmates in English, who told me that Karl's "disturbances" were a creative enlivening of an otherwise dull day that never disturbed anybody's "work."

I decided to see the principal. But when I phoned the school I learned that he was too busy because some arsonist had set fire to his office. That's what I call work-disturbing.

At least Karl didn't get hit with that charge.

November 4, 1978

Noah hasn't been eating his lunch. His teacher thinks it's because he's bored with the same kind of sandwiches every day. We'll have to try to vary his menu.

November 5, 1978

Foumi is going home, returning to Japan tomorrow, in search of fame and fortune there. She hopes to arrange for the publication of her novel. And if grit and determination can do it, she'll score. It will be our longest separation in eighteen years of marriage. It is my birthday present to her. I will run day-care and I will miss her care daily.

At the age of fifty I sometimes wonder what it is I now truly want. What is my dream? I guess it is to write a really good book or two. But mostly it is to stop time, to keep it still. Noah is the ticking time bomb in my life. When it—or he—goes off, when I have to reach a decision about him, my life can very easily shatter.

November 6, 1978

Neither Foumi nor I slept last night. And Noah was up early too. I think he sensed that Foumi was leaving. We made love and then we drove to the airport. Her last words to me were: "Look back when you're changing lanes." Going to the airport I had almost hit another car. But her penultimate words to me were: "Yes. Yes." I had asked her if she loved me. It's harder to get Foumi to speak of love than it is to get Noah to say anything. But there it was: We still love each other. And I guess this separation will show us just how much so.

November 7, 1978

Karl is not alone—I don't like his school either. I went there this morning and met with the burned-out principal, a former math teacher. "Karl is manipulative," he charged. "What kid isn't?" I replied. He said: "Karl must like and respect his teachers." I said: "'Like' is not important and respect has to be earned." I don't mind the principal and me locking heads; after all, we're both theoretically adult and if I worry about the creative aspects in a kid and he is concerned with the practical job of running a school program, we are entitled to our differences. But what distresses me is that the school seems to set up an adversary relationship with the student. That's ridiculous.

November 8, 1978

Karl is trying to write an essay. He is not very good at analytical thinking. But I did get a page out of him. I wish I could get him to think more logically, though. But I'm not a very good teacher. I'm too far down the literary path to know how to double back and really help him.

November 9, 1978

I miss Foumi. I cannot sleep with the place next to me in bed empty. I also miss her managerial skill. One of the parents of our day-care kids had told me her daughter would not be coming today. Which meant I didn't have to schedule an extra worker. Then this morning she discovered that there was no school in Santa Monica and said she would be sending her daughter. I said: "No way. Not unless I can dig up an extra helper." She became angry with me, upsetting me so, that I finally said: "No way, period. I'm not even going to make a phone call for you." Foumi would have handled it much more diplomatically, I'm sure.

November 10, 1978

I'm still not sleeping well. Every night I feel as if I am going to bed in a motel room that happens to be in my house. I stay up late, half watching Johnny Carson and half reading at the same time, falling asleep for only an hour at a time at best, and in the morning I get out of bed completely unrefreshed.

Noah misses Foumi, too. Last night he refused to eat his dinner and began to babble what sounded like "ma ma ma ma" to me. Lately he also has a new habit. He puts his thumb up against the roof of his mouth as if he were trying to vomit. Is he trying to tell me that his throat hurts? Or that he wants to speak?

November 14, 1978

The "60 Minutes" segment was aired. I felt Imre and his crew had done a fine job. They caught the sense of unfullfilled dreams in Foumi's life; they showed Karl as a teenage malcontent but at the same time managed to make him the hero of the piece; I came through as a hyperactive spokesman; and Noah, of course, not speaking for himself but just being himself, was eloquent.

I am curious about the third-person reaction but there have been few phone calls. I guess, as my agent said to me this morning, "It wasn't exactly the kind of thing that you called up about and said, 'Congratulations!'"

Off camera, Reva is back at work at our day-care sentence—Freudian slip: center—and I am pleased about that. Karl has not become involved in additional school troubles that I know of. Noah, for the most part, remains blissfully unaware of Foumi's absence. Grandma has been most helpful. And Foumi, hoarse from all the talking she has been doing with her friends, called happily over the weekend. It seems that a Japanese magazine might be interested in her book.

November 15, 1978

Grandma reminded me this morning as I was dressing Noah that today is Foumi's birthday. Perhaps I should send her a telegram? But where? I can't quite recall her schedule. Anyway, in Japan it's already a day later.

November 16, 1978

It was Open House at Noah's school. How many of these damned things have I had to attend over the years? How many times have I had to listen to a teacher go through her act, showing how much Noah—and his classmates—were theoretically learning. Last night his teacher did it with great energy. But it all boiled down to this: Noah was still learning A and B, but not C; he was still learning the concept of one and two, but not three; he was still learning finger painting and managing to draw jagged connecting lines between dots. It was all déjà vu for me—and perhaps even for him.

November 17, 1978

The only problem I've had running the day-care center in Foumi's absence has been with one of the parents. She never tells me whether or not her daughter is coming. She also treats the staff peremptorily, barking out orders to them. She tries my patience and I'm liable to bark out an order or two at her before Foumi's return next week.

Karl's report card—except for some of the usual U's in conduct—was not bad at all: D in Graphic Arts and C in P.E. Otherwise, A's in Typing and History, and B's in English and Algebra.

It is only when I leave Noah alone and unattended that he does his mouth jobs, chewing up blankets and shirts and licking the wallpaper.

Foumi returned. The rainiest day of the year. I missed her, yes, but I also, to give the truth equal time, enjoyed her absence. She can really troop through the house like a pocket general, barking maternal commands, handing out assignments. Her presence is immense for a person so seemingly small.

This morning Foumi asked me why I've been so "hostile" since her return. What gave rise to her question was an argument over her insistence on starting a new container of milk whenever she prepares Noah's lunch. Which ensures fresh milk for Noah but also means there is now an additional container of milk that is a candidate for spoilage. In similar situations I usually put up with Foumi's foibles. But I guess I was out of practice. Also there is a very thin line between idiosyncratic preparation and paranoia. And sometimes the paranoia wins out in my diagnosing machine. Especially on days when I'm a little paranoid myself.

Of course, I ducked Foumi's question. But I admit I do feel a hostility toward her. She had deserted me for two whole weeks and I resent it.

Meanwhile, hostility or not, we did celebrate a version of Thanksgiving. I bought a hen, which Foumi roasted, and some yams and some instant stuffing, which I made in a saucepan. Karl and Grandma, good eaters both, were delighted. To Noah, of course, it was just another meal.

Today is Karl's fourteenth birthday and I worry about his self-proclaimed expertness in everything: Football. Space. Tolkien. American history. You name it. But he can't clean up his room. I also worry about his smart-ass way of challenging all adults. I can see why teachers get down on him.

For his birthday I took him and four of his friends to the movies. We started out intending to see *Lord of the Rings* but somehow wound up at *Animal House*. And then I took the brood of boys out to dinner. They're all really getting older. This year they thanked me.

November 27, 1978

These days as I drive about in the California Indian autumn I remember how bright and clear and vivid it all seemed to me when I first arrived here—as if I had on a new pair of glasses. I will have spent almost all of the seventies in California. But I think the whole decade thing is a mark—or a marking—of the young anyway. We always tend to set our youth in boldface type.

November 28, 1978

I noticed last night that Karl is now taller than Foumi. Soon he will be taller than I. And next it will be Noah's turn to pass us both. I wonder if we are trying to hold on to Noah too long. Eventually, we have to pass him on anyway. But when and where and to whom? I have always thought religious zealots—rather than those people who have earthly motivations—would be his ideal caretakers, but a week after Jonestown I am no longer sure.

November 29, 1978

How hard it is to begin a new project, to start a relationship, to renew and resume a marriage. Foumi's return has been marked by unrest. Some of the mystique of our togetherness is gone. I can get on without her—and even with Noah—while she can get along very well without me. She had a good time in Japan and she constantly talks of wanting to return there. She experienced freedom again and it's a tough taste to give up. She even talks of painting again. Oh that she would! I don't believe in art necessarily anymore, but I do believe in her art.

Now we are picking on each other. Her booming voice upsets

me, her habits seem more wearing than endearing. We have to be careful with each other, very careful.

November 30, 1978

Noah has been difficult. He wants to sleep on the floor. Last night we gave in to him and he finally slept. He is also putting his hand deep into his mouth. Foumi, as always, thinks it's because his teeth are bothering him. I think it's because he yearns to be able to talk. But I also know we're both wrong.

Karl is the epitome of the lazy kid. He does not do one more measure of anything than he has to do. He even stops his piano practice in the midst of a song if the half hour is up.

Grandma is getting ready to return to Japan next week. I realized when Foumi was in Japan the house was quieter, and it will be quieter again after Grandma leaves. She actually makes so little noise and takes up so little space, but the act of living itself is a noisy, space-consuming process.

My fingers are still idle. But I edge toward poetry. One begins as a writer with poetry, full of dreams and vagaries, and so one ends with poetry, too. I understand now *The Tempest* and *Peer Gynt* and O'Casey's late plays, the move to the surreal as life edges toward what one hopes at best is finally just another vague dream, death itself. Anyway, no workaday prose has escaped from me this week.

December 1, 1978

Carlos is becoming violent both at school and at day-care. In fact, the school director told me that Carlos's days there are numbered. Which suggests that Noah's countdown is next.

Karl had a new velour outer shirt. Seventeen bucks. He wore it to school for the first time yesterday. And it was stolen. The school says there is nothing that they can do about a theft. It's not like "talking in class," which they know how to crack down on.

December 2, 1978

Now that Carlos is acting up and I know that Noah is next, I am beginning to think of Noah as a ball player in terms of the Branch

Rickey dictum. I mean: It'll be better to unload him a year too soon rather than a year too late. In other words, while he is still more child-cute than adult-grotesque. And if the truth be told, we are tiring of him and perhaps it's time for some other people to take over with new and fresh energy.

December 3, 1978

I spoke with a lady from the Bay Area. She has had her son at Sonoma State Hospital since he was five years old. In the state hospital he began to talk. Then she brought him home because she was "afflicted," she said, "with 'rescuitis.'" At home he stopped talking completely. After she returned him to the institution, she said, he started speaking again.

December 4, 1978

Last night Karl told me he planned to do his Christmas shopping early this year. He's going to get a beanbag toy for Noah but he doesn't know what to get for me. "You're a problem," he said. "You're the man who has nothing because you want nothing. It's much easier to get something for the man who has everything than anything for a man who has nothing."

December 5, 1978

I'm still betwixt and between professionally, productively. I spent all of last week writing a single paragraph. And, so far, I seem to have spent all of this week misplacing it. Perhaps it is the half cold. The California half cold. The days are fine: Clear air. Blue skies. Deep breaths. But at night I lie in bed half awake, half dreaming, half cold.

December 7, 1978

Today Karl announced his official Christmas gift list. In print shop he will make business cards for me; he will buy a cuckoo clock for Foumi; and he will pick up a beanbag toy for Noah. Sometimes I get angry at Karl for having no money sense, for being such a spendthrift. But I must also realize that he is a generous kid who enjoys spending money. Which is more than his dad does. If it were just spending money and not spending time in the process as well, I might not be such a Scrooge. Anyway, it is always Karl who manufactures the Christmas spirit around here. In fact, in our house he is the Kid Who Invented Christmas.

December 8, 1978

A letter came from a woman in Canada who has a seventeen-year-old daughter stricken with both Noah's brain damage and severe physical handicaps as well. Sometimes, she writes, she is almost glad that her daughter can barely move. I can understand her feeling. How healthy Noah seems, especially in his down jacket. How normal Noah seems, especially when I bathe him and see his pubic hairs coming into place and the beginnings of a mustache. Now I can push him around physically. But a day of reckoning is not too far off.

Noah does know verbs. I should try to teach him nouns. Patiently, without rewards and punishment, just by coaxing him, letting him provide his own motivation. I will say the word and make the sign and the hell with behavior modification.

December 9, 1978

I miss the East, the soft snow, the well-heated house, the fog before my mouth as I walk through the front door. But before I run away with myself I must recall the gray December days. December is the saddest month, just because unhappiness and malaise do not seem to go well with it. Every December I feel a lack in my life. A lack that goes back to my Jewish childhood and the Christmas season I was never a part of. I would press my little nose against a Christmas display window, knowing none of the silver-sprinkled gifts, sitting on neatly bowed red and green boxes as if they were already packaged, could possibly be for me. And not all the rich-tasting potato latkes and dreidel spinning and Chanukah gelt could ever make up for that. Yes, for me, the non-goy, December is the saddest month.

December 10, 1978

My TV adaptation of "Lovey" is coming in on sneakers. The work will have as little effect as a conversation near a waterfall in the middle of a storm. Oh well, the wages of television are not instant respect but immediate money—and lingering regrets.

Someday I would like to write a book about men who love— and use—each other without a sexual overtness. The love between men is something that is very difficult to deal with because it knows no standardized form of expression. It is the silent love that becomes the awful fury. Noah I can still hug and kiss—if even against his will—but there is no way I can still express love for Karl physically. I'm not talking about sex. Sex is not the only expression of love any more than love is the exclusive expression of sex. Sex is an expression of sex, and nothing else. Which is something most cruising homosexuals know.

December 11, 1978

Yesterday I saw one of those pictures that convinces me anew that movies are no more an art than an election is—or a dream. It was a sincere attempt by artless people to load guns that do not exist and then fire them.

When I took Noah for a walk this morning he was in a great mood. Until we came upon a dog. Then I had to coax him home to avoid his having a tantrum. Noah can usually spot a dog blocks away. His perceptions are very sharp when it comes to personal danger.

December 12, 1978

Last night once more Foumi began complaining about how I wasn't doing enough for day-care, and soon we were in a bitter argument. Karl, who was attempting to referee the rhubarb, finally suggested: "Why don't you two divorce?" To the California-bred kid it seemed the obvious solution.

Tonight is the Christmas show at Noah's school. Instead of a cause for celebration, I fear, it may turn out to be a distinct pain. They want Noah to dance, and Noah doesn't want to dance.

Noah did not even want to go to school today. He signaled that by returning his lunchbox to the kitchen counter this morning. He can signal most of his desires if he really wants to. But he also has an infinite capacity to do nothing. Oh how I wish he wanted to do something.

December 13, 1978

Foumi's eyes have been troubling her and now the eye doctor has suggested allergy tests. The allergy question again opens up the possibility that Noah might be an extreme case of allergic reactions. To something as simple as bread or milk. And perhaps we ought to subject him to the endless series of allergy tests. But somehow I just can't believe an allergic reaction can be the root cause of Noah's extreme behavior.

Last night Noah was dragged onto the stage screaming. So much for his participation in the Christmas show. Even without him I didn't like it very much but the teachers are young and need parental feedback, so I told them how wonderful it was.

Tonight's my night to be onstage—or rather on screen. "Lovey" will grace the tube.

December 14, 1978

Noah was up most of the night. Did he anticipate bad reviews? I know I felt relieved. Jane Alexander was wonderful, the film was moving, better than most television, and I didn't think there was anything in it that I would have to apologize for to parents and Special Education teachers. It showed the "miracle" within a context, and the parents were not ogres but human beings. I think I did *la causa* a service. I just wish I could have felt the kind of high I experienced when I first saw *Harry and Tonto* in public or had my first play produced in Washington. But how high can you get in your own living room anyway?

December 15, 1978

I feel guilty about one of our day-care kids' mothers. I called her last week to find out if her daughter would be definitely attending day-care that Saturday. I was calling her because I was having a hard time arranging the coverage. But then she began giving me a hard time on the phone, finally saying that she was paying for her daughter so that I better make sure an extra aide was there whether her daughter attended or not. I became furious with her. She wasn't paying for her daughter, the state was. But that wasn't the point. I said, "Don't you ever mention money to me when it comes to day-care," and hung up. Foumi later called her but she did not return the call. A call finally did come from her baby-sitter saying that the child would not be attending on Saturday.

I know I was wrong to explode. I am always wrong when I explode. But I was turned against the lady anyway. She treats our aides and teachers terribly, as if they are some hired hands from some lower species. But she is widowed, and there is her daughter to worry about. A brain-damaged kid should never have to suffer just because his or her parents have little brains and less grace. Still I am angry with the woman. All the time Foumi was away, this woman never volunteered to help. But I should accept the fact that in day-care—as in any area involving Noah—we're involved in a no-win situation.

December 16, 1978

How my days are shaped: *Variety* liked "Lovey," Karl received a good report card—his only U in P.E.—and Noah suffered from diarrhea at school. Two out of three is not bad.

December 20, 1978

Noah is jolly, happy. Just like an ordinary kid who is off from school during the holidays. Karl is miserable, down with a bad cold. Just like an ordinary kid who has had too much holiday already.

December 23, 1978

How Karl loves to hear stories of my childhood. In relating them to him I realize that even more magical than one's own childhood is the childhood of one's parent. That's the real magic time, the time out of place, the time from before "I" existed, the time that is pre–personal history. Noah, of course, has no history. Pre, personal, past, or present. When I came home last night I found him having a tantrum. I didn't know why. And today, I'm sure, neither does he.

December 26, 1978

Last night, Noah cried until one o'clock as I tried to sleep. At this point I just want to get through each day and into each night having as little to do with him as possible.

But after every holiday, after every close encounter with Noah of an extended kind, I come to the same inescapable conclusion: I have to decide what to do with him in the long run. Perhaps thirteen should be his cutoff date. Because the longer I wait, the less of a kindness it might be to him. Who, for example, would want a pimpled, gangly sixteen-year-old who can't wipe his own ass?

How did we spend our Christmas holidays? Sunday, Wildcard Sunday, went mostly to football. And Monday went to Christmas. Karl was delighted with his gifts. (He should be, he promoted them.) And somehow just hanging around the house with the family—even with Noah—no place to go and no people coming, was good enough for me. I do not envy anybody the busy social life.

December 27, 1978

A burden shared, so goes the saying, is a burden eased. Well, there was a lot of burden to be shared last night—Noah was up to the wee, wee hours—and neither Foumi nor I feel very eased this morning. Holidays should be called Halfidays. Since there is no school Noah does not leave the house until ten to go to special day-care sessions. We pick him up at four. Leaves a short day. But thank God—and Foumi—for day-care.

December 28, 1978

I've been leafing back through these pages and came upon two entries I don't think I ever culled before. "I'm falling into the trap: One loves what one knows; we're all creatures of habit, and love is a habit. The longer Noah is with us, the harder it will be for us to bear his leaving us. It's all like that game the Germans played with Jews in the death camps: They would make those on line choose going to the right or to the left of a fork in the road without their knowing what fate lay ahead for them in either direction, though both directions led eventually to the gas chambers. Meanwhile, as each individual came to the moment of choice he agonized over it, families split up in hysterical argument, and everyone lost out anyway."

"I've been thinking about Noah. There's really not much to think about. There's simply the fact that, no matter how I slice it, no matter how incomplete he is, I love him with a wholeness I have never loved anyone or anything with since my childhood."

I wish I were so sure of my love for Noah now. I wish I were not forever fixed, standing in that fork in the road.

12

This morning I studied Noah as he prepared to leave for day-care. He is getting thinner. And taller. Almost as tall as Foumi. With his acne and facial hair he is becoming a young man, one old enough for a boarding school—or a religious setup in which the people are philosophically interested in his soul because they believe in souls. Perhaps there is the theosophy of Rudolph Steiner in his future.

I think of Freud and Marx, the twin Victorian gods who are still failing, but people believe in yet. In our search for answers we come up with new vocabularies and jargons that we confuse with explanations. "Autism" is such a discovery. If you believe in Freud, or Marx, your belief is real—or as real as any other belief system. But that does not make it the truth. Truth is that which is beyond belief's way.

December 31, 1978

Karl still can make me laugh. He told me that he wants permission to change his name to Mohammed Abdullah. "Why Mohammed Abdullah?" I asked. "So I can become six feet, eight inches tall," he replied.

January 2, 1979

Once more on New Year's Day to the Rose Bowl and once more we left Pasadena in defeat. Oh the adversity of Michigan! But this time in a rec home, which I decided to rent, and it worked out marvelously. It was a joy to watch television before the game and after the game, tailgate-partying in the parking lot, and perhaps it would have been better to watch television during the game or the game itself on television. There is something to be said for the blue-collar life.

I also do relish being in a crowd, looking through binocs, sloshing down beer. During the game, as we sat in the very top row, Sandy and Rick Schaefer, their sons Erich and Max, and, of course, Karl, I felt a tremor, as if an earthquake were taking place. And, indeed, I later learned there was one. A small one. Enough to frighten Foumi and further spoil an already bad day at home with Noah. Which fact she apprised me of immediately as I walked back into the house. It seems Noah had celebrated the start of 1979 as if he were the New Year's babe himself, constantly tearing off his clothing and stripping, even when Foumi tried to take him for a walk.

But, as I say, going to the game was fun for me—and for Karl. I enjoyed watching him with his friends, hearing his teenage brand of humor. "Let's go blue," was the Michigan cheer called out. "Let's go gray," Karl shouted back. "For the color-blind."

And in the rec home, while we were lunching on the delicious chili that Sandy had prepared, Karl, whose usual response to Foumi's cooking is a succinct "This sucks!," turned to Sandy and asked politely: "May I make a constructive criticism? I think there should be more beans in the chili." Which wowed me enough to make my year.

January 5, 1979

Noah, Noah. Trouble, trouble. When I picked him up at day-care he had a tantrum; he had another tantrum at dinner. And another while I was trying to bathe him. When I finally put him to sleep in one of my old winter underwear tops he seemed very tired, as if primed for sleep. But that was misleading. He was up half the night. Whether it was because of the new material to chew—I eventually changed him back into one of his thermal underwear tops—or because he had had to go to the bathroom I do not know. But he was up. And soon Karl was up too, informing us that he could not sleep because of his noisy brother. And then, at last, when it seemed we were all blissfully asleep, the phone rang. It was Karl's friend calling to tell him that they would have a ride to school. I looked at my watch: six o'clock, but I managed to fall back to sleep. Then another phone call at 7:15—from New York. And so after a day that never ended, a new day began.

January 7, 1979

Adele Mortin, Noah's former teacher, visited our day-care center. The moment she walked into the room Carlos positively glowed, flashing a smile of boundless happiness. Noah responded in his usual way, shyly tucking and averting his head. Noah does that whenever an old friend—or parent—returns. He is angry for having been deserted in the first place. At the same time he is quick to show his independence, the fact that he no longer needs you anymore. Oh what these children know and how deeply and purely they feel.

January 8, 1979

Karl pleases me in the way he can now understand abstract concepts, philosophical issues. For example, yesterday I was able to explain to him how God could be a symbol of morality in much the same way a king serves as the symbol of a nation.

January 9, 1979

I think I can face the truth about Noah better than Foumi can. Noah is profoundly retarded and will require custodial care for the rest of his life. There will be no miracles for him. Autism is currently being redefined from a disease to a syndrome. Which is something that I've been saying for years. But no one ever finds a cure for a syndrome. Headaches are a syndrome, feeling dizzy is a syndrome. I gather now that research supports the notion that the syndrome of autism is caused by some form of brain damage in the left temporal lobe. Progress. But really of no matter as far as Noah is concerned. The cause of whatever ails him is not as important at this point as the place where he can receive the best custodial care. So it's just a question of when we transfer that burden off our own shoulders.

Foumi keeps saying I can't make a decision. But whenever I make the decision, she wants to delay. For example, when I mentioned the other day that I wanted to go East and look at Camphill, the Rudolf Steiner school in Pennsylvania, she said: "Just because we're not happy with Noah's school is no reason to put him in an institution." But that's not the point. The point is, I'm just getting tired of Noah. I have work I want to do, vacations I'm entitled to take. I want to get on with my life without the weight of a constant anchor.

January 10, 1979

Perhaps Noah again requires "straightening out," as the behaviorists say. But Foumi thinks force of any kind is not only useless as far as he is concerned, but also counterproductive. I don't know. But I also don't know what else to do about his deteriorating behavior. Even though bad behavior may be his only form of communication I can't stand it. Foumi is more willing to suffer him, to accept what he does as the best he can do under the circumstances, in other words to "spoil" him.

Dinner usually goes something like this: She prepares his food. He sits down. He takes one bite or taste and runs out of the room. After a few calls he returns and sits at the table again. Then suddenly he gets upset, hurling the food to the floor and spilling his milk. Because it is too hot or too cold or there is not enough rice or the bread is too hard. Who knows why? Then off he runs and Foumi tries to woo him back. I berate her for doing so, I criticize her cooking, she criticizes my criticism. We give up waiting for Noah to return and sit down ourselves and half eat, half battle our way through dinner. Noah eventually returns, the damage having been done, and eats. So goes an evening with the Greenfelds.

Foumi and I are both tired. I'm sick of dealing with—nay, living with on a daily basis—all the philosophical questions that Noah makes me heir to: What are the responsibilities of parents to their own progeny? What are one's duties and obligations toward a member of one's own species? What is human? What is man? What is animal?

This morning Foumi and I visited Nora Sterry, an L.A. public school for special children. The autistic class there seemed better than the one Noah is now in. So we do have a local alternative in terms of Noah's schooling.

This evening we saw on a newscast that the state's North Desert Regional Center was withdrawing its support from OCC, the Operant Conditioning Center. It seems the "autistic" people keep shooting down their own planes.

January 15, 1979

A wintry weekend, rain and wind in the crisp air, we all have—or are expecting to have—colds. On Sunday Karl and I went to a movie, the animated *Lord of the Rings*. A lousy picture but he got off a good line: "This is more slow motion than animation."

He has been getting off a lot of good lines lately. And why not? He's almost fourteen and a half. And, if I recall correctly, I thought I was quite a wit at that age too.

I still do. The other night at dinner some people were discussing a movie that is supposed to be about friendship—or "male bonding," as it is now called—which had been made by one of the local industry blackguards. I said his producing such a movie was like Hitler issuing a treatise on the aesthetics of Judaism.

Anyway, it sounded funny when I said it.

January 16, 1979

The L.A. public school system cannot promise a place for Noah at Nora Sterry beyond June. After that, because of his age, he would have to go to a school that is over an hour away.

Karl really wants to get away from the family and go on his own. He is in a rush to grow, to go forth into the world, and college seems like an acceptable way station. I fear for him, I fear something might happen to him, I fear irony with a vengeance.

January 17, 1979

Noah is in a good mood but I still have to find a place for him in the long run. But how to get away and look for one as long as

Noah is here? Foumi just can't deal with him by herself for a single day.

Last night at dinner Karl and I had one of those father-and-son altercations. I had sharply criticized him for his refusal to eat with chopsticks or to accept any rice on his plate. And suddenly he was shouting: "I hate this stupid family. You and Foumi are idiots. Wasting your lives because of Noah. Picking on me because of Noah. You should have put Noah in an institution years ago. He's going to wind up in one anyway. You're both fools and take it out on me."

And it is true that while I was asking Karl to eat his rice with chopsticks, Noah was clutching at various foods with his hands. But I did think Karl understood that there was no other place for Noah we know of at the moment. Foumi, of course, was soon in tears.

And I, who think in terms of humane treatment for Noah, was scarcely humane toward him later in the evening. After his bath as I was trying to wipe him he began to pinch me. When I brushed his teeth he poked his hand hard into my face. I slapped him. Not hard, but a mistake. He was up protesting my act of injustice until long past midnight.

The only way to treat Noah is by lavishing appreciation upon him whenever he does that which is good and proper and appropriate and simply to ignore whatever he does that is bad. My belief in behavior modification has slipped—or elevated—to that. But I know one must never get excited with Noah, always address him in low, calm tones. He catches the nuances, overreacts to loud tones and hints of hysteria. The hardest thing to accept about Noah—as about Hollywood—is that like everyone else in this town he is doing the best he can.

I have a horrible sore throat. I'm depressed. I feel as hemmed in by family and environment as I did as a teenager. I am restless. I want to burst out. I have energy that needs recharging, replacing, renewal. I yearn to get away for a dramatic change of venue. I want a happy surprise tomorrow morning. But fat chance.

January 21, 1979

Karl is funny. But in the wrong place and at the wrong time. The other day his math teacher asked if Larry Zabriskie was in the class. "What's the middle initial?" Karl called out. The kid is like me, someone who would rather play than work. I hope he can find an escape hatch for himself.

January 22, 1979

I have a slight flu, Foumi's eyes are bothering her, Karl is having difficulty with algebra, and Noah's just been generally impossible, up all night keening.

January 23, 1979

We met with Noah's teacher and the director of his school and if not disarmed we are at least defused. They may not be doing very much with him at this time but who knows what anyone else could do either. And to change schools now would be an enormous problem.

We did learn something from our meeting. According to the director there are twelve-year molars, the last teeth to come in before the wisdom teeth. And perhaps that's what's distressing Noah at the moment as he teethes on everything he can lay his hands on.

January 24, 1979

Day-care continues to be more of a boomerang than a tool. There are always people to be hired, forms to be filed. Just taking care of Noah each day was easier.

January 25, 1979

One of our neighbors has been sick for over a month. And she hasn't even seen a doctor. I prevailed upon her husband to let me speak to our doctor. I set up an appointment but she could not get to the office. Our doctor agreed to make a house call. But now she's in the hospital and he'll look in on her there. Old people. We always seem to have to look after the old people around us.

We've arranged for Noah to go to the Spastic Children's Foundation for four days. We have been preparing him, telling him he's going on a sleepover, so he knows something is up. But it is all so absurd. Because we're sick I have to send him away. The survival of the fittest. But, as I say, we simply cannot manage him any longer. We need a rest. I do not know if we will go away for the weekend. I prefer quiet in my own house to driving hundreds of miles for it. I really want to stay home alone without Noah.

This morning I tried to take him for a walk. Already his face has the institutional-holocaust look: hollowed cheeks, dazed eyes, deep-set in their sockets but still flashing anger. He kept spitting at me when I put on his shoes. Outside on the lawn he lay down and unzipped his jacket and began a rolling, kicking tantrum. I took him back into the house. Whether it was his sense of leaving that caused another leaving of his senses or a howling wind I do not know. I know it is time to make a move in terms of Noah. And, as usual, I am paralyzed by the hideous prospects before me.

I feel like a Chekhov character. I want to cry out: "There can be no good news in my life as long as Noah exists. Nothing can produce intense happiness for me any longer. Everything pales for me because of Noah."

Why must I cry out in translation?

We drove Noah to the Spastic Children's Foundation in the early afternoon. He did not seem upset when he saw the building. He walked into it willingly and sat in the lobby. He became a little difficult when we entered the social worker's office for the intake interview. But otherwise, he docilely accepted his fate. We accompanied him to the ward and showed him his bed—the same bed he had had last August—and he lay down on it quietly as if he were testing the mattress in a motel and found it satisfactory. I had the feeling we were all going through some rehearsal.

When we returned home there was a painful silence in our house. I hope this respite of four days can keep us going for another four months.

Karl's report card was a pleasant surprise. Just one U and that in P.E. Otherwise, he had A's in History, Printing, and Typing, a B in English, and a C in Algebra. I rewarded him with a trip to Westwood to see the new Clint Eastwood.

Sunday we slept late and entertained friends at dinner. Monday we slept late too, allowing Karl to stay home from school, as we declared a vacation for all while Noah was away. But in the afternoon we drove out to Ojai to look at a residential group home there. It was clean but a little crowded, considering that it had eighteen "clients," and seemed to provide very little in the way of a program of activities. Still it's something. Yesterday we enjoyed sleeping late again, lunching well, and then driving out to the Spastic Children's Foundation. Where we were shocked.

When we walked into the day room Noah was lying sleepily on a couch, one shoe on and one shoe off. I went over to him. His lips were gray-white dry and his teeth were covered with a butterscotch-yellow patina. He smelled vile—or of bile. He wore no undershirt. His eyes were rolling upward vacantly. Even his hair seemed to have been cut close like that of an Auschwitz or Buchenwald denizen. It was obvious—as we soon learned from the aides—that he had scarcely eaten in four days.

We packed his things and hurried him out. Ashamed of ourselves. All the positive effects of our own respite were immediately dissipated. We should have phoned there, checked him out. But we had decided not to. Afraid perhaps that we might be told there was a problem.

In the car we fed him three Japanese tangerines. At home he was ravenous, downing bowl after bowl of rice and over a quart of milk. It was as if we had found him floating on a raft somewhere in the middle of the ocean. And we were left at sea ourselves. All during his four-day stay there we had been congratulating ourselves on how relaxed we had become, reminding ourselves that we would have to do it again soon. Well, the next time we need a vacation we will find help we can hire to come into the house. And then we will go away. I will not put Noah in such a place again. Two more weeks and I am sure he would have lost his toilet training.

So the search never ends, the anguish always continues. A persistent voice within me nags: "Find a school, start a residence, build an organization." But at the same time the experience of my life in general and our little day-care center in particular also counsels: "You are not a team player. Neither are you a leader, a pioneer, or an empire builder. You are a loner who eschews group activities, a writer."

13

February 1, 1979

Karl writes like a Neanderthal. He has no idea how to shape a sentence or construct a paragraph. Nor has he any real desire to learn either. But why worry about him? As long as he is normal and can fend for himself my concerns about him are—and have to be—minimal. Noah needs my help and my long life.

February 2, 1979

Since his school isn't teaching Karl how to write, I decided I would. I asked him to write a theme a week for me. His first effort wasn't very good and I told him that he had done better writing in the fifth grade. "But that was poetry," he said. "Poetry is easier." "Okay," I said, "then for next week write me a poem." A half hour later he handed me this:

> *The road goes ever on.*
> *Your mind may be weary or your feet*
> *May need rest, but*
> *The road goes ever on.*
> *An endless line of bricks and concrete*
> *That seems never to need rest,*
> *The road goes ever on.*
> *Broken bricks, smashed bottles, rows of debris,*
> *The road goes ever on.*

I immediately praised him, lavishly and profusely. "You know 'the road' is life," he said. "I guessed," I said.

I do like the kid. I just wish he weren't so highly manipulative and could spell better. But then I can't spell either and neither could Scot—or is it Scott?—Fitzgerald.

February 3, 1979

It is ironic: All last weekend we were thinking of Spastic's as a possible place for Noah. This week he is with us, and respite is far from our minds. He has begun to look like himself—no longer like the D.P. he was at Spastic's—and is happy to be home. And we do enjoy his presence because it is so honest. No guile. When he is unhappy he has a tantrum, and when he is in pain he cries, and when he is delighted he gurgles and smiles. Just like a baby. That is his endless attraction and our never-ending tragedy.

February 6, 1979

Haiku thought: Noah continues jolly and happy, glad to be home. Small blessings on a clouded horizon.

February 7, 1979

I awaken these mornings with dreams all around my bed, clinging like granules to my eyelids even as I go to the john to wash, still lingering for a few last drunken moments as I dress. But then, by the time I've said good morning to my family and sat down to breakfast, I cannot for the life of me recall a single image.

Perhaps Noah, too, is passing through a dream season. He loves to stay in bed, chirping away. He really enjoys his breakfast, eats his lunch at school, and dinner is unmarked by a tantrum. Foumi thinks he appreciates our home, his school, daycare, much more now after his being away. He is happy. No spitting, no scratching, just smiles and gentle tips of his head your way. So we're back into a situation we can easily tolerate.

Karl is a pain though: Falling behind in math. Wanting to quit his piano lessons. Avoiding work. His poor—read: nonexistent—study habits. His fear of taking on any new activity. He lacks the competitiveness he would have had with a normal sibling. He is an only child with a lesser brother.

February 8, 1979

Today's thought: When I was young I actively squandered away my time. Now I am concerned with salvaging what little of it remains.

February 9, 1979

I had lunch with my friend Mario Puzo. He told me of disagreeing with a producer on a story point. Finally, he implored the producer: "Listen to me. Just listen to me." "Why should I listen to you?" asked the producer. "Because," Mario replied, "I'm luckier than you."

February 10, 1979

Yesterday, the Godfather. Today God. And I don't know whether that's a step up or a step down. I arrived at Warner's fifteen minutes early to discover that I was fifteen minutes late. The lunch had been moved up to 12:30 without my being told. I gave George Burns a cigar and he in return handed me fifteen pages of suggested changes in my *Oh, God!* sequel script. I looked them over quickly: mostly they were minor, generally they were bad. George had his manager with him, who seemed older even than God himself. His name was Irving and he would cue George on which story to tell. Since Bob Shapiro, the Warner production chief in whose office we were lunching, had not seen the suggested changes, the lunch itself was quickly ceremonial. While God's manager conducted some business with Shapiro in the outer office, George told me he and his writers, whom he employs on a full-time basis, would like to work with me in the same way they worked with Larry Gelbart on the original *Oh, God!* in "punching up" the script. But not to worry: They would never seek credit. And before they departed, his manager repeated much the same thing to me: "George and his writers want no credit. Only a great picture." I will try to take advantage of their input in my new draft. At the same time I must remember that the other characters in the picture have no one to speak for them.

Karl is going through a hate-his-parents period. And since I am one of his parents, I do not find it too pleasant. Especially when he tells me that sometimes he actually wants to kill me. I hope he's being too honest and just overstating his feelings.

Feelings: I actually did hear this sentence on one of those Dr. Lonelyhearts talk radio shows where the listeners call in their problems to a psychologist: "I feel you feel," said the radio fraud, "you're not feeling your feelings."

February 12, 1979

In the morning I tried to take Noah for a walk but he had a bad tantrum. So I took him for a ride. He kept pinching me. I reprimanded him. And he had an even worse tantrum. But then this afternoon I was able to take him for an hour walk.

February 13, 1979

I feel my age most keenly in my memory. Oh I still have memories and reveries of when I was young and the places I lived and the people I knew. But they are losing their sharpness and clarity and becoming blurry now. I guess death is the final blur.

It's also hard to keep my present life in focus. Noah, after a day of scratching, has been tolerable again. But the question is, for how long? And that's always the question.

The paper Karl wrote for me this week was about Dungeons and Dragons, the medieval fantasy game that so involves him. His writing is still a little babyish but it's improving.

February 14, 1979

I long for sleep these mornings. It is as if I want to stay in bed forever. I linger as Foumi rises, turns up the heat, awakens Noah, starts preparing his breakfast. Finally I do get out of bed, dress, and go to the kitchen to help her with Noah. As she makes his lunch I help him finish his breakfast, give him his vitamins, brush his teeth, and dress him.

But this morning I slapped him. For no reason. For something he's done innumerable times and I usually let go unnoticed. What happened was this: He reached across the breakfast table and pinched me. Perhaps simply to tell me that he wanted his bread buttered. I don't know. But suddenly I slapped him in return, almost as a reflex, and he went off bawling. Fortunately, it did not provoke a major tantrum. He was perfectly well behaved as I drove him to school, still longing for sleep.

February 15, 1979

Soon Noah will have a beard, and it will not be easy to shave him. Which means Noah's days of beauty are numbered. Every time I try to settle into a comfortable vision of the future as an extension of the present, as an ongoing routine of daily life, I get rudely disturbed by this inevitable fact: Noah has no future and neither has my love for him. Over fifty, I am on the downhill side of life. Almost thirteen, so too is Noah.

February 16, 1979

California thought: The products with the lowest cultural denominator that come out of Hollywood are not its films but all the nonsense written about them in novels and pop criticism.

February 17, 1979

I read a piece in *Rolling Stone*, of all places, on autism, entitled "The Kids with the Faraway Eyes." What bullshit! The writer mentions Noah, dismisses his history as "a morbid horror story," and then goes on to venerate and esteem all the prophets, false and otherwise, in the field. I guess people would rather believe the testimony of "experts" than the evidence of eyewitnesses. For example, one of the "experts" says that the Noahs of the world can't feel pain. Perhaps that's the expert's way of justifying not treating these kids with more sensitivity. Because Noah certainly feels pain and discomfort. This same expert talks about how a lack of order causes autistics great discomfort. What is pain if not extreme discomfort? Anyway, how the hell does he know what these kids feel?

February 18, 1979

I caught another cold today. When I began to take Noah for his walk this afternoon I felt a chill but I did not turn back. Sometimes I wonder why I so religiously walk Noah every Sunday, giving up the heart of the day to him. I suspect it's because I realize that when he is in an institution I will have to give up all of my Sunday riding out to see him.

February 19, 1979

Foumi is suffering gynecological discomfort. I have a cold. Karl still does not eat properly. Noah is the only healthy one in the family but I am not sure how much longer we can manage him. My instinct, at this point, is to put him as far away as possible and forget about him as much as possible. I know how to treat as dead people who are no longer in my life. With Noah out of the house I could do that. No other way.

February 20, 1979

Television: On Saturday Karl and I were watching a rerun of the Duane Bobbick–Ken Norton fight. As Bobbick was knocked out in the very first round I said: "There goes the white hope." "Maybe your white hope," said Karl. "I'm not white."

Last night we were watching "Roots." A tender scene ended in a kiss and an "I love you." "Here comes a killing," announced Karl, lying on the beanbag next to me. Karl understands the dramatic turns of television style.

February 21, 1979

Larry Gelbart, who wrote the script for *Oh, God!*, tells me that neither George Burns nor his writers rewrote him. "But you have to remember that George was just an eighty-year-old character actor then," said Larry. "And now he's an eighty-four-year-old star."

February 22, 1979

Last night Karl said to me that I ought to write a novel. "Why?" I asked, expecting to hear words of praise about my talents. But Karl replied: "Because you are a lousy nonfiction writer and everybody has forgotten your bad novels already." I really let the kid set me up for that one.

Every night we continue to sprawl in the den and watch "Roots" together. But letting Karl stay up to watch "Roots"— which I think is important for him—means that Karl sleeps late and misses his bus. A sacrifice on my part because in the morning I have to get up an hour early to drive Karl to school. "Roots" is not the history I learned in books but it is a history that he should know. He is a member of a minority. A double minority.

Noah does not worry about his roots. But I worry about his future. And still do nothing about it. As a writer I never can plot well. Plotting involves responsible decision making. And I like to amble along in fiction as in life.

Noah was up before seven, crying because he was hungry. But when I told him to go back to bed he obediently did so. Noah often understands language. He just does not wish to obey it.

February 23, 1979

This morning, while stopping for coffee with a writer couple nearby, I announced: "I am still obsessed with the burning question of my life: What isn't bullshit?" And the writer woman answered: "Everything is." Were those the words, I wondered, of a profound romantic or a deep cynic? Deep cynic, I've decided. Because I still believe there are values that are not bullshit. Only these, of course, are values to be named at a later date.

Noah, for example, has taught me that some states of awareness are infinitely better than others. Yes, Noah still guides my life. Not only because I have to dress him and humor him and monitor his shitting. Not only because he keeps me home, moored to a base. But because he reminds me that life can always be less. And if it can be less it also can be more.

Yesterday Karl was putting down Shakespeare. Shakespeare was not a genius, declared my son, the pop critic, because only a small select audience could have access to him. "A genius," Karl said, "makes everybody understand him." As he ranted on I realized he just might be as smart as he is smart-assed.

Noah was up early, so I got out of bed and gave him breakfast: bagels. He was ecstatic as he hungrily stuffed them in his mouth. Out the window I could see joggers passing by, exercising to stay in shape. I wished I had the time to.

Karl observed later this morning, as I put on a new pair of paisley pants, that I looked like a rock star's agent. The kid may yet be a writer whether he wants to be or not. The family business is always a fallback position. And his writing, the few simple paragraphs I have him do every week, is improving. Like Noah he reacts best to praise. Especially my praise. I have to remember that.

After giving Noah his bath this evening I joined the rest of the family in watching the conclusion to "Roots." Brando was good and Jimmy Jones was moving in the last scenes. But otherwise, most of it was heavy and obvious going. The stuff about being a writer, especially. But I guess writing is a glamorous profession to the American public.

Tomorrow this writer is fifty-one. Realistically, he can scarcely think of it as young. But by dressing as casually—read: sloppily—as he does and having a lousy car and generally considering himself a failure, he can somehow still maintain his own self-image of youth.

My birthday began inauspiciously and lapsed into absurdity. First, Karl showed me this week's composition. Terrible. Sloppy. He had taken no pains and displayed no sense of style. I sought to teach him anew that the secret of writing was the simple telling of incidents and particulars in one's own natural idiom. But naturally I did not make my points with any great patience. So Karl was reduced to tears. Then I worked the rest of my fifty-first birthday on a movie script for an eighty-four-year-old actor. As I say: absurd.

February 28, 1979

Karl, not Noah, is the source of my greatest concern. Like any full-fledged California parent I constantly fear that he will be killed in an automobile accident.

March 1, 1979

Noah and I had a tiff this morning. He reached out and dirtied my clean shirt. I got mad. I owe him an apology.

March 2, 1979

Noah is coughing and Karl is sick and Foumi is suffering arthritic aches and menopausal flushes. There is no rest in my house.

So I turned to television. No rest there either. I came upon a program about brain damage. They showed some idiot savants at Stanford and for a second it was tempting to fall sucker to the "autistic" sales pitch that tries to divorce autism from retardation because of the existence of these otherwise backward individuals who can perform quirky mental stunts. It's easy to forget that just as the blind can hear better, and the deaf see more clearly, in the same way one kind of brain faculty can improve when another is damaged, and that improvement stands out dramatically against a background of social retardation.

March 3, 1979

This morning at breakfast, while Noah was happy in bagel land, Karl informed me that as a conversationalist I rank among the bottom seven of all time. The other six were Ford, Carter, Nixon, Eisenhower, Coolidge, and Max, the kid brother of his friend Erich.

I really hate Sundays. Noah is my Berlin Wall. I cannot escape him. Even if I were to get the best car in the world all I could do would be to drive around the neighborhood.

I shouted at Foumi this morning. No reason. Except she kept harping on about day-care and how it was falling apart. She becomes one-note-obsessive, and it's the one note I don't want to hear.

Bad news everywhere: Our next-door neighbor is dying in the hospital. A friend's four-year-old kid in New York, operated on for a brain tumor, is still semicomatose. And even Noah was up most of the night, coughing and crying. But my constant fear is that something untoward may happen to Karl. I dread the whim of irony more than the wrath of God.

Foumi and I invited Noah's former teacher Alys Harris and her eighty-eight-year-old mother, Josie, to lunch. "Eighty-eight doesn't seem so old to me anymore," Josie told us. But she would not want to live to be one hundred if it meant living with diminished capacities as a vegetable. Sometimes I feel like a vegetable at fifty-one.

When we came home I shouted at Karl. Everybody in our family is mad at everybody else these days. I know my reason. I am in the midst of trying to come up with something to do next. At the same time I am suffering a dearth of dreams: No money. No adventure. No hope for Noah.

And tonight Foumi and I had one more senseless argument. I was giving Noah his bath; he was being difficult. Suddenly Foumi came into the bathroom and made a big deal out of the fact that the heat was not on. I asked her to leave. "Why do you always have to argue?" she proceeded to argue. Then she ranted and raved and I raved and ranted back. Until I felt my heart might break.

March 10, 1979

This morning I lay in bed trying to remember what it was like to be young. What filled my time? What occupied—or preoccupied—me? Mostly, I think, both dreams and dread of the future. I still have a large measure of dread. But my progeny do not encourage dreams.

March 11, 1979

A day of love for Noah. He was so good. Smiling. Happy. Even talking a little: "Good morning." "I want dinner." In his singsong. And seeming to understand even more. I think he likes the weather, the coming of spring.

March 12, 1979

The flutter of the angel of death. Our next-door neighbor died over the weekend. So this afternoon Foumi and I went over to pay our respects to the widower.

March 13, 1979

One of the aides at day-care tells me that yesterday Noah said: "Oh shit!" I don't know whether to believe that. I do know that aside from a daily tantrum Noah has been behaving quite well. Last night after his bath I noticed something in the folds of his penis. To my poor eyes it looked like some sort of infection. Noah is very private about that part and it took me the longest time to examine it closely. It was just a thread.

March 14, 1979

Karl, writing a paper about the play *You Can't Take It with You*, had to cite ten things that were happening in the world at the time of its original production. By and large he chose important events, showing that he does have a sense of history. Which pleased me.

And Noah remains endearing. If it is endearing to strew pillows and chew blankets and cushions and have just a single tantrum a day.

Noah was about to fall asleep last night when I went into his room to check if he was covered. He immediately uncovered himself and raged for a half hour. Finally he went to sleep. But I felt sorry for Karl, having to listen to Noah, as he tried to fall asleep himself after working on his writing.

Karl is so docile with me when it comes to writing. Because he needs my help. And he is not a bad writer—when I edit him. On his own, though, he simply does not make the extra effort that is necessary for good work.

Noah's teacher this morning proudly informed me that Noah now shakes hands. I didn't want to discourage her so I refrained from telling her that he's been doing that since he was three years old.

Barbra Streisand wants to see me about *Yentl*—and I'm not sure I want to get involved with her. One friend advises me in two words: "Stay away." Another friend, who I trust as an accurate reporter, says: "I never met such a self-absorbed person." And a knowledgeable producer who knows us both says: "You can handle her. But don't. You have enough problems with Noah."

Medical report. My cholesterol is up a little: 255. But my low blood pressure ensures the fact that, statistically at least, my cholesterol won't do me in. According to the Framingham study my chances of cardiovascular disease are .4 percent—or 4 in 1,000. But, as I have proved with Noah, I can bring in a long shot.

March 22, 1979

I sat with Karl and tried to plan his program for high school next year. I was dismayed to learn how few "real" subjects are offered in the tenth grade. We finally settled on French and history, in addition to English and math and whatever nonsense course he wants to take.

Karl is getting broader, filling out, all on junk food. With enough Doritos he could wind up a fullback. He is taller than Foumi and soon will be taller than I. He reads books and has strong opinions. The one thing he knows about the future, he says, is that he does not want to be a writer. Yet I suspect that is what he will have to become. Because he is not liable to pick up any other talents with his love-to-play personality.

March 23, 1979

I noticed this morning when he said good-bye, mouthing the words up against her face, that Noah is now taller than Foumi.

March 27, 1979

Foumi and I went square dancing. Most of the people in the class looked old to me. But Foumi says I look as old as they do.

March 28, 1979

I'll try anything: This morning I was annoyed with Noah. As I was lacing his shoes he spit in my face. But I turned my other cheek, let him spit upon it, and then kissed him.

The behavior-modification people would force a showdown with Noah. And no one would win. In fact, something would be lost. My cat snarls when he is unhappy with me and Noah should have the same right.

March 30, 1979

Whenever Noah spits at me I continue to kiss him. It really disconcerts him—my letting him be.

Karl is off to school early tonight in order to work backstage.

But he said he'd be home late because of a cast party. Which means he's ready for beer or girls—or both.

I asked Karl to rewrite the short piece he did for me last week. To organize it better. And he said that I wanted him to write like me. Not so. I just want him to write well.

I went to Vegas for a quick solo vacation. The low point was the few bucks I lost. The midpoint was a massage I received at the Hilton Health Club from a gravel-voiced old man from Chicago named Iggy. He had good fingers and the massage was almost as good as a Japanese one. Iggy said he used to work in Turkish baths in Chicago. I asked him if he knew Saul Bellow. He repeated the name aloud, "Salbella," as if it were an Italian restaurant specialty, and then shook his head. Later, he suddenly stopped working on me and whistled. "What's the matter?" I asked him. "Your spine here," he said. "It's just like Steve Lawrence's. You could be his double from the back."

The high point came this afternoon just after I returned home. Still somewhat in limbo when I picked up Noah at day-care I matter-of-factly asked him if he had missed me. He quickly nodded his head. And at that moment I felt he really had understood me.

14

April 5, 1979

Noah now seems more "reachable" than he's ever been. He listens, he pays attention, he just does not like to be thwarted—or ignored. Like any teenager he mirrors moods, too. Yell at him and he'll out-yell you back. But in little more than three years he'll be sixteen. No longer a child. And Karl will be off to college. What then for Noah? He still may not be able to wipe his own ass. There is no real future for him even if we were to keep him home until we became senile ourselves. Indeed, Noah's presence mocks my future. He removes my right to dream of it.

April 7, 1979

We knew we were going to be busy today. We had a wedding to go to and a kid to pick up at the airport. But we didn't expect to be that busy. We didn't expect so sudden a welcome to the world of teenagers. We didn't expect Karl to disappear.

What happened was this: Last night Karl was supposed to be sleeping over at Erich's house. But at one o'clock we got a call from Erich's parents, hoping Karl was at our house. Because they had come home to find that Karl had left and not returned. We checked and Karl was not home either.

Foumi and I were frightened. Where on earth could he be? Just a few months ago a twelve-year-old girl, last seen in our neighborhood supermarket parking lot, vanished. All sorts of nightmare scenarios raced through our heads. Despite the hour I began to call all of Karl's friends. No one knew where he was.

Foumi recalled that a girl had called Karl twice earlier in the evening. We did not have her number but I tracked down her address and went there. The lights were on. But still I felt like Marlowe when I peered through a window and saw a tall blonde sleeping in a living room. I scratched on the window until she opened the door. She told me that she had been calling Karl to discuss a few parties that they might go to. But no, she hadn't gone with Karl to any parties after all. But maybe Karl had gone with her brother. Where was her brother? She did not know. By the way, where were her parents? Her parents were split and her mother was away, anyway.

It was almost 3:00 A.M. when I returned home. I called the police to report that Karl was missing. The police replied that they would do nothing until Karl was missing for at least twenty-four hours. They told me not to worry and try to sleep.

But we couldn't. Foumi began with her usual recriminations. Why had I given Karl permission to sleep over? I was too lenient. I was always too lenient. And too inconsistent. I told her to shut up and try to sleep. Even though I couldn't. Instead I half drowsed and half worried, full of visions of Karl drunk or run-away or murdered. And if Karl were dead my life would have no meaning. Two sons, one brain-damaged and one dead. How could I go on?

At 6:30 I called the tall blonde to find out if her brother—and perhaps Karl—had come in yet. Her brother had come in, and picked up his board to go surfing, but Karl was not with him. I recited the names of all the kids I had called and asked if I had left out anyone, if there was anyone else I might check with. She mentioned Steve. I called Steve. His sister answered. No, Karl was not there and Steve had gone to a movie in Westwood the previous evening. I hung up and decided to call the roster of Karl's friends again in search of clues. I was on my first call when the operator came on the line and said she had an emergency call. I held my breath and told her to put it through.

It was Steve's mother. She said that Steve had just told her that Karl was probably with Ernie and gave me the number. I thanked her and called Ernie. Karl was there. He said he was about to call me. I was furious and relieved at the same time and told him I would be right over to pick him up.

Not knowing whether to punch him or hug him, I did neither but somehow expressed both. Sitting beside me in the car, he told me that he had left Erich's house to check out a party, got into a game of "Ditch," a form of group hide and seek, and then adjourned to the local Baskin-Robbins, where he and Ernie decided that Karl would sleep over at Ernie's house. Why hadn't he called us? Because he figured Erich's parents wouldn't miss him, therefore neither would we. Which, of course, was a monumental judgment error on his part.

But I did not have the time to unleash my anger at Karl. At home Noah was already chirping away and I embraced him. At least I did not have to worry about Noah's staying out all night. Staying up, yes, but not staying out. I will have to go through the teens with Karl and last night, I know, was just prelude. With Noah I have enough other concerns but somehow I am more in control. But from now on Karl, in a sense, is completely out of my control. He can willfully wander away, disappear, and get into all sorts of different kinds of trouble. Not Noah. The trouble he causes is a constant, not a variable.

April 12, 1979

On Saturday we went to the wedding of Reva's daughter. It was conducted by the most downright honest preacher I've ever heard. "In thirty years," he told the handsome groom joined hand in hand with the beautiful bride beside him, "your wife's going to be disappointing in her looks."

We did not stay for the reception. I had to go off to the airport and pick up Robe. Robe and Karl had been nursery schoolmates and now Robe was coming west to spend his Easter holiday with us. At fourteen and a half Robe is tall and broad muscled and has a slight mustache. He and Karl immediately picked up where they had left off five years ago. It helped that they're both still Dallas and Yankee fans.

On Sunday I took the boys out to Venice and we rented bicycles and rode around the Marina; on Monday Disneyland; Tuesday Universal Tours; and so the week spent itself. I could not get angry with Karl, buffered by his guest. So I think I took it out on Noah. Last night, while I gave him his bath, he spit at me. Lately, I usually ignore it. But last night I lost my cool and slapped him. Immediately, he made me feel terrible by proceeding to slap at his own head. Once more I was detonated.

April 13, 1979

I had Karl working all day, cleaning up around the house, raking out the area behind the carport, as a kind of penance. And he worked with a singular lack of complaint. He was so tired he went to bed before nine without even changing. I still think we should send him to school in the East. I can cope with Noah or I can cope with Karl. But not both.

April 14, 1979

This morning Karl and I wrestled. It is only a matter of months— or perhaps even weeks—before I will no longer be able to assert an upper hand.

April 15, 1979

I turned down a rewrite for a lot of money. But for me the only thing worth writing is still writing—not the rewrite of an action adventure script. But as one gets older I can see how one cares less for the distinctions between good and bad and more for the distinctions between life and death. Look at Olivier and the crap he's doing. But then most actors end up in the gutter of art. They start doing shit in order to have a career and then they have a career in which they end up doing shit. Perhaps a sense of failure is something to hold on to. Because as long as you still have not succeeded in your own eyes, how can you allow yourself to do downhill work?

April 16, 1979

It's always one step forward, one step back, and two steps sideways with Noah. Yesterday he was in a bitchy, scratchy mood all day, suddenly giving himself to tearful tantrums. But he also seemed to understand the concept of numbers for the first time. He placed the appropriate number of objects on the appropriate squares when Foumi worked with him.

The two steps sideways: I've decided it's useless and fruitless for all of us to waste our allegedly hard-earned Sundays taking turns with him. Instead we should hire a companion for him, somebody to walk him and drive him and instruct him and generally baby-sit him through a Sunday.

Karl wrote in his weekly paper for me about a mythological African country. And he did it very well. If the kid winds up fit for nothing else then, at least, it will be with a writer's knack. Thus the sins of the father are visited upon the son. But which son?

April 17, 1979

Perhaps I should take Noah to a hypnotist. His reactions under hypnosis would be interesting. Except I doubt if a hypnotist could get him to go under. Not unnaturally, my hopes are turning to unreal ways. But how long can we take care of Noah? The normal expectation is to be responsible for a kid until he finishes college. That means Noah, who will soon be thirteen, should be entitled to nine more years with us. Which would take me into my sixties. Not fair. I also have entitlements. I am entitled to a decade without Noah. So eventually Noah and I will be at crossed purposes. And he'll have to lose.

April 18, 1979

I was angry with Foumi last night and awoke angry with the world this morning. So when Noah pinched me I almost slugged him. But fortunately, I caught myself and just rapped his hand lightly. If I had hit him he would soon be hitting himself. Every blow I landed upon him would have meant four more subsequently self-inflicted. Whatever the psychological reason—most likely that he cannot separate and differentiate himself from others—the fact remains that his method of handling violence goes even beyond "turning the other cheek." It is not only turning the cheek but slapping yourself upon it. And perhaps Noah's method is ultimately the way to impede the flow of violence. I know it works with me. I cannot bear to see Noah inflicting upon himself punishment that I initiated.

April 19, 1979

Last night Noah had one tantrum after another, constantly taking off his clothes, and pinching and clutching whenever anyone came near him. Mercifully he fell asleep near midnight. But then he was up at three, wailing again. I plugged my ears and managed to sleep a little until I awoke once more. Not to the screeching of Noah but to the sound of crying. Foumi's crying. She was holding her arm in utter pain.

What had happened was this: She decided that perhaps Noah couldn't sleep because he was hungry. She led him to the kitchen and poured some juice for him. He proceeded to knock over the juice and smear it all over the table. She tried to make Noah clean up the mess. Then Noah pulled on her arm hard, hurting her.

What to do with Noah? When he gets these rages not only can't we handle him, but frankly I don't give a damn about him. Let him go to Camarillo, or any state hospital for that matter, and forget about him. He is beyond redemption and if I am to have a resurrection—read: any normalcy—within my own life then I must get rid of him. It's the only way I can keep perspective.

For example, last night I was giving Karl a vocabulary quiz when Noah began having his tantrums. Karl wasn't doing very well but how could I seriously care about his dearth of words. Noah, tearfully exploding before me, has none.

April 20, 1979

Always Noah makes me feel guilty. Last night he was raging again and I put him into a cold shower, hoping to shock him into a more subdued state. This morning his school called, saying he had a bad stomach. Guiltily, I went to fetch him.

April 21, 1979

We are all prisoners to the care of Noah.

April 22, 1979

Karl, now writing on topics of his own choice, displays a talent. He is learning how to create at the typewriter. And if I tend to be too stern a critic with him, he's also always quick to challenge my views. And he's often right. Hell, I'm eminently fallible.

As for his public school education, I wish for his sake that he were in high school instead of still being in junior high. It's such a betwixt-and-between place. I much prefer the eight-four system to the six-three-three system. Why shouldn't high school be as long as possible?

Also on the educational front Noah now definitely understands the numerical concept of three. But he still has trouble sorting objects according to their colors.

April 23, 1979

Noah pinched and scratched me and I was sorely tempted to really haul off on him but instead only shouted loudly and angrily. Still he wailed for a long time, intermittently flailing out and attacking me. No way to win with him. Hit him and he hits himself. Don't hit him and he hits you. Any way he hurts you.

April 24, 1979

The Specter of Noah Department: Carlos, who has been Noah's classmate all these years, will be leaving their school at the end of this year. The director told his parents that they've gone as far as they can go with him. That means Noah is next and we have to come up with a contingency plan other than killing him.

April 25, 1979

No one ever sets out to be a minor writer any more than any would-be baseball player pictures himself winding up as a utility infielder. I remember as a boy growing up in Boston and Brooklyn I couldn't understand the Sibby Sistis and Whitey Wietelmanns, the Oscar Melillos and the Johnny Hudsons, the fifth infielders who would rarely get to play. I marveled at their patience in sitting it out game after game on the bench. I knew I would have angrily slammed my glove to the dugout floor and gone home. How could any one with the talent to reach the big leagues settle for a substitute—or minor—role?

Yet that is the role I have settled for. I've never been anything but a minor writer. And unlike a Sibby Sisti, who became a wartime starter, I have never been a starter at all.

A minor writer waits for assignments, a major writer makes his own waves—or ripples. Too often I've chosen the drone of productivity over the ache of creativity in order to make a living.

A novelist friend tells me he worries about money needs three years in advance. What a luxury! Not only in money terms. I can't worry about anything three years down the line because I never see past a hulking Noah out of control.

This morning Noah woke up with an "I-want-to-eat" whee, all in one long deci-scream. Communicating back to him, though, is still limited to verbs. Like a stroke victim. But now he can also lay four figures on the number 4, three on the number 3, and so on down. A great step forward. But he has also developed the habit of having his evening bowel movement in two sittings about an hour apart. Which means we can no longer rest easy after one bowel movement; another might yet be coming. Last night my cousin, visiting town, was over for dinner and Noah showed great interest in his beard, playing with it as if it gave him the kind of sensual thrill a cat gives you when it stretches against your leg.

Two diverse pieces of intelligence reach me this morning: A married friend, to add to his already considerable woes, has taken on a girlfriend. Another friend of mine is working on a serious piece about Woody Allen.

I live with Noah and marvel at such activities and concerns: To have affairs. To search for "meaningful relationships." To strive for self-expression and heroic fulfillment. Life, as it has to be lived by most of us, is not its infinite possibilities but its limitations and restricted choices. I laugh when I consider those people who know the least about life—the Woody Allens in their Manhattan penthouses, for example—mulling over the problems of our civilization. Never mind the Zabar's–Bloomingdale's–Dry Dock Country world of psycho-bullshit, just tell me this: What will we do with Noah, Woody Allen?

When Karl sat down at dinner he discovered that Foumi had mixed his stew with the noodles. Evidently, he had told her beforehand that he did not want the stew and noodles served together. Foumi was sorry but she had forgotten. Then Karl used such a nasty tone in remonstrating against her, as if she were some lowly servant, that I became furious and soon we were at each other. Finally, Karl said that he did not want to baby-sit Noah as scheduled, that he did not want to do anything for our family. I told him if that was the case to leave, to get out of the house. Somehow Foumi interceded and we managed to get through dinner.

Whatever I do with Karl these days is wrong. If I'm tough, he rebels; if I'm tender, he no longer receives my expressions of love or affection. He constantly tests my attitudes. This morning, for example, he said: "You sympathize with the proletariat. What's so great about the proletariat? You never worked in a factory, so what do you know?" I tried to explain that though I had never worked in a factory it still seemed to me in theory that socialism was a lot fairer than capitalism and that theory was as good a starting place as any.

Karl then complained, in one of those filial non sequiturs I can never understand, that his English teacher was asking the class to look for symbolism while reading *A Tale of Two Cities*. I told him to forget about symbolism and just enjoy the story. If you have to look for symbolism it's not worth finding. Anyway, it's too early to be asking kids to play lit-crit games.

April 30, 1979

Yesterday Karl had a terrible headache. And he was vomiting. I looked up the symptoms in my medical encyclopedia. Not a migraine. But possibly a brain tumor. I pray it's nothing serious. Perhaps he just needs eyeglasses. But I can't help worrying. Once stricken, twice brain-shy, about both my sons.

May 1, 1979

Put a new shirt on Noah in the morning and by evening it is all bitten through as if attacked by a swarm of moths. Foumi says it might be his teeth again. Who knows? But meanwhile he is exceedingly popular with the girls in his school. When I brought him there this morning, Claudia and La Tanya were calling his name and running to greet him.

What I dislike most about Karl is his sullen approach to any activity involving Foumi or me. I guess it's the age—fourteen and a half—impress peers, depress parents.

May 2, 1979

This morning Noah was in a good mood. And, as always, I wondered: Was it because I was in a good mood? Or was I in a good mood because of his good mood? In every family there is a mood setter and in ours it is Noah.

May 3, 1979

Every day Karl's English teacher asks him to shut the door as he is nearest to it. "It is not fair," he complained to me. "I want the door open and, besides, let her ask someone else." I told him to point that out to her, change his seat, or close the door before the class begins. Next case.

May 5, 1979

Karl and I started the weekend with a monumental row last night. I found him idling in front of the TV set and reminded him that he now owed me three papers—two overdue ones plus the current assignment. He claimed he only owed me a total of two papers. The dispute hinged on whether I was including the rewriting of a paper in my count. I said I wasn't. He said I was. He appealed to me. I would not listen. He stamped his feet and jumped in the air. Foumi interceded, playing the judge. Karl seemed to orchestrate a convincing proof with a calendar. But we both lacked exact dates. We continued arguing until I finally conceded—but not very graciously.

And I was even less gracious this morning when I awoke with a sense that I had been cheated and shortchanged. He owed me two new compositions and I told him so at breakfast. Immediately we were at it again. Karl rose from the table and announced that he was on a hunger strike. But soon I heard him typing away and he emerged with one of his "atmosphere" pieces. He handed it to me and gradually communication resumed. At lunchtime when I announced that I would go to Jack in the Box, Karl ended his hunger strike by ordering two hamburgers deluxe, a super taco, a burrito, and a bag of fries. And last night he knocked off another of his assignments by writing an appeal, outlining his case against me. Which was quite good.

I felt terrible arguing with Karl. We both boiled with such indignation. However, mine stems from altruistic purposes while his is derived from a desire to get out of work. I also do want him to think logically. But not so logically as to defeat me.

May 7, 1979

Last Friday was "Ditch Day" at Karl's school, the day the graduating ninth-graders enjoyed a self-proclaimed holiday from school, which Karl duly celebrated. But this morning Karl asked me to give him an absence excuse note "just in case." A display of a lack of nerve and a sign of intelligence at the same time. I resisted being a wise guy and did not write that his absence was caused by the tension of peer pressure. Instead, I wrote the bloody note saying he had a bloody nose.

May 8, 1979

At Noah's school this morning the mother of one of his schoolmates stopped me. All of the teachers were thinking of quitting, she informed me, and suggested that I talk to them. Which I did. The staff was upset because of the director's insistence that some of the parents medicate their kids with drugs; they also did not like her practice of hiring extra aides whenever she knew that monitoring people from Sacramento or Washington were coming. I told the teachers there was little they could do because it was, after all, a private school. But there is something I can do: start a school. If only just looking at a form didn't enrage me so.

May 9, 1979

Last night I was trying to write some checks and fill out a long-neglected tax return. I had the work all sprawled before me. Foumi walked in, wanting to talk. I hate interruptions when I am doing something I hate doing. So I shushed her away. This angered her. Evidently, Karl had acted rudely to her too when he came home from school. And now I was doing the same thing. No one listened to her. We all wanted her to be a kitchen slave. She wanted liberation from the kitchen. It was no fun cooking for ungrateful teenagers. Karl never liked anything offered to him. Not even steak. He was getting to be a bigger problem than Noah. And then off she went off, crying.

I'll take her out to lunch today. I have to make amends. She has a hard enough time as it is, going through menopause. And my temperamentalness and Karl's impoliteness just make things worse. And Noah, of course, doesn't help out either. As I was going through his drawer this morning, looking for a clean shirt to dress him in, I found all of his shirts were so chewed up that they seemed to be woven out of some kind of Swiss-cheese fabric.

May 10, 1979

Karl must have overheard the scene Foumi made. Because yesterday was a flip-flop. He was courteous to the carpenter working on our kitchen cabinets, he helped with the dinner dishes, he practiced his piano without prompting, he even complimented Foumi on dinner. In other words he went from 0 to 100. There must be something he wants. Or the other night really shook him up.

May 11, 1979

Karl brought home his report card: The usual U's in conduct and cooperation and a D in algebra. And afterward Foumi reprimanded me—not him. She said Karl didn't like math because I, his role model, didn't like math. Also that I don't push him hard enough, and without getting pushed, Karl would do nothing. I disagreed. I don't think relentless pressure, the kind Foumi wants to exert, is the answer either. Anyway, I'm sick of worrying about Karl's education too. At this point I'm just happy that he isn't a girl. I know I couldn't handle a rebellious daughter.

May 14, 1979

All Sunday, lolling about the house, all of us except Noah reading and watching television, I literally felt a warm sense of family. It was just too hot even to take Noah for his walk and he did not seem to miss it. We all ignored him and aside from a sob or two of protest, which soon subsided, he did not seem to mind. And surprisingly Karl gave me pleasure. I have him now writing a story, a long short story, and he definitely shows a fictional capability—his ability to come up with the easy lie serving him in good stead.

May 15, 1979

At breakfast Foumi suggested that a change of venue—such as our spending next year in Japan—might stimulate Noah's brain. I would love it. But when I mentioned the idea to Karl he flatly said: "No way."

May 16, 1979

Noah kept us up until after three, running out of his room, crying, stripped naked. Something is bothering him. That his down is getting fuller is bothering me. I will either have to shave him soon or adjust to the idea of having Fu Manchu for a son.

May 17, 1979

Karl has been working on the stage crew of his school's production of *The Music Man*. Last night he was driven home in a new Trans Am by his friend's seventeen-year-old brother. I asked Karl about the show, but he was more interested in telling me about the car. Tonight I will pick him up. Let him talk about my old Mazda wagon.

May 18, 1979

Today's thought: The two biggest threats to any marriage are a suggestion of role reversal and menopause.

May 21, 1979

On Friday night I discovered that Noah had wet his bed. Not too much but enough to soak down to the rubber mattress cover. I changed the bedding and his pajamas and he went back to sleep crying. Later I checked him again. His bed was a puddle. It's the first time in years he's had such a run of accidents. So in the morning we kept him home, wondering why he suddenly had reverted to bed-wetting. One possible cause could be the onset of puberty and a resultant inability to distinguish between a sexual and a urinary erection.

The other pubescent one came home late Saturday night from stage crew because of a cast party and Foumi suspected that he had been smoking grass. Foumi asked him point-blank and he said no. But he also avoided looking her in the eye as he answered. When I mentioned the incident to a friend of mine, he put it all in perspective by observing that he would be surprised if Karl had not been exposed to grass yet.

So the weekend has presented two worries: Noah's bed-wetting and Karl's grass smoking. As usual I have the consolation that Noah in his strange way does not dissemble. I trust his "statements" even if he does not look me in the eye. But on Sunday, as Foumi tried to teach him, Noah was truculent, moody, sullen, difficult, rebellious, ornery—in short, a typical teenager, as if his stricken genes could still instruct that traditional behavior, even though simpler communications are far beyond them.

15

Karl will soon need glasses, says the optometrist, it's a question of time. And the dentist has told us he should get braces because his teeth are crooked. But right now Karl wants neither. But what if Noah were to need glasses or braces?

May 23, 1979

Last night Karl announced, "I have no feeling for anyone in this family," thus sounding for all the world like a psychopath—or a teenager.

The reason for the outburst was another lecture from Foumi on the fact that he should work harder. I told Foumi she works too hard lecturing. But she insists that if she doesn't "push" Karl, he never does his homework. I don't know what to do about Karl's easygoing attitude toward school. But I know that he's bright and that algebra isn't everything. I also don't want to worry too much about his future. I don't want to worry about anyone's future around here.

The flea season is upon us and Noah, as usual, is the number-one victim, bites in his navel, bites under his balls, bites behind his knees. Foumi too is a constant flea target. And for the first time ever they have had the nerve to attack me: around the ankles and under my arms. Still no one is suggesting getting rid of our cat, T.G. However, Noah is apt to blow his cool at any moment

204

because of the fleas, active despair being his only form of urgent communication. But then isn't that so with all of us?

May 24, 1979

The crisis of the weekend seems to have passed. Noah has not pissed in bed and has been generally happy. At least when I'm around. But we are worrying about a school for him next year.

Do I want to start a school? Do I want to start having people work for me on payrolls? Do I want my life to bog down in administrative details? The answer is a resounding no. So far I have managed to keep my life "small," and no matter how events conspire I want it to stay that way.

I'm also wondering what to do with Karl this summer. In three years of junior high he has gone from Advanced Pre-Algebra to Slow Algebra. Since he is still behind where he was at the end of last semester, perhaps the best thing would be to send him to a summer school.

May 27, 1979

Noah, my thirteen-year-old-to-be, is bouncing on the couch restlessly, eating his hat, a beach-sky blue, and wearing striped pillow shorts and a striped terry-cloth shirt. My boy of summer. But he is also the stumbling block to my future. Because of him I live my life on the deferment plan.

May 28, 1979

Perhaps we should teach Noah more of our own private signs. Right now he knows a fist signifies "rice." The next sign to teach him, according to his needs, might be one for "juice."

May 29, 1979

My cholesterol is down to 248. Not great but good.

May 30, 1979

Fractions, when they are laid out in algebraic equations, remain a mystery to Karl. Which worries Foumi greatly. And then when I don't join her in her worries she becomes furious with me.

This morning Karl told me that we needn't bother to attend his junior high school graduation because he wasn't going to go. "And miss getting your medal?" I replied. "What medal?" he wanted to know. "The one given to the best algebra student," I told him, "with a brain-damaged brother, a Japanese mother, and a Jewish father."

I shouldn't have said that. I'm too quick to tease. But let's face it. The immediate problem in my life is suddenly not Noah's brain damage but Karl's algebra. His present teacher has completely destroyed his confidence in his ability to do math. And we've now heard of a special math summer school, scheduled to run from 8:00 to 12:30 daily, in which he can cover a year of algebra and perhaps even learn to understand it. In any case he can thus complete his algebra requirement and move on to geometry, the next necessary step for him on the obstacle course of middle-class life.

June 3, 1979

I took Karl, moaning all the way, to meet the man who runs the math summer school. If Karl learns nothing else this summer he will learn there is no way he can escape his math obligations. Still, I feel sorry for the kid.

June 4, 1979

I've had pains all weekend, pains in my stomach and in my back, pains whenever I try to deal with Karl in the present, pains whenever I consider Noah's future.

June 5, 1979

My back still aches. Other parts of my body also ache. So I made an appointment to see the doctor tomorrow. And on my walk tonight I wondered: What if I discover I have cancer? What would I do? My first impulse was to send Noah away, to make my last days easier, so to speak. But then I thought: No, I want Noah in the house around because he has been such an important presence in the life I would soon be leaving. And I would just want to stay home with my family and continue living—or begin dying—with almost a sense of euphoria. Because I would be free of the problem of Noah at last. And without that problem the rest of my life—and my death—would be light as a feather.

June 6, 1979

My doctor doesn't think my pains are much because they keep moving around. What should I do about them? I asked him. Wait for them to stop, he suggested.

June 7, 1979

We had our annual meeting with the school district to discuss Noah's IEP—Individual Education Program—for next year. I asked that Noah receive special physical training and special signing lessons on a one-to-one basis. But they refused to recommend that. Rather than try anything different they want to continue much the same program he's had this year. I want something different. But at the same time I don't want to have to start a school. I'm not an educator or an entrepreneur. I'm just a lousy parent.

June 8, 1979

Karl is excited about graduating. Last night he asked me: "Did you think my three years in junior high would pass so quickly?" I answered his question with the same question: "Did you?" "No," he said, "it's all gone by so fast."

June 11, 1979

A hot and busy weekend: I bought a new car, a cherry-burgundy Honda Accord; Foumi banged up my old wagon, bending a fender, destroying a headlight; Karl went to a grad party and then to Magic Mountain. But the big news is that for the first time Noah took a shower—as opposed to a bath—willingly. Yesterday morning I did have to all but force him into it. But in the afternoon he hinted that he wanted one by running to the bathroom and turning the lights on and off. And by nightfall, when he took his third shower of the day with me, not the slightest suggestion of force was necessary. The hundred-degree temperature does have its benefits.

The fender bender wasn't Foumi's fault. Somebody turned into her at a light. But she didn't get the license number. When I asked her what kind of car had hit her, she replied, "Big." And nothing else.

June 12, 1979

Sometimes I think I'll never write another word. And it's not because of Noah. Nor because of the hundred-degree heat. But because of the rest of the family. When I came home for lunch at one o'clock Foumi informed me that she had had a nosebleed and that Karl had called from school, where he was sick. I immediately drove over to his school and picked him up in the nurse's office where he was sound asleep. When we returned home Foumi's nose was bleeding again. A nosebleed is no big deal but she is unaccustomed to having one. And she wouldn't follow my instructions on how to stop it. Instead, she insisted that I call the doctor. For a nosebleed? Meanwhile, Karl napped; Noah, who was home from school because of the heat, yapped; and my work day proceeded to fall apart completely.

After Foumi's nose finally stopped bleeding I took Noah to a friend's pool to cool off. Since it was his first pool visit this year he was shy. I mean shy to the water. After tying him into his life preserver and putting a tube around him—giving him both a belt and suspenders, so to speak—I force-led him into the water. And after a few perfunctory shrieks of protest he began to enjoy himself. And so did I. The hell with writing.

June 13, 1979

Last night Foumi had another nosebleed. And then, as if they were catching, Karl had two bloody noses. He also has a cold. He also has been impossible to deal with about his graduation. I dragged him out of the house to buy him clothing to wear to it. But he insisted he wasn't going to attend anyway. We argued in the car. We argued in the haberdashery store. Finally, I told him to walk home. Whereupon he took his leave, announcing, "Screw you!"

Foumi somehow achieved a détente with him. Karl agreed to go shopping with her tomorrow. But he still says he won't go to his graduation because he does not want to shake the principal's hand. "The principal never ran the school for the sake of the kids," he claims. I think rather than possessing such a fine sense of justice—or injustice—Karl is trying to mask a native shyness with rebellion. Because he next refused to fill out the form for summer math school, this time arguing that he did not have to answer any of the questions under the Fifth Amendment. Oh what a night!

Nor did Noah make things any easier. He was irritable because of the heat but managed to fall asleep. But then he awoke early, visiting the bathroom twice and leaving souvenirs of each visit on his bed sheets, his underwear, the living room couch, and the easy chair.

At this point I wonder why I work so hard at keeping our family together. Foumi would be happier back in Japan. Karl would be delighted if left to his own resources. I would be satisfied living out my life as a solitary in a YMCA room of my own choosing. And Noah would be better off in some institutional residence. Aye, there's the rub. I don't think so. I can't kid myself about that. So our family has to endure as monument to him. He is our banner and our glue. But what price family?

June 15, 1979

Last night I had to clean up appalling amounts of excrement and vomit. His body was slumped over the toilet seat and while his intestines ran, he retched. At the same time he was crying and could barely keep himself upright. I had never before seen him so completely out of control, his eyes unfocused, his head wobbling, and I never have felt so helpless in my life.

It was not Noah; it was Karl. He came home last night more sloshed than I had ever seen a fellow G.I. or student or coworker. In celebration of his graduation he had drunk rum at a friend's house. He had also smoked grass. And it was not the first time, I was shocked to discover, that he had tried either. He said both indulgences had a history of over two years—although the history kept changing every ten minutes.

For example, the reason he did not come home that night around Easter when he slept over Ernie's house was that he was both drugged and drunk. He drinks with his friends, he said. They all have tried pot, he wailed. "I'm weak, I cannot control myself," he cried. "I can't go to college now, I've ruined my whole life!"

I don't know if he's ruined his whole life but he has certainly wreaked havoc in Foumi's. She stayed up all last night, bemoaning Karl's future and berating me for my past permissiveness with him.

Last night, as he sat on the john retching, was the first time I had seen Karl naked in a long time. And, despite the dramatic intensity of the moment, I could not help but notice that he did not have a single pubic hair. Noah is more developed than he is. Which makes his drinking and smoking even harder to take. Not only is he only fourteen and a half, but a young fourteen and a half at that.

Karl was right—to some extent—about his graduation being a waste of time. It was in the Santa Monica Civic Auditorium, a building that in the past has even hosted the Academy Awards. And, indeed, some of his classmates came in top hats and tails; others arrived in limousines. Karl, in his hastily purchased slacks and shirt, looked so much younger and smaller than the rest of the kids. But afterward, he sounded so much wiser and more sophisticated as he mocked the valedictorian speeches. I worry a lot about his going to Pali High next year. The only crowd he can move with is the wrong crowd. I wish, instead, he were going to a prep school back East . . . just to get him out of this milieu. I see how vulnerable he is, how amenable he is to peer pressure leadership. But vulnerable or not, as I warned him this morning, I would not let him hurt Foumi. I would destroy him first. And I meant it.

Noah, meanwhile, has been lovely. I think I can hold on to him longer than I can hold on to Karl. The atmosphere of our family evidently is wrong for Karl. But at this point I doubt if the family exists where the atmosphere would be right for him.

At Noah's school this morning as his teacher was telling me how happy Noah had been yesterday, all I could think of was how unhappy Foumi and I were last night. But I guess we should console ourselves that Karl's stoned drunkenness—or drunken stonedness—may have been a sign of his inexperience and that his getting home safely at all in that condition was definitely a sign of some good luck.

Karl has agreed to Foumi's demand that he sign a contract saying that he will not smoke grass or drink until after he graduates high school. I agree with her at this point that Karl has to be frightened. I've warned him that if he breaks any law while living under my roof I'll turn him over to the juvenile authorities. But I don't think anything will work except getting him out of this environment. I'm sick of worrying about his unhappiness anyway. He is a teenager and active unhappiness is its natural condition.

When Karl is at the center of the critical family spotlight—as he was last night—Noah is really happy in his babbling way, as if he somehow senses that for the time being at least, he is off the hook, so to speak.

I had lunch with Barbra Streisand yesterday at her Malibu Colony digs. Like most Colony houses hers impressed me no more than any Far Rockaway bungalow. There is no way these places can be less than tacky being that close to the ocean. And not all the chintzy pillows about the living room could change that. I kept thinking Noah could chew up the place in ten minutes.

Which was about how long I had to wait for Barbra to make her entrance. It was hard to really look her over because she herself kept looking directly into my eyes. But she's taller than I had expected and her bare feet seemed large. Her tizzy hair was red and she wore a black jumper. She projected a feline quality, except it was self-conscious.

"Hello, Josh," she greeted me, "I understand you're in love with *Yentl*, too." Since this is the season of *Rocky II* I couldn't resist joking, "I'm here to talk about *Yentl One*." Not a great joke, but as it went right by her, her eyes blinking uncomprehendingly, I knew I should begin plotting an early exit. Because if we couldn't see eye to eye on humor, then it was a good bet we would not agree on anything else.

She then proceeded to conduct a seminar, her unremitting eyes never leaving my face for a single moment. What did I think of *Yentl?* I told her I thought the only way to do it was with music and the only way to treat the material was as comedic. Her face wrinkled. "This is a serious movie," she protested. I tried to explain to her that comedy could still be serious in message but that gender passing was basically a classical comedic device, from the Greeks through Plautus and Terence to Shakespeare, and it would be a mistake to try and bend it differently.

Still frowning, she wanted to know how I felt about collaboration. Because *Yentl* was something she wanted to work on very closely with the writer; in fact, she wanted to cowrite. When I shrugged and asked, "Can you type?" she looked into my eyes for a long moment and finally laughed.

Then we broke for lunch. A buffet lunch consisting of several terrific salads, cold salmon, and fruit compote. But no wine. No coffee either.

Barbra ate little but talked much. I asked her for some of her ideas about *Yentl* and as she was telling me them, staring directly at me as she did so, she suddenly stopped. "I can tell by your eyes," she said, "you're surprised that they're good." "As a matter of fact," I said, "I am."

And I was. We spent another hour or so together—she picking my brain like any good producer should, me not being that anxious to return home to my real problems—even though we both knew nothing further would come of it. We had not hit it off in terms of temperament and we both thought in different dictions. I did admire her autodidactic zeal to learn, but I didn't care very much for her star-turn way of treating writers. At one point she mentioned disparagingly that she had given Isaac Bashevis Singer a "whack" at writing the screenplay of *Yentl* but that "he couldn't lick it."

June 18, 1979

The image of my drunken fourteen-year-old son, his face caked with blood and unable to walk straight, but still trying to lie his way out of the situation as he reeled in the kitchen doorway, will probably haunt me for the rest of my life. Meanwhile worry about him fills my nights and empties my days. I see no reason to keep our family together if Karl cannot flourish within it. I feel our lives are falling apart. Foumi and I have such divisive theories about how to deal with our dour teenager, who has already turned on more times in his young life than I in all of mine. Who already has become more juiced out of his skull than I've ever been. Indeed, most of his graduation night is still blacked out to him.

But Foumi has reacted so strongly that she leaves Karl no escape path. She has forced him into a contract he can never keep; she wants him to arrange a schedule that he'll never be able to adhere to. In other words, she's trying to do everything at once. Karl refuses to submit to her easily. And I often rage. And it is not even on a point that is important to me. But the problem smolders and we keep fanning the flames with rhetoric. I wish Foumi would let up. And then I could let up too. Which I did for a moment late last night, at the end of Father's Day, when I hugged Karl in the kitchen and told him that whatever he did I would always forgive him. As if I were some sort of God. Who the hell do I think I am?

June 19, 1979

Each day a discovery, another revelation. Yesterday I learned that Karl had a BB gun hidden at a friend's house. He hadn't told us about it because he knew of our aversion to guns. So we had another family tear session. I think we're overreacting. But Foumi insists there is no other way to react, that turning the other cheek—or averting the other eye—would be absolutely wrong. She does not understand the experimentation of the young in this country and I can't always accept her overreactions to a kid's natural curiosity and necessary rebellions. I just wish it weren't coming at such a young age, that's all. Meanwhile, Noah at least remains a constant, a babbling constant, and I suppose I should be grateful for that small blessing: Because if Noah were normal now he and Karl would probably be fighting to the death over a jay.

Things seem to have calmed down about the house—but not completely. It's as if we now take for granted that Karl has tried grass, booze, and BB guns. All forbidden fruits—or weeds—but perhaps necessary sequential steps on the way to maturity for an American adolescent. Still it hurts to think about Karl reaching those steps at such an early age. It's a little like a girl who still plays with dolls afternoons and in the evenings becomes a whore.

Foumi is forcing Karl to keep a schedule so that he can learn to allocate his time properly. And I must say he has been funny about it, for example, refusing to do certain chores because they're not on his schedule. And without his drug cronies, playing only with old friends, he has not been his usual sullen self but rather sweet.

Noah remains sweet too. Though he still tips over tables, jumps on couches, pulls hair, and is just too big to be doing any of these things.

I spoke to Spence, the pastor of the church that houses our day-care, about the possibility of having a school there. He said: Certainly. So Foumi is already thinking of hiring a teacher and getting started. She is a study in action. I am a fugue in inertia.

Karl gave me an oral history: He first tried grass a year ago at the end of June, splitting a five-dollar buy; next around Christmas. Neither outing had any effect. Then he smoked some on New Year's eve; this time it worked. Later he bought a bag of his own. But he really began smoking in earnest on the infamous "missing persons" night. He sold some of his Dungeons and Dragons pieces and with the money made a fifteen-dollar buy. That night he hosted a party in the park before retiring to his friend Ernie's house. He subsequently smoked grass with his D and D friends, these sessions often enhanced with beer and wine. He says he has had many opportunities to smoke during school hours and after school during weekdays but reserved his grass smoking for weekends. The BB gun he purchased from a D and D player for five dollars and it figured in some pot fantasy. He and two friends were going to attack the owner of a grass crop who threatened to shoot at kids. In other words, they would be invoking their own law of the West.

The more people I talk to about drugs, the more widespread I realize it is among teenagers. A friend in Denver tells me he has been through the problem with his sons. Another friend back East in New York tells me his daughters were both into it. Still, I feel Karl has been a little too precocious.

June 22, 1979

When I mentioned that I was thinking of sending Karl to a school back East a friend gave me a brochure on Choate, pointing out that Edward Albee, Adlai Stevenson, and JFK were among its distinguished alumni. This afternoon, our cabinetmaker, who is still working on the kitchen, heard me mention Choate and stuck his head out from a floor cupboard and announced: "My old school. I went there."

Our cabinetmaker's fine example notwithstanding, there are three good reasons to send Karl to a school like that: He will learn manners, he will get a better education, and he will be out of this environment. But it also all seems so simpleminded and stupid to me. I mean, sending the good apple away. I think we should send them both away. After all these years, Foumi and I are entitled to some kind of life of our own choosing.

June 23, 1979

We were sitting about the living room talking—Karl is much more sociable these days since he's been cut off from his grass-root friends—when Noah suddenly streaked by, running from his bedroom into ours. "Get out of that room," Karl shouted. And in the same motion, without missing a stride, Noah turned and beat a rapid retreat back to his room. It was a classic comic moment and we all could not help but laugh.

I have a moral dilemma. I wonder whether I should inform the parents of two teenagers at whose homes Karl has been smoking and drinking recently. Both are single parents. And it seems on the night of Karl's monumental debaucherie, graduation night, the older sister of the teenage host, and her boyfriend, who is in his twenties, were there pouring the drinks and passing around the joints. My informing could cause Karl to develop the reputation of a snitch. Than which there seems to be none lower among teenagers. Not to be a snitch or a stool pigeon, it seems, being the only moral law teenagers live by these days.

June 24, 1979

While I was in the bathroom this morning I heard Karl and Noah fighting. What happened was this: Karl had been reading the newspaper when Noah reached over and poked his hand at it, pushing it down. Karl, like a normal brother, reacted angrily and violently. And soon they were at it, two brothers fighting. By the time I came out of the bathroom the fury was over.

June 25, 1979

Foumi and I went square dancing last night and my muscles are still aching. Dancing is good exercise but I'm not in shape. Noah behaved well while we were gone, according to Karl. Who is still on a kind of grounded surveillance—but is beginning to get restless.

Noah will be thirteen on Sunday. I have already measured out my life to him in countless ass wipes. Still I will try to treat him especially well.

June 26, 1979

Foumi is raging at Karl, because he's not "diligent enough," while Noah, who is not diligent at all, is off on the Universal Studio Tour with our day-care group. Sean Vincent, the cabdriver who usually ferries our kids from school to day-care, is taking them on his day off in his own car. How nice some people can be.

June 27, 1979

When Noah came back from Universal he refused to get out of Sean's car. On the way home, Sean told us, Noah had been kicking and screaming. In the house he continued to have a tantrum. I diagnosed thirst as a possible cause and gave him three glasses of water. But when I left him to answer a phone call, he pulled Foumi's arm and hair and she was a crying mess by the time I returned. What happened was this: She had tried to wipe his face. Her compulsion to clean, her aversion to dirt, had led her to do something she shouldn't have done: gone near him when he was like that. So she blamed me for being on the phone.

June 28, 1979

Last night I played Monopoly with Karl. Beat him. But we argued about the rules. I played according to the rules, block rules—the block being East 46th Street in Brooklyn.

June 29, 1979

We were out at a gathering last night to greet an old friend in from New York. The talk got around to teenage drugs. A woman was discussing her two kids who had gone what she described as "the route," with one presently being on probation in Texas, when the phone rang. I had the feeling it was for us and I was right. "You asshole!" Karl, who was Noah sitting, shrieked hysterically into the phone, "Get home!"

What happened was this: He simply could not handle Noah. He had tried to force Noah to go to bed but had been unable to. Noah had retaliated by pinching and scratching away at him at record clip. And poor Karl. He has not learned the adult art of ignoring.

June 30, 1979

A letter came from a man in Florida who has a son like Noah advising me to "stop worrying about whether Noah is 'autistic' or 'brain-damaged' because all names mean anything and nothing. There is no solution," he writes. "Adjust to it." He has had his Noah to live with for thirty-five years.

Immediately, I could see myself taking care of a thirty-five-year-old Noah, a forever father washing his hair, shaving his face, wiping his ass, as I creaked toward my own seventy-fourth birthday. And so I would totter away, addicted through love or ennobled by guilt, a slave to our species in a sense, a caretaker of one of our rarer specimens.

A life increases in value in ever-decreasing circles. From living room to bedroom, from kitchen to bathroom. The more we meet someone in a limited space, the more we are joined to him in love. As if love is a form that follows real estate.

The fuel crunch fills the headlines of the page-one world. There is talk of solar and geothermal heating and extracting oil from shale and grain. But if I were a businessman I would invest in the fuel of the future: fossil fuel. In the same way, just as cable is the subject of most entertainment news, I would put my money into the medium of the future: network television. Because the future, I am afraid, like Noah, will resemble the present more than we care to imagine.

In celebration of Noah's thirteenth birthday yesterday I took him for two rides in my car. Foumi also honored us with her presence on a walk. And we celebrated his appetites, feeding him according to his tastes. Croissants for breakfast. Pizza for lunch. Japanese dumplings for dinner. Carrot spice cake. Cherries and grapes. And this morning we continued our salute with bagels.

This afternoon they will have a party for him at school for which I will supply more carrot cake and apple juice. Noah is thirteen, a teenager, and I just hope he is not heir to all the additional woes that go with the franchise.

Like this morning Karl woke up at 5:30, instead of 6:30, for his first day of summer math school, just to rouse us early too and give us a hard time. And when he finally went off to class he did so insisting that he would not learn anything anyway.

I don't know what to do about him. I must try to condition him to do right, to instill in him the proper moral values and virtues. I also have to try to build up his self-esteem and to quell his *che sarà, sarà* attitudes. But I realize too that he is constantly trying out poses on us, wanting to show us just how independent he is by taking a stand of his own. For example, guns. He claims a fascination with guns, says he looks forward to becoming eighteen so that he can have his own gun. Foumi, of course, is shocked. And I'm duly appalled. Which, I know, is just the effect he wants. Sometimes I think my mid-life crisis—if I'm having one—is Karl's adolescence.

16

July 3, 1979

I feel sorry for Karl. The summer math school goes for four and a half hours each day. He has the imagination and energy to become very impatient during that period. It must be torturous for him to sit through it.

I have to straighten out the day-care tax situation by filing an amended return. I am angry with myself. For all the doggie work I have to do. For all the real work I don't do.

July 4, 1979

Independence Day, but who's free? We lunched with a lady from the State Department of Education who left us a sheet of instructions on how to open up a special school. We'd have to start by hiring a credentialed teacher and a secretary. And then we'd go first class, putting bookkeepers and all sorts of help into the budget. Still I could not sleep last night worrying about it.

July 6, 1979

Karl was complaining about math school. The boredom is infuriating him. So I promised him a radio-operated glider if he gets an A in the class. I have to give him some sort of positive motivation.

Carlos is getting too big to handle. He's attacking too many people at day-care. Yesterday, he scratched one of our male volunteers. So we're not letting him come today. But his future with us—and our future with ourselves—is in doubt. It gives me pause in starting a school because I certainly wanted Carlos to be one of the students.

I sometimes think of parting with Foumi still as friends and going off on some mid-life adventure before it's too late. But Noah brakes that. How could I leave her with him? And how could I take him anywhere else?

Karl made all sorts of sounds about wanting to go to the beach today. We knew it was because he wanted to meet the fast crowd he had been traveling with before his graduation-night fiasco. He is devious and scheming. Oh that I could plot in fiction as well as he can plot in life.

Just another typical Friday the thirteenth: I awoke at 7:30, sleepy, and drove Karl to his summer school. Next, still sleepy, I drove Noah to his summer school. Then because I was so sleepy I had a terribly stupid argument with Foumi about some electrical problem. I went to my office and wrote letters to our congressman and senators. Our nonprofit day-care center has been getting harassed by Internal Revenue because, it seems, I had neglected to file some form in time.

When I drove to day-care in the afternoon to pick up Noah, Carlos's mother told me she was looking for an institution for Carlos, that he has become just too much for her. Which depressed me no end. Not only because I have come to love Carlos after all these years but because I also know after Carlos comes— or goes—Noah.

He is next. He spits and scratches and clutches. He is unhappy and trying to tell me something. But no matter what he wants to tell me what he is actually telling me is that he is on his way out.

Just the other night I watched the rerun of the "60 Minutes" segment on Noah. How adjusted I seemed. And so much happier. No wonder: I was a year further away from the end of Noah than I am now.

July 14, 1979

Quiz for befuddled parents of teenagers: What do you do when your teenage son's dealer calls?

a) Take the message. b) Get a price. c) Place an order yourself. d) None of the above; just forget all about it.

July 15, 1979

At a party this afternoon I ran into a lawyer I went to high school with. He had a salt-and-pepper beard and looked like a man of fifty, which he was. Which I am. Which is still difficult to reconcile. I am old. I really do belong among the square dancers.

July 16, 1979

I had a great day at the typewriter yesterday in just a few brief hours. Without any special effort either. Today it is noon and I have done nothing. It is because before coming here I first had to run all sorts of mundane little shitty errands. Nobody, Foumi included, understands that if I get involved in the worldly I cannot get untracked into the unworldly or the otherworldly. Not that the act of writing is holy or anything like that. It's just that's the way I am—a hard-wrought empirical fact I've learned about myself.

July 17, 1979

I picked up Karl at math school, took him to lunch, and bought him a bigger "Boogie"—a plastic surfboard. Now he plans to go straight to the beach each day after math school. Where he is having some difficulty as a behavior problem. But that's him. Big-mouthed and with a passionate lawyer's sense of justice. I like him.

I like Noah too. There is a wisdom always lurking within him. I wonder if we should look to find something new to try with Noah. I have been passive for too long. But I never know whether to put my energies into adjusting to things as they are. Or to alter radically the need for such an adjustment no matter how lamebrained or quacky the scheme.

I remember a kid from Rhode Island in my barracks in basic training who used to lie on his sack wondering: "If I adjust to the army, how can I adjust to the rest of my life?"

July 18, 1979

As the summer grinds away, the same questions hover over me: Do we continue our day-care center? Do we start a school? Do we make every effort to find a residential placement for Noah? Should we follow up on "patterning" or a special diet or any other nonorthodox alternative? The hardest thing to accept about Noah is the fact that there is no solution. Optimism is an act of blind will, not illuminating intelligence. It is always necessary but it is also always a terrible energy drain. And I want to use my energy to be more than the father of a crazy kid.

Karl boasts of an impending A in his summer math class. If he can pull a B I will be pleased. And then I have to get him to work on his piano and English again.

July 19, 1979

Last night as we were going to bed Foumi began to cry. And hit me with some facts: She is deathly tired. We cannot go on with Noah too much longer. We must seriously seek to find a place for him. The place has to be within easy visiting distance, close enough so that we can monitor the situation. Starting a school would be just getting on the merry-go-round again with younger children and suffering a similar ordeal.

Noah is acting more aggressive. He has evolved into the most fearful of all species to deal with: a teenager. Normal or special, it seems, there is simply no way of dealing with them. For example, the other teenager is now protesting because we are not making any trips this summer. But where does the kid want to go? I don't think he wants to go anyplace so much as to have gone. I think he is just jealous of his more peripatetic peers.

July 20, 1979

Karl was badly shaken after being caught in a riptide yesterday. As he went under a wave and saw no prospect of coming in, he tells me, for the first time in his life he was prepared to die.

July 21, 1979

I force-weighed Noah. He seemed to hit ninety-four pounds. Two pounds less than Foumi. And he is as tall as she is. In fact, when he looks at her he seems to marvel at how small she is compared to him. He is still afraid of me physically, but he has no fear of her.

July 23, 1979

My typewriter broke down on Friday. I broke down this morning. What happened was this:

I got pissed off at Karl because I thought he had lied to me. I couldn't recall his telling me that the director of the math school had threatened to expel him because of his poor behavior. In fact, I was so furious with him that I knocked him down in front of the math school. A passing teacher thought I was a child abuser and I almost took a swing at him, too.

The guy I should have laid out was the director of the math school. He lowered Karl's grade from an A to a B because Karl was a "disruptive influence." I can't stand teachers who insist on confusing good academic performance with bad behavior, something that dogged me throughout my own school life. So I'm confused. The school no longer wants Karl and I'm not so sure I want Karl to continue in that school anyway. Except for the irony that Karl now does understand something about algebra for the first time. He has also learned again how unfair adults are when it comes to dealing with spirited kids.

What with rigid educational authorities, a crazy brother, an immigrant mother, and an inconsistent father, it will be a wonder if Karl can survive his childhood. But he will. The way we all did: somehow.

Noah has been a joy lately. But that always happens when I'm preoccupied with Karl. Or when he's enjoying regular bowel movements. Then he's like a dog or a cat, happy with the world. Or if we're having good weather, the air clear, the temperature pleasant, he becomes the climate control of our lives.

Reva has the mumps. Which means we do not have enough help at day-care. Especially when it comes to handling Carlos. So once more we've had to ask his mother to keep him home for the next few days, something we hate to do.

I have learned too late that we should have started day-care grandiosely with a huge budget instead of a modest one. But we did want to do something simple and small. Far more difficult to accomplish in our bureaucratic society. Bureaucracies are set up to deal only with each other.

A friend of Karl's was boasting about how well he had coped with the divorce of his parents. "The divorce of a parent at our age," Karl told him, "is nothing." "Oh yeah?" challenged his friend. "You don't know how tough it is. You've never had to go through it." "I've had to handle something a lot tougher than that," said Karl, "living with a brain-damaged brother." "Oh, that's nothing," his friend replied. "You're used to it."

Foumi told me that yesterday Karl drew a knife across his wrist and threatened suicide if she displayed any of Noah's finger paintings. When I confronted him, he said he had only been teasing and had done it playfully. But I did not accept that. Teasing or not, one does not play with weapons or joke about one's own life.

I think of Karl and how we're disappointed in each other. We've both turned out to be less than we had expected. I am not the ideal father and he is not the ideal son and we just have to live with that. But instead we fight. About everything. In the car this morning he told me three times that I should get a new stereo radio. He dismisses what I consider large sums of money as "nothing." He is smart-ass, sassy, ungrateful, impolite, selfish, and demanding. He seems to have nothing to do yet never volunteers to do anything. I fear it will be harder for me to get through his teens than it was for me to get through my own. I was rebellious too, but I was never so close to an edge of violence. But then I didn't come out of a generation of TV watchers.

August 2, 1979

We could never place Noah in a residence too far from our home. First, because of the simple logistics of getting him there. Second, we would have to be able to monitor the facility.

August 3, 1979

Whenever I begin thinking of finding a residence for Noah, something like this happens: A San Diego woman told me she institutionalized her eighteen-year-old autistic son because he was beating her up physically. In Patton State Hospital, she says, he was raped by a fellow retardate. Now she has him in Camarillo. In a good ward, she says. But when the hospital employees threatened to strike recently she was notified to come and get him. So there is no way of just getting rid of Noah. There is only a search for breathing spaces.

August 4, 1979

A therapist called who claims she teaches kids like Noah while they're sleeping by using pressure points. It seems a lot of people would like to take a crack at curing Noah. But no one wants to take care of Noah. There is still no place I know that we can entrust him to confidently. Noah is also, I fear, a dark cloud forever looming before Karl, the reason for Karl's tendency to be so pessimistic and negative. Karl knows too much about life and its cutting edges. He knows more about life than many of his teachers do.

Foumi's arthritis is bothering her again. She cannot lift her arms overhead; she cannot move her hands without pain.

This afternoon we all drove out to Hollywood to pay respects to the family of a friend who died suddenly of a heart attack. And I can't say who behaved worse—Karl or Noah. Noah was constantly eating his shirt. But Karl was just as obviously eating his heart out, not enjoying the company of grown-ups for a single second and rudely showing it.

I awoke in the middle of the night hearing the sounds of Noah. Who else, I thought, has to get out of bed to check a thirteen-year-old? Noah had stripped away his sheet and mattress cover and was lying on the rubber insulating cover we use in case he bed-wets.

Foumi still goads me to start a school. Schools are the easiest way to get funding. Day-care, though necessary, comes at the orphan end of funding programs. What we need, of course, is a place that cares. Really cares. But no one funds caring.

So there is still no place for Noah but with us and no one to care for him but us. It is as simple as that. The kind of care offered for Noah these days is like the workmanship in everything else: Shoddy. Botchy. Make-do.

Noah debunks the traditional Oedipal myth. I can kill him and he can kill me and it has nothing to do with our wanting consciously or unconsciously to sleep with the same person.

Karl takes his summer math final. For the past few days he's been saying he's going to fail. But then he's always negative.

August 13, 1979

Foumi and I had a real to-do yesterday. Ostensibly it was about the new flooring in the living room. But what really upset us was a piece in the morning paper about Metropolitan Hospital, the mental hospital in Orange County, and the deplorable conditions there. Whenever the future of Noah comes into view, because we are at a loss what to do, we slap each other in the face verbally.

August 14, 1979

Karl received an A in algebra at summer school. It's probably the most hard-earned A in the history of grading. Not only did he have to go to school for six weeks, four and a half hours a day, getting up at seven each morning, but we had to get up early, too. Karl is elated and so are we. He is full of talk about the N-gauge railway set he has decided he wants me to get for him rather than the glider I had promised. Now nice it is to see a happy kid! When I was driving him to his friend Warren's house to play this afternoon I had to constantly resist the impulse to reach over and put my arm around him and hug him. He is too old for that. Even Noah is getting too old for that. I have no one around here to hug anymore except Foumi. And even she's threatening to get too old for that.

August 15, 1979

Karl may not have gone away on a trip this summer but he has managed a change in his personal geography. He's switched rooms with Noah. And it's been fun watching Noah's reaction. I thought he'd be greatly upset. But he rather likes it. I guess like all siblings he wants what his brother has. And, in any event, he can't figure out if it's a promotion or a demotion. Karl now has the larger room, which is only right. He does need more space: He has more stuff.

August 16, 1979

Last night Noah shit a little on my bed and on the floor. This morning he bit my finger as I brushed his teeth. But it's Karl who really gives me a pain, the way he's always quick to argue with us. I like his militancy, I admire his rebelliousness. But I'm also afraid that he might be the kind who dies sacrificially in the revolutions of others.

Which ties into my recurrent nightmare. The predeceasing—as they say in wills—of Karl. No matter how he dies. Whether in an auto accident. Drowning. A fight. Then what purpose would there have been in my life? Noah?

August 18, 1979

A son is supposed to give a man a sense of immortality. But Noah instead confirms my mortality. When I look at him instead of knowing that something about me might persevere and endure, I am reminded instead that one day I will cease to be and wonder who will take care of him. Noah is someone to be taken care of. Not cured—just taken care of. So hard for our society to understand. But why blame our society? We all, normal and abnormal, would like to be taken care of.

August 20, 1979

I bought Karl his electric trains over the weekend and now he is completely involved in the world of N gauge. Except I must note that when his friends come over to play with him he acts as if everything about me is a complete embarrassment to him. I would be an embarrassment to him, I'm sure, even if I looked like Robert Redford. In fact, I suspect, even Robert Redford is an embarrassment to his own teenaged kid.

August 21, 1979

To love Noah is to worship man, the species—dumb, strange, inscrutable, unfathomable, defenseless, and terribly beautiful.

August 22, 1979

Yesterday our day-care kids went on a supermarket shopping tour and then cooked a meal. The days are winding down in terms of our day-care and Foumi is still bugging me about starting a school.

Karl is having a materialistic end of summer. All he is interested in is money and what it can buy for him. If he delights in money so, he should start developing an ability that might earn him some.

August 23, 1979

Karl, waiting to go to lunch with me, is lying on my office couch reading a thriller. He is still a child caught between N-gauge trains and grass, D-and-D games and Ronrico Rum. I think chemically the coming of old age and the coming of adolescence must be quite similar, a sort of half dosage of the manly hormones. Because now I dream again of finding magic in life, only this time I know that it is only a belief in magic that makes for the magic.

August 24, 1979

My temper frightens me. Last night I wrestled Karl to the floor and almost slugged him. What happened was this: Foumi and I were about to go out to dinner and he began to insist that Foumi had to wear her gold chain. That unless she did so he would leave the house and not Noah-sit. What really makes his behavior frightful is that when it was all over he said that he had not been teasing. Still I should not have reacted so violently. Foumi says I take him too seriously. I guess I do.

August 25, 1979

I can't stand Karl, his long hair framing the constant look of unhappiness on his face. Only Noah, as if on the other end of a sibling seesaw, is behaving well in spite of the heat. Or perhaps because of it. These hot summer days no one has the energy to force him to do anything he does not want to do.

August 26, 1979

Foumi is tired, overwhelmed with day-care duties, confused as to what to do about Noah. In addition, there's her arthritis, all the normal woes of menopause, and an end-of-summer blues. I want her to go away, to take a trip, to get a little R and R. But instead she insists on hanging around and being indispensable and playing the martyr. The strain is so great that I feel my love ebbing and sometimes I think I'm just waiting for our marriage to end. Because I don't like being afraid that anything I say might set her off. She worries so about everything down to the tiniest detail, asking "What then?" the way a child keeps asking "Why?" There is no solution to Noah and she cannot accept that. She wants me to act when there is no action for me to take. Starting a school just makes no sense to me because then the problem never ends. Getting Noah out of the house is the only way our marriage can last. I guess I will apply for a placement for Noah at OCC.

August 27, 1979

When Karl sides with me in an argument Foumi thinks he is a kid and that she is being outnumbered. But when Karl opposes me she considers him a mature voice of reason.

August 28, 1979

It has occurred to me that I could buy a small house and hire people to take care of Noah. That would require a high income, but I think I could increase my income without Noah around. It would mean changing our life-style, but it could also mean saving our lives.

August 29, 1979

Last night both Foumi and I really enjoyed square dancing. It was sort of a bowling night out together.

August 30, 1979

After Foumi, Karl, and I went shopping yesterday we stopped at the day-care center to pick up Noah and Niko. But Noah was having a terrible tantrum, writhing on the floor. I asked Terry, our aide, to take Niko home. We waited around for Noah to calm down. But he didn't. Every time someone went near him he reached out and scratched or clutched at their clothes. I thought he might be thirsty and tried to get him to drink some water. He poured it on the floor. I tried feeding him a few peanuts, I played some soothing records. But nothing seemed to work. Finally, we offered him some apple juice. He drank three cups, one after the other. He rose from the floor and began to dance about the room. He had been thirsty and just didn't want water. But how were we to know? We live our lives on a rusty razor's edge.

August 31, 1979

Karl and I are always fighting. Which gives me an idea. There is a marvelous comic premise in Jocasta's leaving home because she can't stand the constant arguments raging between Oedipus and his father.

September 1, 1979

Noah is now thirteen, a man according to the tradition of my faith, so it really is time for him to leave home and go off and live in a yeshiva. I also want to get him out of the house soon so that I can get out of the house. I would so like to go to New York. To Paris. To make all sorts of trips. But right now I'm stuck at home because of him.

September 2, 1979

I was furious with Karl last night. He had carelessly taped over a cassette I had been saving, and I sent him to his room. Still angry, I walked into his room and found it in its usual mess. Like a platoon sergeant I ordered him to clean it up. He rose from his bed, his face hardening, and stood up straight. "No," he said resolutely. It wasn't the first time he's defied me but somehow it was the first time I knew that I should not call his challenge. I turned and walked out of his room. He has achieved manhood; he can now defy me and I accept it. Not like it, but accept it.

Noah too is a teenager who has his pride. And I must be as careful with him as I should be with Karl. Yet it is so easy to forget.

My two kids: Karl is rotten and Noah is crazy. Still better than no kids at all. I have to believe that.

September 3, 1979

I brought Noah to my office this Labor Day. His spitting and scratching were getting on Foumi's nerves. And as he sits on the sofa, leaning against the wall, clapping his hands, I realize what would be my "room"—like Winston Smith's "room" in Orwell's *1984* with the rats scuttling about—the room I would dread visiting. It is Noah at twenty-five, pale, snag-toothed, sitting in a ward corner, much as he is sitting now.

September 5, 1979

After serving as a reluctant volunteer at day-care yesterday Karl told us, "Noah is smarter and cuter than the other kids." Perhaps there is more than just fraternal pride in that statement. Perhaps it means we ought to get down to teaching Noah sign language immediately.

September 7, 1979

With our friend Carl Kugel staying with Noah, we've gotten away to Santa Barbara for our annual mini-vacation. The first night Karl behaved terribly. Last night he was a joy. He is a bright funny kid who often gets under my skin because he knows how to. After all, he's one of the world's great experts on me.

I again think of buying a house here. As an investment, a reward, a spur, a necessity. The only trouble is houses here are now double what they were two and a half years ago.

September 8, 1979

No sooner were we in the door than Karl and I were fighting again. When I asked him rather strongly to unpack his suitcase and put it away, he replied, "You're tough." Which immediately infuriated me and I went for him as he kept taunting, "You're tough." I had scarcely inflicted a telling blow when he ran toward the kitchen, saying he was going to call the child-abuse hot line. But when I reached the kitchen he was gone from the house, out the back door. Later he returned and slept in the den.

As we lay in bed trying to sleep, Foumi said I ran too hot and cold with him. That I had to expect him to tease me because I was such a teaser myself. That above all I should not cut off communication with him.

So this morning I apologized to him for my past teasing and he agreed not to tease me either. He was also very good about helping vacuum the house. I guess he must have felt some guilt too.

When I told a friend at lunch today that Karl sometimes makes me so mad that I could kill him, he laughed: "You're so screwed up, Josh, you're liable to kill the wrong son."

17

September 9, 1979

Noah was in a good mood upon our return. And I noticed last night as I gave him his bath that he really has a full cluster of pubic hair. He is physically a man. But definitely not his own man.

September 11, 1979

I woke early to prepare breakfast for Karl. It's his first day of high school. He was so nervous about going into the tenth grade that he even acted quite civil.

In September 1942, thirty-seven years ago, I started my fourth semester, or the end of my tenth grade, at Tilden High School in Brooklyn. I was fourteen and a half, a few months younger than Karl is now. My classes began at 10:45 A.M. and ended at 3:30 P.M. I would work in the morning from 6:30 to 10:00 A.M. delivering milk and rolls and bagels on a pushcart for the corner grocery store. Then I would walk the mile to school, often meeting on the way Miss McKelvie, my Latin teacher, a sturdy old Scotch woman who lived two miles farther away from the school than I did. In addition to Latin I took Hebrew, Modern European History, Geometry II, and Journalism that semester. And it was in the Journalism course that semester I discovered I wanted to write. I wonder what Karl will discover about himself this semester.

This morning I also called Regional Center, the state agency that deals with the handicapped and disabled, and asked them to start the paperwork for Noah to be admitted to OCC, the Operant Conditioning Center.

So Karl has started high school and I have initiated the first steps toward placing Noah in residence. We all have to move on.

September 12, 1979

Reva Jones will soon be leaving day-care, and neither Foumi nor I are making any serious moves about finding a replacement. So our day-care on an every-day basis may soon be over, although we may be able to continue to limp on during Saturdays and holidays.

Today I turned down a TV assignment because it would have meant having to go back East and live in Providence for a week or two. To research the story of a socially conscious nun who became a lawyer and has now been threatened with excommunication as she fights with her bishop. There aren't that many TV projects worth working on. This may be one, but how could I leave Foumi alone with Noah? Who may be the best career guide I have. He keeps me away from projects that could devour me. I mean, I keep thinking about the nun and her love for God and the Catholic Church and her order. All of which are as difficult to walk away from as an idiot son.

September 13, 1979

Karl seems happy in high school. He showed me a composition he wrote for his English class:

Karl Greenfeld English P.2

Liglief Grenoble, otherwise known as Liggy, lived in a house on a hill in a small town. He had few neighbors and no friends.

Liggy was a painter, not by profession but by hobby. He had no means of making money and lived on a small inheritance left him by a distant relative.

Liggy loved to paint. In fact, that was all he did. He especially liked to paint leaves and twigs. He considered himself an expert on the painting of leaves and twigs.

One day he started painting a leaf. It began as a small painting of a simple leaf of no particular type. Oh, how much time he spent painting this one leaf! When Liggy finally finished he decided this leaf was much too beautiful to let stand by itself. Liggy then painted another leaf of near equal beauty. And another. And another.

Soon Liggy had an entire tree that took up nearly all of one wall in his spacious cellar. He kept working at the painting until it was too big to fit in the cellar. He continued his painting in his living room. Liggy now had an entire forest on canvas. He ceased to care about anything besides his painting. He didn't count time, he didn't take care of his house, he didn't feed his animals.

In order to continue his painting, he had to take all his other canvases and attach them to his masterpiece. Oh, how it was beautiful: forest, mountains, animals, flowers, and more leaves than could be counted. His painting took up every wall in his house and even a few ceilings.

He went to bed the night before he expected to finish the painting a happy man, dreaming of how beautiful it was. The vines leaped up myriad, dark brown trunks, capped by a montage of leaves of every possible hue and shade. Above, a solitary white bird streaked across an azure, blue sky.

Suddenly, his dream began to turn into a nightmare. Liggy dreamed he saw a fire consuming his painting. He awoke in a sweat and saw a red glow everywhere. Without thinking, reflexively, he ran from the house.

Liggy watched in anguish as the fire burned the house to the ground. After the embers cooled he went back into what had once been his home. He looked about the ruins, heartbroken. But then, among the ashes, his eyes caught a glimpse of something. Something beautiful.

It was the first leaf Liggy had painted.

I don't know if the story is derivative, nor does it matter if it is. He has an imagination. I hope the teacher is smart enough to appreciate that.

Aside from English he has Geography, French, Health, and Geometry. Not exactly a fun schedule. But I am convinced he is a smart kid and shouldn't feel too much pressure.

Karl brought his composition home from school and all the teacher had written on it was "Amusing—and very touching." But while she had had other kids read their pieces on what they had done over the summer and how they felt when friends moved away, she had not asked Karl to read his.

"See," said Karl, "it's not so good. You don't know anything about writing."

Noah has a new teacher and I'll withhold judgment. The most important thing anyway is not my reaction but how Noah reacts to her. He always has very definite opinions about people.

Two letters: One from a child psychologist who said he grew up with a brother like Noah in the home and that it was not worth it. He said his brother is in a good residence now. I should write and find out the name of the place.

The other from an Irish writer friend worrying about the reviews his new novel is getting. Hell, all he has to worry about is the fate of his book. I have to worry about the fate of Noah.

We're in the midst of a smeat—smog and heat—wave, and I wonder once more why school in Southern California is not off in September rather than July. The smog has blown in from the valley to the coast, and my sinuses are aching and it's just too hot to go outside. Naturally this weather bothers Noah. He has nothing to do and there is nothing we can do to entertain him. Not even take him for a walk.

I'm tired too. Plumb tired of taking care of him. Also tired of Foumi's being angry with me for not starting a school. But I just don't think a school would ultimately be such a good idea. I do not want to end up dedicating my life to the care of retarded kids. I want to take care of myself for a while. I have let my own body run downhill. As I say, I'm tired.

I keep saying I am tired of Noah. And I wonder if that means I am tired of keeping our marriage together. I am not afraid of killing Noah with a gun anymore. I am afraid of destroying him by walking out on our marriage.

Yesterday, in the heat and smog, we scarcely left the house, lying on the floor, watching TV, listening to news of brushfires. Suddenly the engines were roaring down our street. Temescal Canyon was ablaze, the brush burning down near the end of Asilomar, less than the length of a football field away. The Fire Department quickly put it out. And then came back at 11:00 P.M. to check. Not a calm night for us.

September 18, 1979

At lunch Foumi spoke of the irony confronting all parents of special children: As the kids get stronger and more willful, the parents get weaker and more tired. I pointed out that that holds true for the parents of all kids.

September 19, 1979

Perhaps the cumulative effect of all the smeat, perhaps a collective payoff for all my procrastination, but Foumi and I were shouting at each other all day. And after coming home from school, Karl, wanting money to buy more trains, joined in the general discontent. Only Noah was in a good mood. Upon his return home I showered him and took him for a walk. He was not upset because of the lack of day-care.

Foumi is tough on Karl, while I am difficult with him. Anyway, adolescence is never a picnic. I try to remember my own adolescence. My only dream then was to grow up and get away from home and be on my own. Adolescence, like childhood, will not have been the happiest stage in Karl's life. But he does have an imagination, one even more playful than mine. In the third grade his teacher called him a nonfiction kid. He is no longer that. He has an active sense of the bizarre. And why not? Aren't we the family bizarre?

September 20, 1979

I spoke with the people at Cal State Northridge. They will send deaf tutors to teach Noah signing. I want Noah to learn that he can communicate to us without having a tantrum. Both Foumi and Karl are dubious. They insist that Noah does not have the gross motor skills necessary for signing. Haven't I yet learned, they argue, that professionals know nothing? I know it's a long shot but I'm willing to give it a try.

Anyway, everything that is happening with Noah seems to be déjà vu. I think no new thoughts about him. Find no new places for him. I can only keep trying, against all logic and despite all past experience, to have faith in a new approach whether it be diet or megavitamins or signing. But I've got to keep trying. And even that notion reeks of déjà vu.

September 21, 1979

A cab now takes Noah to school each morning. But it's a mixed blessing. The cab was late this morning and the driver seemed uncomfortable with Noah. So we were quite worried until we heard that he had arrived at school safely. But the cabdriver did report to the new teacher that he almost had an accident because Noah kept sticking his hand into his face. Foumi felt the cabdriver did not want to carry a kid like Noah from the moment he saw him. If so, I'm sure Noah sensed that and did his stuff.

I read yesterday of a movie about a fifty-year-old retarded person, *Philly*. His parents had kept him home until the father died. Only then, although she did not wish to do so, did the mother finally put Philly into an institution. And Philly was happy there. That's what the review said. I just want to put Noah in OCC before I die and see what happens.

September 22, 1979

Karl gets little homework from school, and that bothers Foumi. Not me. I think high school is a waste of time anyway. Karl has decided to change out of Geography into Biology. And that's okay with me. His program then would be: English, French, Biology, Geometry, and Health. Which should be a modicum of work. But still, Karl says, there'll be little homework.

Karl really wants my approval. Last night when I told him that I didn't think he made a good deal in buying a certain N-gauge engine from another kid, he was so annoyed that he punched me. Playfully, but hard.

September 23, 1979

Now that I've acknowledged to myself that my youth is over the memory of it seems to have deserted me too. Or is it Karl who is robbing me of my own true memories? Because every time I try to remember myself as I was, instead I see him as he is.

September 24, 1979

Karl's finding high school no better than junior high. He has no single class he can look forward to each day. He's also getting in trouble for speaking out and arguing with teachers. And if high school is no treat for him, I am afraid it means that it will be no treat for us either.

September 28, 1979

We took Noah to the Regional Center offices for an evaluation by their psychologist. As usual he was untestable. And it looks like our Regional Center will recommend an institutional or residential placement for him.

September 29, 1979

Noah had a tantrum yesterday and badly scratched the bridge of his nose. Karl's school called: His French teacher does not want him in her class for a few days because he's disruptive. Ho hum.

September 30, 1979

Today is our nineteenth anniversary and perhaps the best gift I can give her would be the end of our marriage. Foumi is just too nice and too pure to have to live with someone like me.

October 1, 1979

Where is the ghost of Yom Kippurim past? I would have to sit up front with my father, who was the secretary of the synagogue. He loved Yom Kippur. It was the day he worked for all year round: auditioning cantors, buying pews, selling seat tickets, arranging appeals. He was in heaven, proud of my company, exerting his fatherhood proudly, while I was in hell, squirming beside him, plotting rebellion. Sons and fathers. I make the same mistakes my father made. I too yearn for active expressions of father love from my sons.

October 2, 1979

My great signing experiment has begun. A large deaf girl came to tutor him. Noah was intimidated by her size. But they didn't do very much. Foumi and the tutor spent most of the afternoon furiously scribbling notes back and forth between them.

Karl too needs a tutor. For geometry. I'll have to arrange that.

October 3, 1979

We took Noah to Regional Center for a physical evaluation. He tore their doctor's shirt. "I admire your patience," the doctor told us and tried to smile professionally. The shirt Noah had torn looked like a silk one to me.

Regional Center will definitely recommend a residential placement for Noah. And it's much simpler to place him in an existing group residence than to start one.

October 4, 1979

My great signing experiment isn't working out. Another deaf girl came. But she could not handle Noah at all. She was too small physically. But I'll give it one more week.

October 5, 1979

Sometimes I wonder if the books I've put together about Noah—even more than Noah himself—keep Foumi and me together and our marriage going. The books, the lingering shadows of a reality past, determining a present reality.

October 6, 1979

A friend has breast cancer. Another friend's son broke his hand playing football. Life is full of agonies and I don't have a complete lock on them.

I love Noah on Sunday mornings. He is the first up and I am next. I let Foumi sleep and go down and make him breakfast and we eat together, a small community of the real crazies in our house.

Karl is having a terrible time in biology. Just can't understand it at all. And Foumi doesn't understand why he can't understand because she doesn't understand how poorly most sciences are taught in American high schools.

Last night Foumi began bugging Karl about not studying enough. I told her it wasn't the time. She then accused me of always defending Karl, of always joining forces with him against her. At this point, Karl wisely fled the house. But Foumi continued on, lacing into me for raising Karl to be a sexist. I fled the house too, taking a long walk along the bluff and down to the ocean. But somehow after dinner the hubbub was over and I was even able to joke: "This family could be worse. Noah could be normal."

Our square-dance class held its "graduation." All very formal, what with scrolls and all. But it did represent some sort of achievement. Somehow we have learned to square dance. And to enjoy it. Karl, as usual, Noah-sat. If it weren't for him we never would have had nocturnal freedom.

Karl showed me his latest composition. The kid has a good style. Given his character, a combination of bluster, impatience, and shyness, perhaps he will become a writer after all. What else can he do?

At a meeting at Regional Center they tried to talk us out of applying for OCC. Their psychologist argued that OCC does not have enough positive rewards in their behavior-modification program. In rebuttal, I made an eloquent speech about the difference in various levels of behavior and that getting a kid who functions at a low level to stop hurting himself is positive enough. I know I won them over. I also know my eloquence stemmed from the fact that we have to get Noah off our backs soon.

It's Noah's pubic hairs that are doing him in as far as I'm concerned. Every time I bathe him or wash him or wipe him I realize that we have a man on our hands. A child I can deal with. But not a man.

Karl has a personality that is still very boyish: his interest in model trains and football and movies. But Noah has only a physical being. And now it is that of a man. And Noah as a man I cannot deal with. Because that's a life sentence.

October 12, 1979

An individual requires a family. Even a family with Noah. Almost any family is better than no family. Even for Noah.

October 13, 1979

I canceled the deaf tutors. It was not working out. It also meant that Foumi had to deal with two handicapped people instead of just one.

October 14, 1979

With a cat, with a kid like Karl, with Noah, ours is no house for a fine Chinese rug and Persian carpet. But Foumi fell in love with them and they arrived today. Already Karl doesn't like the idea of having to be so careful and tentative in the living room, and I agree with him. But I also think Foumi deserves the indulgence.

October 15, 1979

Karl will be fifteen in a month, and I shudder for him. He has so much yet to live through. Noah is thirteen. He has nothing to live through. I shudder even more for him.

October 16, 1979

We hired a young man, Bruce, who was on the staff at OCC, to work with Noah. He reminded us that they squeeze muscles and scratch palms as aversives. Such deterrents would backfire with Noah because he would only imitate such actions.

The parent of a brain-damaged child who is not at OCC but is familiar with them did remind us that they would take into consideration Noah's dietary likes. For example, she said, if Noah goes there we could make sure he was getting daily portions of his beloved rice.

October 17, 1979

I have noticed this: The more resigned I become to Noah's imminent departure—and it will happen in a matter of months—the more I become resigned to the fact that I can do very little to resolve Karl's problems either. At the moment, he is failing geometry, finding biology difficult, and in constant trouble in French. Only in English does he seem to be keeping up. He'll be lucky if he winds up with a C average. So much for his dreams of college. I don't really care if he goes to college or not. But he does need to spend those four years maturing someplace.

October 19, 1979

Noah's impossible to teach. He just isn't motivated. Like most incurable maladies his involves the spirit as well as the flesh. And there is still just no way to light a fire under Noah's ass. We accept that.

In the same way, I tell Foumi to accept Karl's failing in school. But she can't. Foumi believes in being tough. But I'm afraid we might just tough him out of going to college. We have given him a hard schedule for the tenth grade. Perhaps we should have made it easier for him. No, what am I saying? With Karl as with Noah it's all a question of motivation.

October 20, 1979

Last night, while lying in my bed reading, I asked Karl to see what Noah was doing. A few minutes later he handed me the following typewritten report:

NOAH: HIS ACTIVITIES AT TWENTY OF NINE

At approximately twenty of nine, Noah Greenfeld was sitting in a living room. Not a normal living room, but a living room with two valuable Asiatic rugs in it. On the walls hung five paintings painted by Foumi Greenfeld. On the rugs were a love seat, a sofa, and a white chair. This was the living room, the same living room that Noah Greenfeld was sitting in at twenty of nine.

October 21, 1979

A friend called me. He and his wife were having lunch with Princess Margaret and then dinner with Norman Mailer and another dinner with Tom Wolfe, and then on Friday his wife would have a D & C. Some schedule. But as Foumi pointed out, without Noah all schedules are easy, any social or medical activity is possible. Meanwhile, I live the social-climbing life of my friends vicariously.

October 22, 1979

Karl is in trouble in school again. His French teacher has reassigned him to her first-period class. It seems he laughs too much in his current third-period class.

Bruce, the former OCC worker, took Noah to the high school track and tried to get him to run around it. All he got for his efforts were pinches. And I am afraid he pinched Noah back in the OCC style. I wonder about OCC now. Noah, like everyone else on earth, need not be instructed in the ways of violence.

October 23, 1979

We were invited to a dinner party for Norman Mailer last night at the Bistro Garden. Norman has aged and a lot of the piss seems to have seeped out of him. He said that I never change in appearance. I wish that were so. But the mirror on my bathroom wall, this hung-over morning, tells me different.

I spoke with Karl's French teacher. She seems to like him but she feels he was the catalyst of all the misconduct in her room. Which is why she transferred him. He acted childish and immature, she said, giggling and making noises and all kinds of animal sounds. Animal sounds? Karl? But it is time for him to grow up.

October 24, 1979

Bruce asked us what to do when Noah had a tantrum while he was trying to teach him a task. I told him to tell Noah to go to his room. Foumi corrected me. He should walk away from Noah himself. Then when Noah calms down he can recall him to the task at hand.

I'm not expert at handling Noah anyway. Last night he lowered his head and pinched and scratched me, clutching both skin and shirt, tenaciously. But I also made a mistake and cocked a fist at him. Which only enraged him more.

October 25, 1979

Noah and I quarreled again last night. When he poured his apple juice on the rug I swatted him across the behind. He took the blow without complaint. Just went to his room and lay down on his bed. Obviously, he was still angry with me. Because later, when I bathed him, he gave me a hard time.

October 26, 1979

Sometimes Foumi cannot understand simple things. We have a cat. We bought lovely carpets. And the cat scratches them. I had told her we would have to choose between a cat and the carpets. As it turns out our cat has expensive scratch pads.

October 27, 1979

We have help but Noah is still tough. My fingers are lined with cuts from the scratches he inflicted while I washed his hair last night. Still I'm not sure I want him out of the house. I am a fool, a self-enslaver, unwilling to surrender my yoke.

October 29, 1979

I visited an old high school friend I had not seen in years. He has angina and high blood pressure. My cholesterol should be lower. High school kids become old men.

October 30, 1979

I watched Bruce teach Noah to put his finger above his chin as the sign that he wants to eat. And Noah should soon be able to indicate the drink sign too. And then perhaps we can all be merry.

October 31, 1979

Karl's going to the optometrist to pick up his first pair of glasses. I suppose he can break them in as a Halloween mask.

I will allow him to go Halloweening tonight but with an early curfew. Because he has been honest in telling me that he will not be out collecting candy but rather egg throwing and shaving-cream spritzing. Neither of us mentioned drinking or smoking, which is my real fear.

November 1, 1979

Halloween has passed without incident. My car got shaving-cream splattered; kids came to the door for tricks and treats; Noah was gurgling happily; and I picked up Karl at a friend's at 9:30—according to curfew—and brought him home safely.

November 4, 1979

Foumi is angry with Karl, who spent all afternoon playing with friends in his room. She is concerned about his future. Who cares about Karl's mythic future? At least he's got a present. Which is more than Noah has.

November 5, 1979

Art is what you die for, commerce is what you kill for. George Burns is ready to murder the script for the *Oh, God!* sequel. Gil Cates, the director, called to tell me that George had taken a hard-line position. He would only do a version of the script his writers had "punched up." Gil didn't like their changes. But he also didn't know what to do. I thought about it for ten seconds and gave him a *te absolvo* return call, advising him to go ahead and direct the "punched up" version because we weren't talking about a work of art. Just a piece of commerce that if George, having finally achieved stardom at eighty-five, was willing to kill for I certainly wasn't ready to die over.

More important, Karl was immensely pleased last night. He received an A on a geometry test. Which brings his term average up to a D.

November 6, 1979

As I read in *Newsweek* about some new miracle brain drugs, once more the thought crossed my mind. Perhaps I have not done enough for Noah? But then I recalled—or reckoned—that while the acceptance of death is considered heroic, the acceptance of the ravages of life aren't. To accept Noah as he is takes more, far more, courage than to accept Noah as he might possibly be.

November 7, 1979

A UC Davis doctorate student in clinical psychology came to see us. She had studied with Ivar Lovaas at UCLA. Now she wanted to know what professionals could do for the parents of the developmentally disabled. We told her: They had to level with parents about the degree of hopelessness. They had to realize their help was often a hindrance. And they also had to accept the hard fact that the parents were often a mess themselves.

November 8, 1979

Autistic children are not supposed to give affection. But no one can communicate more than Noah can with a smile. He comes to Foumi and rubs his face against hers in a way that says: "I love you more than all the words in the world." Thirteen and a half, the down forming on his upper lip, his body broadening into a squat, solid mature build, Noah is still a love child. Our love child.

November 9, 1979

Karl is involved in Dungeons and Dragons again. With squinting eyes he's always painting miniature figurines. Foumi's afraid he'll get headaches again that will keep him from his schoolwork. She still doesn't realize that the headaches he had were probably drug-related.

I love Saturdays. Bonus days. Gift days. On my walk to work this California crisp morning I passed the high school field where the girls were playing soccer in their colorful uniforms. Kids look better playing soccer than any other sport.

My kid's in trouble in school again, having once more committed that terrible crime of "talking in class." Now it's his Geometry teacher who wants to see me. And he must be in more trouble than he is letting on. Today he actually volunteered to help out at day-care, which is down to just a Saturday program.

In English he was assigned a paper: "Write about members of a family who live under different roofs." Karl wrote of a salesman of roofing material whose various family members were allergic to different substances, resulting in a house in which one room had a glass roof, another a tin roof, a third had a roof of tiles, and another had pine-scented wooden shakes. Karl's paper is quite funny. The teacher found it "hostile."

Karl, like me before him, has a way of evoking the antagonism of teachers. He's not exactly a kid teeming with control and his tendency toward moderation is in no way excessive.

November 13, 1979

Noah, who has not had a bowel movement in days, had a terrible tantrum at school.

Karl is reading *Black Mischief* and thoroughly enjoying it. How many kids in his school can go to Waugh at his age?

November 14, 1979

Karl was all charm when I bought him another model engine for his trains. But he still has roller-coaster mood swings. I wonder if he's on drugs again. Though he swears he isn't.

November 15, 1979

Karl's report card: F in Health. D in Geometry. C in Biology. And B's in English and French. There goes Harvard again.

My other great yellow-and-white hope finally shit after five days and is intensely lovable. Right now he's my favorite son. No tantrums. Just smiles.

Foumi's birthday yesterday passed with little official notice around here. Forty-nine. But I'm sure we won't escape Karl's birthday that easily next week. Fifteen.

Trying to expose Karl to anything worthwhile is always dicey. Last night I took him to see a marvelous production of *Pacific Overtures* that both Foumi and I had enjoyed. But he was a constant crank, more destructive than enthusiastic, no doubt feeling that we were trying to force something down his theatrically illiterate throat. But I still think it's a good thing for him to have seen.

Karl bellyaches every once in a while about our imposing a curfew but he doesn't seem to be *that* unhappy about it. I think he knows his own weaknesses when it comes to drinking and smoking and wants us to protect him from himself. Foumi objects to his hobbies, his trains and D and D figures, and how expensive they are. But if like a curfew they keep him out of trouble, then the cost is cheap.

Foumi wasn't feeling well so I gave Noah breakfast, dressed him, and put him out to play in the backyard while I watched football with Karl. I called Noah in for lunch and fed him. Then we went for a long walk and a ride. In the afternoon, as Karl and I watched some more football, Noah chewed his shirt. Sunday: a blank of football games and a blur of warmth with the boys. My boys.

A friend tells me the average father spends just twenty-five minutes per week with his kids. This morning I exceeded my quota.

Karl wanted to leave the house without eating breakfast and wearing just a T-shirt. Foumi didn't like that and she roused me to give her support. Foumi also didn't like finding his room a mess, full of toys. She thinks he's too old for toys. But what's the alternative? Alcohol. Drugs. Sex. And she's unhappy that he's failing in Health.

What is Health? It's a subject in which he's learning the seven methods of contraception. But he failed a test because instead of answering "coitus interruptus," he wrote "withdrawing cocktus erectus." In Health class the girls ask if the pill is chewable. Coed classes. What mysteries are left? Who wants to dream of "coitus" rather than of getting laid? Who says good clean sex shouldn't be a little dirty?

Regional Center has stopped shuffling the papers on Noah's placement. We don't buy OCC completely but we will be able to place Noah there. Do we want to part with Noah so soon? We have to. It will be best for Karl. Some of the pressures he bears will disappear—or at least lighten.

Yet I really cannot picture our family without Noah. He is the linchpin that holds us together. Without him we each may go flying off in different directions. But Noah's going into an institution is inevitable and we might as well let his world with us end with a pre-set whimper rather than an unforeseen bang.

And nothing is forever. We can always take him back.

November 21, 1979

I awoke with a dream involving a daughter who had run away from home and was wandering near the Columbia University campus. I had books to return to a library there but I wasn't sure which library. I also had a class to get to. I came upon my daughter playing with dirt and placing gooey stuff on her hair. (Last night I saw a documentary on television in which the boat people were washing their hair with a lice disinfectant.) I went over to my daughter, who could only communicate in a most torturous manner. "Can't talk," she finally said. "I want to go home to Mommy." But I had the library books to return, the class to get to. I was trying to figure out how to manage to do everything when I awoke.

November 22, 1979

I've been asking myself all sorts of questions. These are some of them:

Noah has defined my life by giving it limitations. What will happen once he is in OCC? Do I, without a center holding so to speak, go floating off? If I can assign away my responsibility to Noah, can I do the same with Karl and Foumi?

How long will OCC last? Who knows? There are no guarantees. So if Noah's stay there turns out to be a temporary one what happens when he returns home? He has no school and we've let the day-care support system wither away. Are we back not to square one but to square minus one?

November 23, 1979

A quiet Thanksgiving Day. Woke early and gave Noah breakfast. Walked him. Watched the Dallas game with Karl. (Wearing his new eyeglasses, Karl can't help but look like a more serious person.) Went out and got a fast-food lunch for the family. Took Noah for a ride. And then in the evening we had our turkey-day dinner, a cornish game hen for each of us—little birds for little people.

November 24, 1979

Karl worked at day-care along with a volunteer who was taking the kids to Marineland in my wagon. I'm not too sure of the brakes and so I worried all afternoon about the possibility of an auto accident on the freeway, both Karl and Noah killed. But there was no terrible tragedy. They both bounced back into the house this evening, Noah happier than Karl.

November 25, 1979

Karl has been campaigning so long to see *Apocalypse Now* that I finally, dutifully, took him and a friend of his to the film. It turned out I liked it a lot more than either of them, Karl calling it a "Vietnam rock concert."

But Karl is a problem or a fool. After Foumi told him that she did not like a particular friend of his, Karl repeated that to him. As if he did not know where his loyalties lay. As if he would betray his mother for the friendship of a peer. He seems to lack completely an understanding about the way the world works. He is an innocent with habits that quickly offend people. One of them is an utter honesty that somehow seems devious in its applications. Another is an expectation that people will act consistently. Is he just like his brother, nothing but a baby with the balls of a man?

November 26, 1979

In the movies they pay first the face that is up there on the screen, the actor. Then they reward the body whose stamina upholds that face—or persona—the director. But the writer, who may be the spirit and the soul behind it all, is treated literally as no body at all.

November 28, 1979

In Brentwood last night I parked my car in a spot reserved for Pioneer Chicken customers and went into an art-supply store next door for a few minutes. When I came out my car was gone, towed away in a bucket-shop towing operation. I called a friend, who picked me up and drove me to the garage where I could pay the ransom to retrieve it. I thanked my friend profusely. And this morning when I told Karl what had happened I moralized: "Friendship is a bond that makes life easier. See how important it is to have good friends."

"No," said Karl. "If he was a good friend he would have punched out the guy who ordered you towed away."

November 29, 1979

We signed all the papers and Noah can go to OCC anytime after the first of the year. I look forward to it and I dread it. I know I should feel that Noah's out-of-the-home placement is part of a process as inevitable as each receding wave. But at the same time I fear a whole new sea of troubles rising.

Yesterday Noah was volatile, one moment almost throwing a

tantrum, and the next laughing and giggling. But last night he was difficult. He was sleepy, I suspect, because of the Santa Ana winds that enervate us all. When he came out of his bath he lay on the floor and wouldn't get up. Finally, I wiped his body—still on the floor—and maneuvered it into his p.j.'s. And then I force-brushed his teeth. By the time I got him to his room he had all but passed out in a drowsy stupor. But in the middle of the night he awakened me. He was lying on the rug beside his bed. For the first time in months he had pissed in his pants.

18

December 1, 1979

I watched this afternoon as Foumi was treated by an acupuncturist. The needle heads gleamed like rhinestones. Foumi looked like a hybrid animal, a porcupine with peacock feathers. She reported that only the insertion of the needles hurt. And her sinuses felt better. But not her arthritis.

December 2, 1979

Noah has been very disagreeable. Karl thinks it's because he knows he'll be leaving home. And I have informed Noah of that fact many times. Somehow he always understands more than we have any right to assume.

I was particularly sharp with him this morning when he clawed and spit at me. I was also very upset with Karl. He kept using the expression "All's I have to do," despite the fact that he both knows better and knows it offends me. After the scene with Karl I imagined I was having chest pains. Either kid can yet be the death of me.

December 3, 1979

I called four employment offices in search of workers for the day-care center during the Christmas vacation. Lately we've been operating on Saturdays but I want to try to keep open throughout the holidays. I want Noah home this Christmas.

December 4, 1979

We have a little wicker chair that sits in our entrance hallway. I picked it up in a Yokohama department store when we were leaving Japan in 1965. We were planning to take a boat back, and it was for the nine-month-old Karl to sit upon. We never did take the boat and I can remember carrying it onto the plane that brought us back to America. Foumi, with her trim ass, can still sit on it. So can Noah. He sits down in it whenever we put on or take off his shoes. And I've always wondered what we'd do when Noah became too big for the wicker chair. The solution of using another chair, an ordinary chair, never seemed right. But perhaps I've always secretly suspected that when he became too big for the chair I would simply put him in an institution.

December 5, 1979

Karl woke up this morning with a headache. But after he napped he decided he was well enough to go to school. I wonder if the headache was caused by the Santa Ana winds, which feel like a blast from an opened oven, drying the throat and clogging the sinuses? By an impending French test? Or by renewed drug activity?

December 6, 1979

Karl has been arguing against Noah's leaving the house, claiming that Noah has been behaving well lately. And it's true that he has. But Noah has to be leaving us one day and it is time to make the break. I'm getting older, and without being morbid about it, one day he will have to live on without me.

December 7, 1979

The Special Education community is small. The word is out that we'll be sending Noah to the Operant Conditioning Center. And one of Noah's former teachers called us. She has a friend who taught at OCC and has told her horror stories about the place. Could he talk to us? Certainly, I said. He called but he would not reveal anything over the phone, not even his name. I told the parent who is the Administrative President of OCC about the former teacher. He said he couldn't imagine who it might be. Anyway, Deep Autism is coming over to the house Sunday night.

A crisis day. Our day-care aide called at ten to ten this Saturday morning to say that she wasn't coming in. Karl was lying prone on the floor of the den at the time, watching the Dallas game. I suggested that he might volunteer, which elicited a mini-tantrum from him. I drove with Noah over to day-care to tell the other parents we couldn't have the program.

So far today Noah is the only one who is behaving decently. Because Foumi is moaning about Karl. That he has no schedule, does no homework, displays no drive, has little ambition, and does not contribute to the family. But what Foumi cannot appreciate about him is that he has a sense of humor and that he will work with a passion when it finds expression and direction. She worries too much about him because of Noah. Instead of enjoying him.

December 9, 1979

I took a walk with Noah and loved the camaraderie of being with him. Now I am confused. Why do we have to part from him? Why not wait a few more years? Why break up the family?

December 10, 1979

Deep Autism, the former employee of OCC, came over last night and had only terrible things to say about the joint: They were short-handed, the morale of the staff was poor, there was no real curriculum, it always beastly hot in summer. As I listened to the disgruntled former employee I wondered if I should go through with Noah's placement there.

But an ideal place for Noah will not be found that easily. There is no simple resolution to the problem. Or even the promise of one.

How much I love Noah! How impossible it is for me to be logical or judicial in making any decision about him. I barely slept all last night. And when I did sleep toward morning it was only with an undertow of bad dreams about Noah and his future.

Bruce, who has been working with Noah every day, is also a former employee of OCC and a much more gruntled one. He paints a far rosier picture of the place. I also spoke with the Administrative President, whose own son is a client there. "Do you think I would keep him here for one minute if the conditions were bad?" he asked pointedly. I didn't see how I could argue with that.

Meanwhile, Foumi is not feeling well. Pains in her stomach. Pains in her shoulders. "I think I have cancer. I think I am dying," she said to me this morning. I think the pains derive from the fact that she and Karl are at each other constantly, having the traditional parent-teenager run-ins. I used to have them with Karl. Now it's her turn. She's very concerned about Karl's watching too much television. But I also note that he stays up late reading, which is fine with me.

The disgruntled former OCC worker wants to give me additional negative reports about the place. But I don't really want to hear them. Noah is getting too big for us. Too much of our time is devoted to dealing with him. Directly and indirectly. We're all bothered. Karl included. Once Noah is stashed away we'll all feel better. At least of a Sunday morning when we'll be able to sleep late.

And Noah won't miss me. I dress and feed and bathe him, in other words, I take care of him—but we have no real interaction. If I were to hire someone to take care of him in our home it would be the same thing as far as he's concerned. It would not provide him with any more learning experiences than he is getting now.

I hate operant conditioning. But better for him to do the right thing automatically than to do nothing at all. Better to have a robot that can dress itself than have an independent animal that shits all over the place.

We took Noah out to OCC yesterday afternoon. The Executive Visiting Adviser was waiting for us with the rest of the staff.

Unfortunately, she seemed more interested in finding out what the former disgruntled employee had said to us than in Noah himself. But finally, she did get around to Noah. How far were we willing to go when it came to the use of aversives? she wanted to know. The time would come, she was sure, when she'd want to be able to utilize her whole program, which included pinches and muscle squeezes.

I did not quite understand why she wanted to talk so of pinches and muscle squeezes. Because they're not allowed to use them anyway. Right now, under some special dispensation of the law, the only aversives they can apply are water squirts and spanks.

She gave me some papers to read but still did not pay much attention to Noah, who was bouncing on the couch. However, she did impress me by having another autistic kid I know stand quietly at attention. The kid certainly seemed to be under her control. But I was dismayed to see that all the other children there were skinny, skinnier than Noah. And skinny is the mark of regimented eating—or not eating.

On the way home Foumi mentioned that the Administrative President had told her in an aside that no matter what the Executive Visiting Adviser was saying, it was much too early to talk of pinches and muscle squeezes and they certainly would not be used on Noah.

December 15, 1979

The OCC facility is a large house on a very pleasant street and does not reek of an institutional setup at all. But the Executive Visiting Adviser does loom as a problem. She is a humorless, inflexible ideologue who believes in behavior mod as a gospel. I am no believer at all. I give some lip service to it but I am really sending Noah there for custodial purposes. That is the lure. Of course, I would be delighted if they could obtain good results using their methodology—but not too stringently. In no way will I allow Noah to become the recipient of pinches or muscle squeezes. Such aversives are too hurtful and too dangerous. If they try to inflict them on Noah I will immediately withdraw him. All that, of course, is down the line and on the down side. Meanwhile, if we can get two weeks of respite out of the whole deal, I will be happy. After that I'll worry.

Now I just want Noah at home over Christmas. It is a family time. The Swiss Family Greenfeld. Oh what holes there are in our cheesecloth of happiness.

December 16, 1979

I secretly count the days now until Noah goes to OCC. I look forward to it the way a kid anticipates a summer vacation.

December 18, 1979

For a few weeks, at least, OCC should do Noah good as a kind of basic training for him. He does need shaping up. His behavior has broken down as surely as his zits are breaking out.

December 19, 1979

Karl did not go to school until 10:30 this morning, complaining of an upset stomach when he awoke. Then he later said he felt better. I have a hunch he wanted to miss his first few classes. Probably a test in French.

He's not a bad kid. He's just not a good kid. Last night he reached across the table and swiped a piece of Noah's barbecued chicken. I get awfully angry with him for taking such advantage. But Karl lives with all the disadvantages too.

December 20, 1979

I went to a holiday party out in Hollywood. One of my old army buddies showed up with his eighteen-year-old daughter, with whom he was sharing a joint. Another old friend, I learned, had just gone through eight thousand dollars' worth of coke, free-basing in a period of three days. I retreated to reality and came home to find Foumi in a state. Noah had been attacking her and Karl. And it was all my fault, she insisted. I go out one night in three months for four hours and get the complete guilt book thrown at me.

December 21, 1979

Noah's school this morning had their Christmas music program. The school now has just eleven kids. Ten took part in the program. One stood in the back with his teacher: Noah.

At breakfast I had a run-in with Karl. He was staying home from school because of a headache. But he joined us at the table with Frances, our once-a-week housecleaning helper. And at one point I said something about Karl never listening to anybody. Whereupon he screamed, "I hate you!" and ran from the room. Immediately I told him to get the hell out of the house. He left in his stocking feet. And wouldn't return until I went after him. He's a kid who loses control easily. Just like me.

After Noah's school's music program I stopped at my agent's office to leave Christmas presents for his staff. One of the secretaries told me that both of her sons, regular grass smokers, had dropped out of school. She further advised me that "kids will turn out like you no matter what you do." If she's right we're in for a lot more trouble from Karl.

December 22, 1979

A broken Saturday. This morning we had some new people working in day-care, and Foumi became concerned when no one was answering the phone there. I drove over with Karl to find the phone out of order and Noah pulling a new aide's hair. I returned home, brunched with Karl, quarreled with Foumi, and then chauffeured Karl and his friend Stefan over to the hobby shop in Santa Monica and left them there. Karl had thirty dollars in his pocket with which to buy Christmas gifts. I expect the money to melt away by evening. But it is his money and he is entitled to spend it as he wishes.

December 23, 1979

Noah pissed in his pants last evening, and then again last night on the rug in his room after a prolonged tantrum. Foumi thinks it's because he's still confusing the pangs of puberty with the hints of urination. Bruce suspects it might be his rebellion against going into OCC. I wonder if it's because he noticed how much time I've been spending with Karl. Anyway, problems with Noah, problems without end.

December 24, 1979

I awoke dreaming: Foumi stood at the top of the stairwell that led to our first apartment in Brooklyn Heights. She was in charge of a psychiatric ward that was overflowing with patients, some of whom were playing football.

December 25, 1979

Christmas Day: Karl was unhappy because somehow we haven't gotten around to getting him anything yet. Noah was unhappy because that's the way he's been lately. Foumi was unhappy because of her painful arthritis. Fortunately, by evening we were all in better moods. Even Karl, who was joking about how neglected he was. I played checkers and chess with him, beating him at both. But then he trotted out his electronic games and I couldn't come close.

Karl is just an inch shy of me in height now but worlds away from me in personality. He possesses one of the two qualities that most attract people: danger. One can never foresee his reaction to any situation. It may be ironic but it is also a fact. Danger and its polarity, rocklike stability, are the qualities that are the most magnetic.

December 27, 1979

Noah still scratches me, Noah is a strain. No way could I keep him home much longer. If not OCC, I would have to put him someplace else. Almost anyplace else.

December 28, 1979

Today is really Christmas: At day-care this morning, Richard Davis, a Special Ed teacher from Utah who runs a residence for retarded adults in Provo, visited us with his wife and baby daughter. What a nice man! Along with the deadheads, the field does manage to attract some living saints.

In the afternoon we managed to go shopping and finally celebrate Christmas for Karl. Got him a down jacket and a Swiss Army knife and a D and D set. By evening he was still purring with happiness.

December 30, 1979

Noah continues his scratching and pinching. Seems to be treating me as if I were an enemy. I wish I could treat him as an enemy.

263

Or just not care about him. As long as I care about him I'm a setup to lose.

December 31, 1979

When Noah pinched me as I was brushing his teeth this morning, I gave him a whack across his ass. But he did not have a tantrum. He took his hit like a man—as if he knew he deserved it.

January 1, 1980

Last night some friends came over, bearing champagne and sushi. A lovely way to start the new year—in fact, the new decade. Until Noah suddenly tore off his shirt, had a tantrum, and scratched me fiercely. Karl was smart, he spent the night at a friend's house, and did not show up here until lunchtime today.

January 3, 1980

What I see most clearly in Noah's face is his down, each hair like a spike nailing down his own coffin. For when his beauty dies, so will he.

January 4, 1980

I turned down an assignment, writing the book for a musical. It would not only have gotten me back to theater but it also would have involved me so completely for the next few weeks—and months—that it might have insulated me from the trauma of parting from Noah. But Noah has been trying to make it easier for me. By spitting and scratching up a storm.

January 5, 1980

Bobby, one of Noah's schoolmates and day-caremates, went into a residence yesterday. Foumi called his house. His parents were not there but his twenty-year-old brother answered the phone. "I miss Bobby already," he said.

Foumi called there again tonight and got through to the parents. They were crying. And I suspect we'll be crying here next week, too. And I don't know what will be worse. Living with Noah or without him.

But I do think with Noah gone Karl can't help but become more adult. It must be awfully hard trying to leave your own childhood behind when your sibling's childhood is perpetual.

January 6, 1980

In a little more than a week Noah goes to OCC. I am nervous. I shouted at Karl for not setting the lunch table. He shouted back. He must be nervous too. Foumi joined in. Soon we were all shouting at each other. We're all nervous.

January 8, 1980

Noah, the sonofabitch, was in a remarkably good mood last night, laughing and smiling infectiously, a complete joy to be with—except for the guilt he was instilling.

January 10, 1980

Whether I planned it this way or not, Noah is spending most of his last few days with us—or rather with me. Foumi is sick with the flu. And this morning Noah's school called: His teacher was out with the flu. Could we keep Noah home from school?

January 11, 1980

Noah's last day at school: I arrived late, after all the other kids were gone. The teachers were still there. Noah was sitting on the floor. The school director gave me a card, an oversized construction paper folded in two. On the front was a drawing of the gingerbread house that is the school. Within the centerfold was printed: WE'LL MISS YOU, NOAH! All the kids and teachers had signed their names. I had to leave quickly because my eyes were welling up. All the way home I had to fight back tears. And for the rest of the day.

January 12, 1980

Foumi still has the flu. And Noah goes to OCC after the weekend. I am sure that he will come down with the flu before he leaves. Bound to happen.

A bloody bad day. A terrible start for Noah with OCC. The Executive Visiting Adviser, the Administrative President, and a treatment worker came to the house. They brought a camera and lighting equipment with them, which they began to assemble and set up. If it was to establish a baseline, I asked, why didn't they use videotape? Because videotape was too hard to edit, answered the Executive Visiting Adviser. When she asked me to talk into a microphone and describe Noah's "inappropriate behaviors," I told her I would do no such thing. If she wanted promotional pictures or movies, I said, she wouldn't get them from me. "Then there's no point in going on," she said, and packed up and left.

In other words she had a tantrum. In any case, today, Noah's last day home, was not the day to play around with us. Both Foumi and I have constantly been on the verge of tears. Karl has tried to joke his away, insisting that we should feel sorry for him because of the trauma he is undergoing. Foumi is afraid I may have loused up Noah's future at OCC.

A gray rainy day, an easy-to-cry-upon day. Thirteen years, six months, and thirteen days we have been a four-person family. And now we will become a three-person family. And oh how greatly diminished we shall be!

19

Morning: Another rainy, gray wintery January day. Today Noah
leaves for OCC. I am upset, I have misgivings. But I also have had
enough. I only wish he still weren't so cute and cuddly. As he was
today when I fed him a bagel breakfast. And afterward, when
I brushed his teeth, no spitting, no scratching, no hair pulling,
just cute and cuddly. But that's the reason he must go. Because
he can still be so cute and cuddly. Something Karl can never be
again.

I do not cry yet. I know there will be crying later. It is good that
Foumi will be with me. If she cries, I cannot. One of us must
remain dry-eyed in the presence of the other—and of Karl. He
will be with us because I think he should see where we are putting
Noah. He should have the same misgivings we have. Noah is an
experience he will share with us until our deaths. And then, even
to his greater misfortune, afterward.

Meanwhile, I try to tell myself I am sending Noah to a military
academy from which he can be withdrawn at any time. Foumi is
busy with details, labeling and packing Noah's clothing. She
thinks of everything. Overthinks. She is even washing out the rice
cooker we're contributing to OCC.

Oh the future! Today is the first day of it.

Evening: Noah got into the car as if he were just going on
another ride. But when I picked up Karl at his school, Noah immediately attacked him in the backseat. I pulled over and freed

Karl. Then we waited for Noah to calm down. Finally, after twenty minutes, we were on our way, this time with Noah in the front seat beside me. Neither Foumi nor Karl was willing to sit next to him.

At OCC we filled out many forms, signed papers galore. One of them gave permission to use aversives on Noah—but not the muscle squeeze or the pinch. There are four other boys there. Noah will share a room with one of them. Foumi had cooked a stack of dumplings for Noah, which we left behind along with a rice cooker and a twenty-five-pound bag of rice. I showed the staff how to use the rice cooker. Noah jumped and flopped about and waved a desultory good-bye to us.

Karl behaved well. When he was introduced to people he mumbled but was never downright rude. He just took me aside and told me he did not like the place, thought the program was too strictly structured for Noah. But he agreed that it was the best place for Noah to be at this time. On the long ride home, on the freeway, we all quietly cried.

I am still on the edge of tears. Parting, as they say, is a hint of death, a preview of the inevitable and the unbearable. But I refuse to feel guilty. Not about Noah. Not anymore. I just hope I don't feel guilty about how I invest my new freedom.

I remember when I was twenty years old in the Rehabilitation Hospital recovering from polio and I had finally progressed to the point where I was going to be allowed out of bed for ten minutes a day. The orderly brought me a wheelchair. "From now on," he said, "no bedpans for you. I expect you to use this chair to go to the toilet." I had been flat on my back for months. But I said, "Take the chair away. I'm not getting out of bed just to shit." In the same way I am now wary of using the gift of normalcy just for shit purposes.

January 15, 1980

Woke up with an aching sense of emptiness, missing the white noise of Noah's insistent presence. How still it was all last night without him here. The house has never been so utterly quiet. It is truly amazing how much noise the act of living makes even without the emission of words.

Day Two Without Noah: A parent who long ago placed his special child in an institution told us that within a week we'll be wondering why we had not done so sooner. He's wrong. I won't wonder. I know precisely why. Because out of sight not only out of mind but also beyond responsibility.

We think of Noah constantly. He is the unspoken thought that fills all the silences. How long the evening seems to wear on. When Noah was home there was never time to do anything in the evening. Now it seems there is too much time to do anything.

Lots of phone calls. From friends who call with the voice of condolence expecting to hear sniffles in our replies. But the truth is we feel like the family of a long-suffering cancer victim who has finally succumbed. We are too relieved to be distressed.

Meanwhile, at OCC they tell us all is going well. Noah is sleeping well and eating well. Except for his salad. Foumi thinks that might be because they are cutting it in pieces smaller than those Noah is used to.

We are limiting ourselves to one phone call a day to OCC. At four o'clock. Each day I wait for the phone call the way a prisoner must wait for mail. So far the reports are good. Noah eats, sleeps, and has an occasional tantrum.

Noah's schedule: Up at eight. Breakfast. School with rest periods. Lunch. School with rest periods. Free play. Dinner. Walk. Shower. Bedtime at ten. School consists of constant behavior modification. And since I can live with it, I hope he can. I look at behavior mod not as an etiology or belief system that I am committed to but rather as a way in which attention is paid to Noah. I believe if someone pays enough attention to Noah he will improve. But deep down I don't pray so much that he improves but that he doesn't deprove—or regress.

I myself am in a strange limbo. I feel I have suddenly been discharged from the army and it seems more appropriate to celebrate than to become a civilian again just yet. Last night, for example, we picked up Karl after his French lesson, went into Westwood to see *Kramer vs. Kramer*, and then had a big Indian dinner. We joked about a Greenfeld vs. Greenfeld in which no one wanted custody of the kid. Truly, *Kramer vs. Kramer* for me was the other side of the coin. I really have been living in another world.

I must say, with Noah gone Karl seems more relaxed, less moody, and happier. It is as if a great burden has been lifted from him. Or am I simply being more patient? Or just projecting? But I do enjoy Karl more.

Foumi too. She looks better and our marriage feels better. And I even have time to worry about the Afghan invasion and the possibility of America's withdrawing from the Moscow Olympics.

January 18, 1980

Stan Nakao, our man at Regional Center, visited OCC and liked what he saw. Said Noah seemed to be doing well. The staff, when I spoke with them, said the same thing.

January 19, 1980

This afternoon one of the workers at OCC told me Noah was giving them difficulties on walks. I immediately briefed him on the fact that Noah does not like to be held by the hand. He likes to assume the guise of manly independence.

I took a walk this evening. Down familiar streets. Along Asilomar and then up Muskigum to Sunset and then back down El Medio. It is the route I usually take with Noah on Sundays, walking up ahead of him and then patiently waiting for him to catch up to me. Suddenly, I found myself crying.

Foumi, too, was crying today. While we were preparing the salaries of our day-care workers. We both cry at odd moments. We hear sounds in the house, sounds that we assume are Noah. And then, of course, we realize that they cannot be Noah because Noah is not here.

The days are quiet and the nights are long without Noah. My guilt cushion is gone but so too is my love object. I think I love Noah more than any woman I have ever known and more than any friend I have ever had, more than I loved my own parents and more than I love my own wife. After all, he has never betrayed my love a single second.

January 20, 1980

The recurring image I have of Noah at OCC is a tricky one. Suddenly it is my father I see there. It is an image I do not like. It means I have placed Noah among the dead.

January 21, 1980

I feel bad. It seems Noah shit in his p.j.'s in bed on Saturday night. And I thought he had been making the adjustment well. A toilet accident on his part is a bad sign.

January 22, 1980

Last night I helped Karl with a book report. That's the hardest writing I ever have to do. And the least rewarding. He doesn't appreciate my help at all. We argue. But at dinner tonight he happened to relate how he had helped another kid at school write his book report by passing along my advice: Start with a general statement and then apply it to the book.

January 23, 1980

We're all going out to OCC this afternoon. It's nine days since we've seen Noah. And I have a hunch that it's been harder on us than it's been on him.

January 24, 1980

Noah has the institutional look already; the baby—or home—fat in his face is gone, and he seems paler. When he saw us he came out pinching. But somehow he also did seem to accept the fact that he is at OCC. And so, too, must we.

To be sure, there are faults with the setup. Like most group residences its size, only one person is on duty after midnight. And Foumi feels that in case of fire, for example, it would be difficult for just one person to rouse and guide four or five Noahs to safety. I find the desert heat there oppressive and wonder how Noah will be able to stand it in the summer. But we have to take what we can get. I know of no other choice.

Karl did not come with us, backing out at the last minute because he feared that Noah might be jealous seeing him leave with us. He still thinks that somewhere in Noah there is a thought process similar to his own. And perhaps there is.

I still act as if our separation from Noah were no more than a hiatus. I treat myself as if I were on a vacation, lingering in bed each morning. I had thought putting Noah in an institution would suddenly release a parcel of energy. Instead, it has released a parcel of tiredness. A thirteen-year tiredness, explains Foumi.

January 25, 1980

We went out to dinner last night with five adults. And Karl, acting his usual mean and sullen self when he is with us in public, addressed Foumi as an "idiot" and me as an "asshole." It must be uncomfortable being a kid among grown-ups but still he doesn't have the foggiest idea how to behave properly. I didn't get as angry with him as I should because I know he must be having a difficult time with the absence of Noah. The spotlight is now too much upon him and he does not bask in it gracefully.

Nor should he, considering his grades. Foumi perhaps made a mistake in forcing biology upon him. He could have waited before taking his science. I had forgotten the greatest single lesson of my school years: Put off the subjects you do not like as long as possible.

January 26, 1980

A friend asked me how we were getting along. I told him I never realized how much of a pain Karl was until after Noah left home.

January 28, 1980

I still feel as if I've just been discharged from the army—the army of parents with disabled children. With Noah out of the house I am indulging in all the little things I could not do when he was home. I sleep late, I eat out often, I enjoy silence. Eventually I might even be able to go into his empty room. Right now no one goes there. Except the cat.

Foumi and I began to take a sign-language class. If Noah will learn signing at OCC, as they claim he will, then so should we.

Karl surprised us last night. He cleaned the kitchen beautifully. But Foumi no longer has to worry about dinner, anyway; we can always go out. The house is clean; the living room is a cinch to keep in order. We can all sleep through the night without interruption. And theoretically, since I have more hours to work, the pages should be piling up on my desk.

But what I look forward to most at the moment is Noah's return home for a weekend visit. Institutional workers, no matter how kind, I know can never be as warm and as concerned as family. I hate to use the word loosely but I think both Noah and we must be suffering from the same lack at different ends: love.

After lunch we go to pick up Noah. And for the first time ever we're in a "can't lose" situation with him. If he acts terrible this weekend then we know we did the right thing in getting him out of the house. If he acts good, behaves beautifully, it simply will be a joy to have him home.

Karl is behaving better on his evenings out with us. I think Noah is still a problem to him when he assays the future, reckoning that he will always have to take care of him. And that is not so. I don't know who will have to take care of Noah eventually, but I am determined to see to it that Noah not be Karl's worry.

Karl has a diction, a teenage 1980–post Salinger diction, that I can't always catch completely. I notice it particularly in his writing, which shows a fictionalist's flair. I wouldn't be surprised if he winds up a novelist.

A case of nerves. Ours. On the drive out to OCC, Foumi and I argued constantly. But anything to do with Noah has always induced arguments. And now we both feel so guilty about not having him in the house any longer.

But at OCC, Noah was a delight to see. He did not look at all like the emaciated D.P. I had picked up at Spastic's. Though pinching, he was smiling. When I put my hat on his head, he immediately knew where he was going, and he sang—or chirped—all the way home. When we arrived at the house I told him, "Go into the backyard," and he eagerly ran there. When I later took him for a walk, he clung to me tightly, shyly hiding his head in his jacket, his fingers digging into my elbow.

Except for puckishly pouring some of his juice on the table at dinner, Noah ate beautifully, sitting up on request. And afterward, when we cut his hair, the problem was Foumi and not him. I sat with a bag of potato chips ready to reinforce him as Foumi snipped away. But she said "good sitting" when he wasn't. Which confused him because he then expected a reward he wasn't entitled to. And when I would not give it to him he pinched me. I became unduly upset and slapped him back. But he did not cry and just sat there. Despite Foumi's dumb behavior and my subsequent dumber behavior it was the easiest haircut we've ever given him.

This morning Foumi and I fought all through breakfast. We're both feeling so nervous. And guilty. And crazy. The argument began over the freshness of the chicken I was putting into Noah's lunch sandwich and soon escalated—or descended—into the very depths of our personalities, raging on and on. After I finally dressed Noah and brushed his teeth and got him off to day-care, I realized he is better off at OCC than he is with us. I no longer have any patience, I raise my voice too quickly. And Foumi is too much the paranoid perfectionist for any brain-damaged kid to live with. By worrying about everything she becomes a worry herself.

February 3, 1980

Foumi and I are still on each other's cases. But Noah has been eating like an army recruit home from basic training. (And shitting like one too: three movements in three days.) I took him for a long walk this morning and a car ride this afternoon. He's also been playing in the backyard, sitting on the lawn and investigating it, as if counting the blades of grass to see if any are missing.

In other words, mostly he's been Noah, ignoring us as we ignore him. He has chewed on the edges of our bedspread and on his T-shirts. He has eaten his quilt and his pajamas. But he's been relatively easy. As I say, Foumi and I have been the problems. Foumi says she picks up the cues from me. But I think she has her own guilt just as surely as I have mine. On Friday when I took Noah for a walk I suddenly began to cry. And I guess I must expect tears to sneak up on me at odd moments for the rest of my life.

Right now Karl is sleeping on one couch in the living room and Noah is sprawled across the love seat. And I'm angry with Foumi again. When I mentioned that Karl and I might go to a movie this evening she exploded: "Then why have Noah home?" I tried to explain to her that having Noah home for a weekend shouldn't mean our lives have to come to a complete stop. But she would have none of it.

February 4, 1980

A day of peace. Noah did not protest much when I drove him back to OCC. It was as if he were returning to a dorm after a weekend at home. I will be curious to see how he reacts when he comes home next weekend. And how we react too. Some of us might even be able to go out.

When I described to a friend yesterday the constant state of apprehension and edginess in our house, he explained. "Of course, you have a guest in the house." And I guess Foumi is a better host than I. Anyway, the weekend was a success. The arguments notwithstanding, guest or not, Noah can go home again.

20

Having Noah home over the weekend showed me nothing has changed. I am forever bound to Noah. But what's the big deal about that? I am also forever bound to Karl. Every parent is inextricably and irrevocably tied to his offspring. And vice versa. Normal or special. And yet the energy necessary to maintain that involvement inevitably somehow decreases. Except with a special child.

Even Karl keeps worrying about Noah. Part of his projection of himself as an adult involves taking care of Noah. He would like to have a great deal of money, he tells me, so he could start a school for Noahs.

He also might start a better school for Karls. The high school he goes to looks like a prison with its cell-block-like corridors, and treats the kids as if they were cons, with its checkpoints for passes. It is an atmosphere loaded with aversives. Which means Noah's school with its behavior modification punishments and rewards more closely resembles the way we treat ordinary children than we like to think. But I'm still not sure about behavior modification in general and OCC in particular. I can't believe that food is the only reward and physical hurt is the best aversive.

February 7, 1980

Karl is in the coin business. He goes to school each day bearing rolls of old silver dimes and somehow comes back with more. I hope he isn't gambling or dealing and just has something his old man lacks—business sense.

February 8, 1980

There is a flu over my cuckoo's nest. Foumi is sick with it, so we won't be taking Noah home this weekend.

February 9, 1980

I am now typing in Noah's room. His playthings, which he never seems to play with, are all about me. I have my notes, my folders, my pads, my own playthings all about me.

When Noah was around I would grab any opportunity to get away from the drudgery and obsession of having to take care of him. Even writing was an activity I looked forward to. Now I look to get out of writing. My negative source of motivation has gone but a positive one has not yet emerged.

February 10, 1980

This morning I was flipping the television dial and stopped at a college basketball game between Connecticut and Rhode Island. Just that moment Karl came into the room and asked who was winning. I shrugged. "Want to bet?" he asked. "Sure," I replied, "a million dollars." "I'll take Rhode Island," he said and sat down to watch as I continued to joke. When Rhode Island did win he turned to me and asked for his million dollars. He was serious, too, and became very upset, calling me an asshole. He worries me. Can he really not tell the difference between make-believe and reality? Or is he of the television generation that blurs the distinction? Or was he, I hope, just pulling my leg?

February 11, 1980

I missed Noah all day yesterday. In the afternoon I decided to go out to OCC and visit him. But when I called there I was told he was at the park. His absence preyed on me for the rest of the day. And I awoke in the middle of the night crying.

I drove out this afternoon to see Noah. He was performing a perfunctory matching task when I walked in and he seemed glad to see me. I took him to a nearby park. We walked around for a while. I let him play on a swing. He took off his shoes and clutched and pinched at me. In other words, he was his usual self. After I bought him some popcorn I took him back to OCC. I liked seeing Noah again. But in all truth I was also glad to take him back after an hour and get away from him.

Seeing Noah at OCC was like seeing him with a frame around him. A frame that describes his present and predicts his future. The frame does not include home. Once Noah has been out of my house for a significant period, it will be as if he is gone forever. He leaves no real signs of life behind, no toys to trip over, no artifacts of his interests. Karl's room is an obstacle course. Noah's room is that of a transient.

Karl received his report card. Three C's and a D. He tells us he hates school, is bored by his subjects, and even feels constantly victimized by some black students who are much bigger than he is. I can't do anything about his size or the race problem and I don't know how to react to his low grades. If he is a confused teenager, I am a confused parent. I do not believe in grades but he has to know that his are scarcely the kind that will get him into a decent college.

I find it increasingly hard to justify myself without Noah. Noah would allow me to do trash, to make do. He gave me a value system that I could easily live with out here. Now I am confused.

And distracted. Karl is as much a worry as Noah. He has profligate—if one may use that word for a teenager—tendencies. He also evinces—and it seems all too familiar—an inability to live up to his potentialities. I was the same way. So it is even more disheartening to see it in him.

Foumi seems better. At least she had enough energy to be all over Karl's ass because of his lousy report card. But once more it occurs to me that maybe I sent the wrong kid away.

When I picked Noah up yesterday he looked lighter; I assumed that was the institutional cast, which makes all kids look slimmer. And he was not exactly a pleasure to be around. He pinched and kicked at me all the way to the car. On the ride back he whimpered and then reached over and started clawing at me. I began to wonder if that was going to be my absurd end—death in a crash on the San Diego Freeway after being attacked by Noah in my own car. For more than a few miles it did not seem such an unlikely fate.

At home I weighed Noah immediately. He was down to ninety-five pounds, five less than when he entered OCC. If he continues to lose weight at this pace, I decided, then we'll have to get him out of there and just be glad that we had some respite.

Noah pinched throughout his dinner, even as we were stuffing him, and then still wasn't satisfied when he was told that he had had enough. He had consumed dozens of pork dumplings, bowls of rice, platters of salad. Yet he still wanted more and had a tantrum, crying, tearing at Foumi's hair. Finally he subsided.

When I gave him his bath he also acted up, constantly pinching me as I washed him. Nor would he get out of the water when I asked him to. And he gave me a hard time brushing his teeth. It was all part of an ordeal I had so easily forgotten, an ordeal I can so easily live without. I don't know what's worse: keeping Noah in a residence and not seeing him but wanting to see him all the time. Or having him home, knowing he's home, and not wanting to see him at all, just wishing he'd go hide in his room.

Which is what Karl did. He was in his room all day. He came out late for dinner and barely acknowledged Noah's presence.

If Noah has been losing weight since he left the house, then I've been gaining it. I'm up to 145 pounds, as much as I've ever weighed. But then I've been ignoring my low-cholesterol diet and doing very little exercise.

I am working at my novel again. And a book, I've decided, even a movie, yes verily any work of art, should never be an illustrated *anything*, like a Q.E.D. mathematical proof, but rather a discovered *something*, like a sudden realization or insight.

February 18, 1980

All night it rained. All day it rained. And when it rains in tropical L.A. it really rains. As I started to drive Noah back to OCC last night the deluge came and Sunset Boulevard was cut off from the world. But instead of turning around I went by way of the canyon. I decided it was best to take Noah back to OCC while we were still enjoying him. Because by Sunday he was through testing us and was really happy to be home, beginning with the two and a half bagels he devoured at breakfast.

But when I deposited him at OCC he seemed glad to be returning there too. Immediately he sat down on the couch and even turned his head occasionally toward the TV screen the other clients were watching.

The drive back without him was boring. And I could see how life without Noah might become very bland. But I'll still take my chances on terminal boredom.

February 20, 1980

When Noah is home with us, after a few moments it seems that he has never left the house. When Noah is gone from the house it seems as if he has never been with us. He leaves no imprint of his stay except a chewed blanket and a frayed pillow. Activity is the indelible ingredient of memory.

February 21, 1980

Foumi has three main gripes with OCC: (1) The treatment workers—in other words, the psychology students—rather than specially hired people, do the cooking. (2) They lack a disaster drill.

(3) The Administrative President never seems to be around when she wants to get in touch with him.

February 22, 1980

Karl can be wonderfully funny. The other night he was watching the beginning of a Goldie Hawn–Liza Minnelli TV special. When I came into the living room they were dancing with a chorus to that "YMCA" song. "How is it?" I asked Karl. "Gay-wise," he replied, "not bad."

But he also can be very troubling. Last night he admitted to me that in the process of coin dealing he had stolen a valuable dime from a fellow student by palming it. He did so, he said, because that kid had previously stolen a quarter from him in the same manner and it was the only way to get even. The morality—or amorality—deeply disturbed me. What engendered the confession was his disclosure that his badminton racquet had been stolen at school. The loss of the racquet is of little moment but his cavalier acceptance of that fact upset me. "Report it," I suggested. And he only laughed and confessed his own thievery by way of argument.

And when we went out to dinner last night he gave me the usual hard time, constantly finding fault with me: the way I dressed, the way I drove, the way I ate, even the way I ordered. As if my very existence were a constant source of embarrassment to him. In other words, the sonofabitch treats me as if I'm a teenager. Which I'm not.

February 23, 1980

When we picked up Noah at OCC yesterday afternoon Foumi noticed that the matching tasks they had him doing were tasks that he's always been able to do.

This morning we sent Noah off to day-care. And then Karl, Foumi, and I went to the funeral of our pediatrician, Gunther Bick. Gunther never made us feel we were imposing upon him the way so many other doctors had. He had simply treated Noah with a matter-of-fact dignity.

The church was full. In fact, I never saw a funeral service with so many kids in attendance. And the kids behaved appropriately too, crying and wailing.

February 25, 1980

When Noah is home with us it seems the most natural thing in the world. When Noah is not home with us it seems the most natural thing in the world. This morning I took him back to OCC.

February 27, 1980

A historic day. My fifty-second birthday. How old fifty-two once seemed to me. But I'm not really old. Not me. Not this kid. Didn't I start the day discussing a sitcom with a producer over bagels and lox at a local delicatessen? Scarcely the behavior of a grown writer.

March 3, 1980

We spent the weekend in Eugene, Oregon, at a conference of parents with special children. We enjoyed the sharing of experiences but I felt a little bit of a cheat—and a large sense of irony. We were there because of Noah, but because we were there Noah was spending the weekend at OCC.

As always before a trip, Karl was difficult. But once we got to Eugene he settled down and I could regard him almost objectively. I delighted, for example, in watching him order escargots and beef Wellington in our hotel dining room. But I know if I treat him as an adult I am as mistaken as when I treat him as a child. He constantly flits between the two states. And whenever I think he's in one place, I soon find out he's in the other. He is like a radio station I can't quite tune in fully, forever missing the exact frequency.

I liked Eugene, the college-town ambience, and the hills above it, sort of a Croton of the Northwest. I could easily fantasize a pleasant life of retirement there, if not for Noah. But if not for Noah I can easily imagine a pleasant life anywhere.

The honeymoon is over. Noah's weight is eight pounds less than it was six weeks ago. So we're back to worrying about him again, wondering whether we should withdraw him from OCC.

Last night I dreamed I had climbed a fire ladder to the top of something. But there was no way I could get down. Because the fire ladder had been removed. I was offered instead a stringy, tattered-looking rope ladder that obviously hadn't been used for a long time. I agonized over what to do until I awoke.

And I don't have to be a Joseph to understand the parable.

March 5, 1980

We have decided to go into New York over Easter. We owe ourselves such a holiday trip before making a final decision about bringing Noah back home.

March 7, 1980

I picked up Noah at OCC while he was having his lunch. And he looked terrific. Bigger. Taller. And not at all emaciated. He was ninety-seven pounds, I was told, up five since Monday. And he was in a good mood, eating by himself and chirping away. He waved to me and I waved back as I patiently waited for him to finish his lunch.

March 8, 1980

A good night with Noah. A bad night with Foumi. Because of Karl. She's convinced that he's on a cholesterol death march, the way he eats rich, fatty things, and that there is no way to head him off. He's also not doing well in school despite all our badgering and tutoring.

I just don't know how to make that kid wake up. Either he's pissing away his future or he's a lot smarter than either of us. Foumi and I take the bourgeois tack with him. Trying to encourage the traditional values, the eternal virtues. Even though he knows we're quite independent venturers ourselves. But the unhappy result is that he has become a strange creature philosophically, a political conservative fascinated with destruction and violence. Either out of rebellion or simply because he's another bad seed. And with our record that is a legitimate possibility.

March 10, 1980

Noah is still an albatross, no doubt about it. After a day of his constant spitting and pinching, I wasn't too unhappy returning him to OCC last evening. Nor was he too unhappy either as he lugged his suitcase out to the car. And when we arrived back at OCC he seemed quite at home as he quickly appropriated a place for himself on the couch there. Perhaps he knows better than we do that he belongs there. Perhaps the transition is over and we all have come through.

But I don't know how I can adjust to Karl. At breakfast he announced that he wanted to eat sushi for dinner. But in the evening, as we were about to leave for a Japanese restaurant, he suddenly complained, "Why do we always have to eat in Oriental restaurants?" I became furious. Where did he expect to get sushi? In a bistro? A pizzeria? A delicatessen? After I had shouted at him, he decided not to come with us. But Foumi, the Japanese mother, brought him back some sushi anyway, and later, somehow, this Jewish mother—read: "father"—was broiling a steak for him.

March 11, 1980

OCC tells us that Noah had a tantrum shortly after he returned there Sunday and had three more tantrums on Monday. They're blaming the tantrums on our taking him home. But they seldom take him anywhere on weekends. And he has to leave the joint, otherwise he'll go stir crazy.

Foumi and I have decided that Karl is simply not a bright kid. He doesn't even know how to tear off a piece of Glad Wrap, he uses far too much toilet paper, and he has no great passion to learn anything. He does nothing particularly well but talk. He has good reason to have low self-esteem. He remains a likely candidate for drugs. He gives me a pain.

I also have another pain. When I walk. In my heart, across my chest. Or at least I did yesterday. I don't know whether it comes from an incipient heart condition or because Foumi had me read a long piece in Sunday's paper on the anatomy of a heart attack. Anyway, I scheduled a physical.

March 12, 1980

Today's definition—or rather distinction: Marriage is an act of will, whereas divorce is an act of won't.

March 13, 1980

I shot some baskets with Karl. My, how he has improved. He has a jump shot, he can pass off, and he has become a decent school-yard player. Last night I thought he would beat me for the first time in Horse. He even scored the first two letters on me. Then he choked. But any day now he should beat me. Sic transit gloria pater.

March 15, 1980

Foumi and I went to the wrap party of *Oh, God! Book II*, as it's now called, at the Friars Club. I glared at God and his manager and they glared back.

Karl sat with Noah, home for the weekend. They were both still up at midnight when we walked in the door. Karl, sleepy-eyed, watching TV in the den. And Noah, in his p.j.'s, perched on the couch as if waiting for me to provide a cue. I did: I told him to go to the bathroom. Which he immediately did and then ran off to bed. I covered him and kissed him good night. It was good walking into the house and finding both my boys there. When Noah is home we are a family again. Even Karl seems better be-haved. I went to sleep happy.

March 18, 1980

I took my annual physical this morning. When I mentioned to my doctor that I sometimes felt a burning sensation in my throat and occasionally had chest pains, he suggested I take a treadmill test at the hospital. Otherwise, all seems well physically.

We drove out to the desert for a meeting of OCC parents with the Administrative President last night. I had thought the purpose of the meeting was to give the parents an opportunity to voice their concerns. For example, Foumi and I still worry about their lack of a disaster plan and their failure to hire a cook. It turned out the purpose was to pledge undying support to OCC and to talk about fund raising for them.

On my walk this morning, I noticed that whenever I strode briskly uphill, I felt a burning acidy taste in my throat and suffered a shortness of breath. Probably too much coffee. Or too much breakfast. Or I'm coming down with a cold. But, whatever, I am glad that I have scheduled a treadmill test after our trip to New York.

A weekday update: Noah was a terror over the weekend, pinching and spitting—especially spitting. His increased spitting may have been caused by OCC's use of the water squirt, a spray in the face like the kind one puts on a shirt when ironing, as an aversive. But what Noah sees, Noah does, and they may have inadvertently encouraged him to use his own water squirt. Anyway I did not enjoy having him at home. Foumi and I still fight over how to handle him—whether it's to cut his hair or just get through a simple meal.

Happily, we'll be in New York next weekend, and I won't miss him. Those days are over. If truth be told, I count the minutes until he goes back on a Sunday.

I look forward to New York. We've been invited to a seder at which my Uncle Philip will preside. Whoever thought Uncle Philip, my mother's kid brother, would be the last patriarch of the family? Foumi doesn't want to go. Neither does Karl. But I think it will be good for him to meet my last blood uncle and to see some sort of religious ritual in action.

We had a marvelous time in New York. The apartment we borrowed was beyond our wildest expectations, big, comfortable, and ideally located. We saw old friends, went to the theater, museum-hopped, and ate many fine meals. A producer friend of mine took Karl backstage in a Broadway theater and showed him the light board. But the high point for me was the seder at my cousin Tovah's. We arrived late. But Uncle Philip, well into his eighties, immediately rose and came toward me. "Since I heard you were coming, Josh," he greeted me, "I have been dreaming of your mother all week." We hugged each other and cried. But neither Foumi nor Karl was so happy about the seder. They kept casting me dirty looks from behind their Haggadahs.

I go for my treadmill test tomorrow and I am more than a little curious. Because in New York I noticed that whenever I tried to walk a little briskly, my breathing came hard and I felt a strain. In fact, I began to wonder if I was enjoying my last hurrah.

21

April 7, 1980

This morning, when I took my treadmill test at St. John's Hospital, they stopped the test early because of irregularities. I was having that pain in my throat again, and I guess the wiggly lines were confirming a reason for it. But they would not tell me the reason. They just told me to talk to my doctor.

Which I did this afternoon on the phone. He said an angiogram was in order and that a bypass might be necessary. I asked if I could go square dancing tonight as Foumi and I had planned. "Better not," Jon advised.

So I've been in a state of shock all day. While in New York I was looking forward to getting back to my book. Now I just want to stay in my life. And even though in the past month I sometimes did experience a shortness of breath, I never really thought it might be due to a heart condition. What a bum rap!

April 8, 1980

My first day as a heart patient is over. And it's been harder on Foumi and Karl than me. Foumi barely slept last night, and what a difficult time Karl must have had behaving so wonderfully: obedient, considerate, just a good son. The worst thing that has happened to me is that my few remaining hairs have literally turned gray overnight. I would even cry except I understand that irony is at the root of life. I mean, I finally find a place for Noah and my heart may be ready to give out.

288

I never knew there were so many "heart men" in Los Angeles. Each friend recommends a different cardiologist to see for second opinions. Meanwhile, this afternoon, I'll see the man my doctor is referring me to. At least in this way I can get a quick reading on where I am, how bad my condition actually is. Because my symptoms have become much more pronounced since I discovered I had the problem. It is as if I am so conscious of the presence of my heart that it begins to hurt.

April 13, 1980

On Tuesday I went to see the cardiologist, Howard, a nice young man from Great Neck. He said that there was little doubt that I had some blockage in my arteries—it was this blockage that, by depriving my heart of oxygen, caused my breathing pains—and that only an angiogram would reveal the extent of that blockage. I watched a videocassette explaining the procedure: A catheter would be inserted in a blood vessel on the inside of my groin and directed toward my heart; then a dye would be pumped through it. The dye would enable the doctors to see exactly where the blockage was. I wasn't so sure I wanted an invasive procedure. In the meantime he prescribed a medicine that, acting like a thermostat, keeps the heart from pumping too fast and demanding too much oxygen; and some nitroglycerin pills to take in case of pain. They would dilate my blood vessels, he explained, and thus relieve the discomfort.

I picked up the medications at the druggist's and went home. I couldn't concentrate on any work so I began to fill out the mounting pile of health-insurance forms. While doing so I felt chest pains. I knew they were psychosomatic. But still they hurt. I popped a few nitroglycerin pills. The pains did not go away. I called my doctor. He suggested I check into the hospital right away.

I drove there with Foumi beside me and was admitted to the Coronary Care Unit. Immediately they plugged me into an EKG, drew some blood, took my blood pressure, and x-rayed my chest. The pains persisted that evening and I slept badly all night. In the morning I was informed that I had not suffered a heart attack. But since I was in the hospital anyway I might as well schedule my angiogram for the next day. I agreed.

That night a male aide came into my room, checked the I.D.

tag on my wrist, and began to shave me. First with a dry razor around my pubic area. Then he lathered me and shaved me again there—this time tipping my penis the way I might push up my own nose to get to hair beneath my nostrils—until he had removed all my pubic hair, my first badge of manliness, leaving me looking like a boy, like Karl of just a few months ago. I now had the least pubic hair in my family.

A female nurse came into the room. She asked me if I was a bit frightened. When I admitted I was, she told me that was quite natural and suggested I take a sleeping pill, which I did.

In the morning I was not served breakfast. Instead I was given a shot of Nembutal and then wheeled into and out of an elevator and through labyrinth-like corridors to the Cardiovascular Room. Although I was drowsy I recognized Howard, my cardiologist. I was also a little bit distressed to notice for the first time that he was left-handed: I know the gadgets and tools of the world are designed for right-handers. But the angiogram went without incident. I felt no pain and was lucid enough to cough and breathe according to directions during the catheterization. It all seemed to go quickly. Even the moment of extreme discomfort when the rush of hot iodine dye flowed through me. And that was it. I relaxed and began to tell jokes.

Later, Howard showed me the rushes. My right coronary artery is completely blocked. But evidently I have developed some natural collateral arteries. It's as if the body has come up with its own natural bypass. But I don't know yet if that's enough.

April 15, 1980

Both my doctor and the cardiologist agree that I do not require surgery at this time, that medications can help ease the blockage problem. It was good to hear that, and I feel better. Foumi and I went square dancing last night and the only thing that bothered me was the swelling in my groin where the catheter had been inserted.

I feel fortunate to have Noah in OCC. Otherwise, with my newly discovered arteriosclerosis—heart disease—we would be in real trouble. Yet I miss him. And I feel guilty about not seeing him for three weeks. As if I have deserted him. Even though I do have an excuse.

I don't think I would miss Karl, though. I'd like to send him off to a prep school in the East. He needs the enforced maturing process and I need to escape the pressures of living with him. I'm particularly upset about his nutrition. With his eating habits and patterns he is headed for the kind of decline I'm in.

Meanwhile, my groin still aches and a drowsy anger fills me. For getting myself into this position.

April 16, 1980

Karl's English class surprises me. They're teaching the kid "Prufrock." He likes "The Highwayman" better. And perhaps rightly so. It's a lot more fun as a poem, and he is still closer to junior high school than he is to college.

April 17, 1980

Noah was home today. OCC was good enough to drive him to the house for lunch. We enjoyed having him and I feel awfully relieved. He's big and fat and still has his baby face despite his adolescent zits. And he was affectionate to Foumi as we all took a walk on the cliff. He stayed for two hours, which was about the right time span.

April 18, 1980

I saw my cardiologist again this morning because the groin swelling has not gone down. Howard looked at it closely and assured me it was not an aneurysm. He also assured me that my heart problem is not in the gray area. I have no delimiting symptoms other than those in my head. I can have a normal life, as matters now stand, for another twenty years. And since there is no proof that a bypass would prolong my life anyway, why consider surgery?

A friend of mine once said that the moment you talk about the truth in L.A., people say, "Don't be negative." But I really do think in a positive sense that the discovery of my heart disease might save me from wasting too much time writing movies. Because I am forcibly reminded of what I really want to do: work on books.

April 19, 1980

Second thoughts: It has occurred to me that when a doctor says that you have every chance to live for another twenty years, he's also telling you that you might die tomorrow. Anyway, one does not like to be confronted with one's own mortality. Especially with Foumi as a dietary consultant. She frowns on every cholesterol-laden bite I'm tempted to eat.

Even with a doctor present. Last night we had dinner at a friend's. Among the other guests was his doctor brother, a heart man himself, who drank and smoked and made light of the perils of cholesterol, not a Pritikin atom in him. But as for me I'm going to monitor my diet strictly and start exercising regularly. If you run as much as Karl does, for example, use as much physical energy as he does, then perhaps you can eat anything. The system can handle it. It's when you are as sedentary as I've been that you get into trouble.

So I've become like my father was, like my uncles were, just another old Jew worrying about his health. As Mel Brooks's 2,000-Year-Old Man says: We mock what we are yet to be.

April 20, 1980

Knowing the likely cause of one's own death removes much of death's mystery. But it is still hard for me to get my priorities in order. What do I want to do now? How do I want to dedicate the rest of my life? To do something good. But the only truly good thing I have ever done was to take care of Noah, and now he is out of the house.

April 21, 1980

I saw Jon, my regular doctor, this morning. He said the draining in my groin wound is normal and that I should still wear the dressing and bandages for another day or two.

I am touchy with Foumi. I want no recriminations for my bad diet or failure to exercise sufficiently in the past. But she insists on dishing them out. When she brought up the subject at dinner, I cut her short. She replied that if she had to worry about what she says, she might as well leave me.

April 23, 1980

Today I thought I could walk for the first time without the steps of an invalid. The bandages were off my groin and I tried to walk briskly along the cliff. But then I suffered the hesitancy of the invalid, the hypochondria that has a reason—I imagined I felt a burning sensation in my chest again.

In addition to moving slowly, I still sleep badly and dream worse. Last night I awoke AWOL from the army and unable to return because I could not find a uniform. Once awake I resolved never again to write the pilot for a sitcom. I would not want to die while working on one.

April 24, 1980

We rarely venture into Noah's room. It is an ignored monument. Foumi has moved the table that was there into our room and made it her desk. There she works long hours on her writing. Longer hours and more writing than I produce.

April 25, 1980

This morning I walked a half mile with Foumi and found a turtle. In the afternoon I read a book about the heart and decided to avoid stress. But this evening at dinner I exploded at Karl. He was too loud. He was not respectful enough of Foumi. And most aggravating was his unhealthy diet. The kid has no sense of longevity. But then what kid has? Still he should act intelligently about his own potential genetic problems. Between my heart disease and Noah's condition, he has a lot to act intelligently about.

Karl placed the turtle in an aquarium in his room, atop his trunk, dislodging his electric trains. I am also happy to note that he has left the silver market to the Hunt brothers. Instead, now he is cataloging his old baseball cards, having read that they have value. The kid wants to accrue collectibles. I just wish he'd accrue a little more self-protective intelligence.

April 26, 1980

We didn't go to Glendale to watch Noah participate in the Special Olympics as we had planned. Because when Foumi began to make noises about whether I was up to driving there, I exploded. I can't stand her erring on the side of overcaution. What I don't need now is someone to remind me to be careful. My body will do that for me, thank you. So Noah's track feats will have to go unwitnessed by us. Still it is good to know that he is involved in such activities.

Instead today I staged my own special Olympics. I walked twice, doing two miles in forty minutes each time. Which is pretty good for somebody about to enter a cardiac-rehab program.

Since the center of my life is now my heart and how to take care of it, I no longer seem to worry so much about Noah's head and what to do about it. I just keep repeating to myself mantras like: I overcame polio, I've managed to deal with a brain-damaged son, I can survive a blocked coronary artery.

April 27, 1980

Noah marched with his group, we're told, at the Special Olympics and finished his race, albeit in his own time. I'm sorry we didn't get to see him live but we will be able to watch him on film as OCC recorded it.

I walked two and half miles this morning and another three miles in the afternoon. I grew tired but was never short of breath. My walk this afternoon was with an old friend who dropped in. He now weighs more than two hundred pounds and complained of a chest pain as we walked. But I'm not sure whether or not he was doing that just to make me feel better.

April 28, 1980

I went over to St. John's Hospital to enroll at their Cardiac Rehabilitation Center. The nurses walked me through it. It's like a small health club, only the patients—or members—wear telemeters so that their heart rates are constantly monitored. There were two distinct groups of patients: those with clean chests and those with "zipper jobs," the open-heart surgery alumni. I'll be using exercise bikes, rowing machines, treadmills, weights, and ergometers for hand exercises. They told me they would try to build up my capacity to exercise and increase my confidence in myself physically. I enrolled immediately, grabbing the few open slots they had in their schedule. I'll go there three times a week.

I don't like walking around with a blocked artery in me, feeling I have to restrict myself in every way. But so far I don't miss sweets, I don't miss fats, and I suspect I'll even enjoy an exercise regime. And if it does kill me at least I'll be in the right place.

Damn it, though! I used to pride myself on the fact that I was slim. I would make fun of the fatties jogging, joking that it added five years to their lives—only at the wrong end, meaning they might have to spend five more years in diapers. Well, evidently slim ain't necessarily trim and now I hope to be a jogger. That's a comeuppance, as Penrod used to call it.

April 29, 1980

How selfish we are as people. Or I am as a person. Since my troubles I find myself thinking completely of me and scarcely of Noah at all. But I do look forward to having him home this weekend. We will take a long walk together at his killer pace.

April 30, 1980

I did not take my morning walk until eleven o'clock—some two miles and change—and so I did not get to my office until after noon. Which is better than yesterday, when I did not get here at all. But I don't care. I feel no internal pressure to work. The only pressure I feel is to exercise, to eat well, and to stay healthy.

There is obviously a big difference between death and dying. But what strikes me these days is that while living with death in vague terms usually causes depression, living with dying in a specific way can be exhilarating almost to the point of euphoria. Because it is so dramatically clarifying. The world is not anxiously awaiting the next outpouring from my typewriter. I have to take six months off to reclaim my body—and I will.

May 1, 1980 (Afternoon)

I feel so Jewish now, like my grandfathers, but without a beard. Like theirs, my life is one of ritual, which does not allow for much in the way of worldly activities. Their day was structured around prayer; my day is built around my exercise regime. In the morning I walk for forty minutes; in the afternoon every other day I exercise for an hour and fifteen minutes at the Cardiac Rehabilitation Center; and on the days I don't go to the hospital I take another constitutional, leaving me little time for mental loitering. I don't know how much healthier I'm getting but I do know I can now calmly recognize my own angina. It comes in the neck in the form of a burning sensation. And when I feel it, I pop a nitroglycerin pill.

It happened last night at the Laker play-off game. Karl was beside me in the smoke-filled upper reaches of the Forum. All of a sudden I felt the twinge of the burn. I took a nitro and Karl gave me a long look.

As we drove home I asked Karl to consider going East to school. I'm not sure I want him to decide to go. I prefer his staying at home with us and not putting me through any gyrations. But that's too much to expect. At the same time prep school would be a difficult adjustment for him; the first year at any school always is. Ultimately, I guess, with Karl as with Noah, since whatever we do by definition is wrong, whatever we do is also right.

May 1, 1980 (Evening)

I ran away from home twice tonight. What happened was this: After dinner Karl showed me something he had written. I read it and told him he had misused the word "patter" and should look it up in the dictionary. He point-blank refused, I became furious, and nearly strangled him. My pulse was over 120. I left the house in a rage.

When I returned home later I was more than conciliatory. "I'm sorry that I burst out at you," I apologized. "I don't want to talk to you," he replied and walked away. Whereupon I exploded again. At this point Foumi interjected herself. "You need a psychologist," she said and then invoked my past history of high cholesterol levels and heinous dietary crimes. I became pissed off with her and walked out again.

May 2, 1980

Last night I told Foumi that I had decided to move. She broke down and cried. She really does love me and worry about me. I overheard her telling Karl that the medications I am now taking might be the cause of all sorts of psychological side effects. Karl said someone should have told him that sooner.

So I did not pack my bags. And things are better with the family today. But I don't feel so good myself. Walking to my office I felt angina, and then while napping here I had another burning pain in my neck. Each time I popped a nitro.

My moods roller-coaster from a kind of euphoria over having been released from the "fast lane," as it's called out here, to a gloom about death. Not that there is much more that I want to achieve personally. But I would like to see Karl mature, making his way in spite of me. To see Noah permanently taken care of in a setup I can trust. To see Foumi realize her literary aspirations.

May 3, 1980

Foumi and I picked up Noah at OCC and brought him home. He's behaved well. Better than I've been behaving. He had just one tantrum and that during his haircut.

May 4, 1980

Is it the medicine or is it me? Again I exploded last night. Twice. First because Foumi began to reindict me for my nutritionally criminal past. How many times do I have to hear about it? And I have improved my diet. Though I still refuse to believe that Pritikin is the sole possessor of nutritional truth. I don't want to wind up a complete food faddist. So I had tantrum number one.

But no sooner had I calmed down than Foumi announced, "If I want to sleep I'm going to have to drink a lot of liquor tonight." As if I were driving her to drink. Which provoked tantrum number two. This morning our arguing raged on so that I left the house with her in tears.

I should move out, go away, until I get my physical confidence back. Meanwhile, I want to be neither babied nor blamed. I am angry and I want to be left alone. Why am I angry? Because I do not like feeling insecure about my life and having to worry about the effect of my death on my family. "Poor Karl," Foumi cries to me every once in a while. What about poor Josh?

Is it the medications or is it me? I will join a heart patient's group forming at St. John's. The participants will meet every

Tuesday night, along with their spouses, to discuss common problems. Foumi insists that I am suddenly irrational and out of control. I want to discover if my behavior is a side effect of medicines or the result of her constant nagging. She thinks needling is a wifely office. But so too is praising and reassuring. And that she rarely does. She offers me no emotional support now. Rather she wants me to feel sorry for what she's going through because of me.

Once again the mystique is leaking out of our marriage. If it could produce first Noah and then a heart-diseased me, what good is it?

May 5, 1980

I live in a war zone, a civil war zone. Foumi did not speak to me when I came home yesterday evening. Each of us, Karl, Foumi, and I, prepared separate meals. Karl went to his room, theoretically to study, Foumi adjourned to the den to watch her Sunday-night Japanese television, I read the newspaper in our room. Foumi spent the night in the den. And this morning she went about her activities wordlessly.

At my exercise session at Cardiac Rehab I spoke with one of the nurses about my problems, my tendency to be irritable and explosive. Could it be the medications? No, she said, but perhaps I have been overexercising to the point of fatigue. And fatigue does cause irritability.

I have been pushing myself hard. I do get more tired as the day wears on. But I still think the core of the problem is Foumi's damned oversolicitousness. I just wish she'd leave me alone.

May 6, 1980

I spoke to my cardiologist. We'll cut my medications in half and see what happens. I'm sure much of my behavior lately is an aftershock to the disturbing reminder than I do have a closing time. And I should treat the whole incident as a five-minute—or twenty-year, for that matter—warning. I just have to get used to living with a certain fear instead of with an overwhelming anxiety.

Meanwhile, it is amazing how out of shape I had allowed myself to get. So when I have pains in my chest now I'm not sure whether it's angina or whether I've stretched a muscle that I haven't used for years. Or decades. At Cardiac Rehab I exercise for just three minutes at a time, keeping my heartbeat between 90 and 100 beats a minute. Not very much when I see folks a lot older than I hitting 125 for a half hour straight.

May 8, 1980

I live in a limbo. I have little desire to work more than an hour a day. I find it hard to get excited about anything. I rise in the morning and doodle about my coffeeless breakfast. After my exercise period at the hospital, I lunch, nap, and soon my day is over. At night I watch television or read a magazine—not even a book. I have little patience with fiction. I have no desire for anything hinting of art. I watch Clint Eastwood movies. I look forward to no social activity. I just want to relax, to be comfortable, to escape. Sometimes I think that part of my mind has left me. Money is of little concern to me. But if at one moment I feel extremely mellow, I am still apt to explode in the very next. The slightest pain in my neck, in my chest, in any muscle or rib, frightens me. I have absolutely no faith in my body. On what side does my ambition now lie? Tipped over.

May 9, 1980

A friend will pick up Noah and bring him home to us for the weekend. Noah deserves a break. And I'll try to be calm. Usually, when he is home, Foumi and I are constantly quarreling. This time I vow to be submissive to Foumi's will in all things. I have learned why they call a sick person "patient." He has no choice but to wait to be better.

For the time being I must learn not to listen to Foumi. What I mean is this: Right now when I tell her I don't want to talk about something, she takes it as a putdown of womankind, Asian civilization, and the entire non-Caucasian population of the world. So I should let her talk on, make believe I'm listening, but tune out and actually pay no attention to what she's saying. It goes against my grain to participate in meaningless conversation but in that way she'll leave me alone, happily thinking she's achieving communication.

Noah came home with marks on his ass and I do not like them. It looks as if he's been beaten there. We spoke to another OCC parent. She said her son has the same markings. I called the Administrative President and queried him about it. He promised to look into the matter. If Noah is getting beaten at OCC then I will have to withdraw him as soon as possible. His conduct has not improved since he's been there anyway. His scratching and spitting, for example, have in no way decreased. And although I do not like the constant state of alert his presence demands, I'd certainly rather have him in the house than have to worry about his getting beat up. I am wary about the future. Both his and mine.

22

May 12, 1980

Mother's Day was no great joy for us. We worried all weekend about the marks on Noah. I wanted to withhold any discussion about it until we heard the Administrative President's explanation. Because until then there was nothing we could do. But naturally, Foumi wanted to do nothing but talk about it. She simply has no control. She kept trying to bring it up but I would not talk about it. The result: constant tension between us. And the one thing I'm trying to avoid: stress.

Today when I took Noah back to OCC I checked his behavior chart. The only time a spank is supposed to be administered as an aversive is when he scratches others. Foumi spoke to the teacher at OCC over the phone. It seems that Noah was scratching the other kids. And several male staff members did spank him. Hard. Now we really have to worry. The trouble, as always with corporal punishment, is, where do you draw the line? And the people at OCC evidently do not know.

May 13, 1980

I could not believe the Administrative President. He said that if we couldn't take the beatings—"spanks" was the word he used—that Noah was receiving, then perhaps OCC wasn't the place for him. I was further amazed to learn that according to Noah's program he can be given ten spanks during any five-minute period and that he had received fifteen spanks last Wednesday and an additional seventeen spanks on Thursday—all for scratching others.

I had assumed that the Administrative President would show a parental sensitivity since his son too is at OCC. But he didn't. Nor was there any hint of apology or admission of a possible error. Not a conciliatory note. Just a very tough attitude. I could only conclude that both he and the OCC Executive Visiting Adviser have decided to get rid of Noah, whatever miracle-worker designs they may have once harbored for him having come to an end.

Right now I'm obviously in no condition to bring Noah home. But I also cannot bear his being maltreated a single moment. What to do?

May 14, 1980

This morning Foumi wanted to do nothing but talk about Noah. I told her the only thing to talk about at this point is how to stop the beatings immediately. But soon we were shouting and yelling at each other. Another day, another holler. But before fleeing from the house I did call OCC. And they told me Noah had been taken off the spanks and put back on "water squirts" as aversives. A water squirt is a spray in the face from a bottle of cold water. I can't see any harm there. Especially on a warm day.

May 15, 1980

The parent of Noah's roommate at OCC tells us she's discovered that her son once received seventy-seven spanks in one day. The fact is that had I taken Noah to a doctor he might have considered him a battered child. We can't ignore the situation. We really should take Noah home now. But we'll wait for the weekend.

May 16, 1980

Now we learn from his mother that Noah's roommate was spanked not 77—but 177—times in a single day. They've stopped the spanks. But I can't imagine what kind of people we're dealing with.

No easy chapters in my soap-opera life. Heart condition better; Noah situation worse. And I worry about Karl. That shoe has to drop. Last night I coax-coached him into rewriting a paper for English—the only thing I did with my writing energies all day—but otherwise we have not been paying enough attention to him. Each weekend, for example, he disappears.

May 18, 1980

When I picked up Noah at OCC yesterday the teacher told me they were terribly understaffed. And when that happens everyone has to work overtime, their jobs become merely custodial, and morale goes down.

I didn't take that news badly. If they're presently understaffed and merely custodial, it means they cannot apply their aversives that diligently, not even the water squirts.

Noah was happy at home and behaved well. But, as usual, there was constant tension between Foumi and me. She is such a perfectionist, for example, constantly washing Noah's hands. I keep telling her how dirty his hands must get all the days she does not see him, but to no effect. And I am too quick to yell. The drugs are doing the yelling. My heart and blood vessels are doing the yelling.

May 19, 1980

Every pain is a scare but I continue on my exercise program to the point of fatigue. Oh, how tired I get! Each day I'm so tired.

I wonder whether I should continue with Foumi. For what reason? Her crisis management. I guess I'll let her decide the fate of our marriage. The decision to end a marriage, just as the decision to start one, essentially belongs to the woman anyway.

May 20, 1980

After all these years I still don't know what to do about Noah. Perhaps I should forget all my principles and look into the group residences run by the group of "autistic" parents whose self-aggrandizing insensitivity I deplore. Principles may be a luxury I can no longer afford.

Karl and I stood back to back comparing height. He is just a half inch shorter than I. I tried on his sneakers this morning. They are too big for me. These days he stays after school, working on the stage crew for the senior show, *The Pajama Game*. He cares little about the show; he's fascinated with the technical aspects of setting up the light board.

He's also become a morbid wit, a black humorist. Last night as Foumi and I left the house to go to my heart group, my wise-ass son asked, "What time will you be back from the death class?"

I have switched to another heart medication, a different beta blocker, and I feel better.

I still wish I had the courage to run away—or, at least, to walk away—from my family. But I also know that if I did I would somehow probably wind up with another domestic life that is even worse.

Karl was very nervous this morning. It seems he had scheduled a grudge match in badminton with a kid who teases him badly. I told him not to be so thin-skinned and that, anyway, games are not worth it. This evening I asked him the result: He told me he had won the match but that immediately his opponent took his joy away by saying he had not tried at all. Karl still has a lot to learn about gamesmanship.

Foumi thinks Karl is smoking grass again and I suspect she's right. There is something behind his frequent surliness besides just ordinary adolescent rebellion. It's also that time of year: the end of school, the sniff of summer freedom in the air. And he has it too easy. This morning he asked me for money so he could go with some friends to Westwood and see *The Empire Strikes Back*. How much did he need? Twelve dollars. Twelve dollars? Well, they'd be eating lunch too.

When I was his age, fifteen years old, during the wartime summer of 1943, I worked a five-and-a-half-day week for a salary of just eighteen dollars in downtown Manhattan delivering heavy office typewriters through the subways. And on Sundays and holidays I worked at Ebbets Field hustling, "Cigars. Cigarettes. Candy. Peanuts. Chewing Gum. Scorecard. Pencil. Scorecard." And if I earned twelve dollars that was an exceedingly good, but unfortunately rare, day. I gave Karl the money anyway.

I still have wildly fluctuating mood swings. This morning after exercising I felt wonderful, full of hope for a fine day. I stopped in the supermarket and picked up a low-cholesterol soup for lunch. But that's where I went wrong. Going home for lunch. Because Foumi was complaining about the post office, how it had returned a short story she had sent to Japan for insufficient postage, one she had tried to send off as "printed matter." And now she was accusing the postal-system people of picking on her, singling her out, because of her Japanese script. Didn't they always allow my manuscripts to go through the mail as "printed matter" or "Special Fourth-Class Educational Mail"? The post office was discriminating against her.

I didn't want to hear any more of her paranoia so I went into the kitchen to heat up my soup. But it turned out I had bought the wrong can of soup, potato rather than split pea. And from then on it was all downhill. Foumi suddenly decided she wanted to go shopping. We had to buy baby and wedding gifts for friends and she wanted to pick up a pair of "walking shoes" for herself. It seems we always have to go shopping to buy her a pair of "walking shoes." I deferred shopping until tomorrow. And instead, sat myself in front of the television set and tried to watch Douglas Fairbanks and Mary Pickford in *The Taming of the Shrew*. Not much escape there. And soon I was depressed, engulfed by worry. About OCC. About Noah. About our marriage.

May 25, 1980

There are no two ways about it. I think our marriage has finally dissolved. There is only the formal act to follow, the ritual of trial separation, and then finally divorce. Because Foumi and I do not please each other any longer. Instead, we now goad each other, getting on each other's nerves, harping on each other's failings, faults we both readily abided on better days.

I realized this clearly when I returned home from my exercise walk this morning. Foumi was standing in the doorway, shouting. I could not hear what she was saying. I assumed someone was on the phone, something important, long distance perhaps. But when I came closer Foumi was saying, "You're late. One hour." I almost expected her to extract a gold watch from her pocket and hold it up to me like a sweatshop timekeeper.

It seemed I had agreed to go shopping with her at twelve o'clock and she had been waiting. Well, screw her. I was so angry at being treated like an exploited employee that I went into the house and exercised for another half hour.

When we finally left to go shopping I was still angry—I hate shopping—and I continued to spew out my venom until Foumi became hysterical, screaming that she wanted to get out of the car because I would kill her the way I was driving. And, I guess, I did have the look of a madman. I was that angry.

I parked at the foot of the canyon until she quieted down. But once I started she was again pleading, "Please take me back! Please!" I turned around and returned home.

In the house we continued to tear at each other. She was crying, tears pouring down her cheeks: She did not know how to live with me, she moaned, she did not know what to do, I was impossible.

I tried to explain to her again that I still had no confidence at all in myself physically and was therefore very confused.

"What about me?" she replied, pushing herself onto the center of my stage. "How do you think I feel wondering whether I can hear your breath in the middle of the night?"

I became angry again. She was not listening. I was trying to tell her how *I* felt. Not argue. She wanted to argue. She always wanted to argue.

The real trouble is that I have become a cantankerous old Jew while Foumi has evolved into a traditional old Japanese lady, tough and mean, and neither of us is willing to budge very much. Our life of compromise is over. Which means our marriage is too.

I don't know what I expected of Foumi. But I guess I did expect more of a nursing patience. Anyway, we're finished.

But wasn't it this morning that we awoke cuddling in bed, embracing each other dreamily?

Last night I penitently apologized to Foumi for my bad behavior. She tearfully did not accept it. But this morning we have been talking to each other and this afternoon we might finally get to go shopping. But as Karl said to me at breakfast: "In order to live with Foumi, you always have to say you're wrong."

Karl's presence fills the house. He is a baby man. Yet I can still bring him to tears with my rage. Noah is a man baby. He can still bring me to rage with his tears.

What can I do for Noah now? I am not happy with OCC. But I just don't have the energy to do anything about it. This heart problem has me depleted. I am always tired. And irritable.

It's hard not to be irritable when I've always perceived of myself as young with my life ahead of me and suddenly I have to figure out its finish and how to end it properly.

Yesterday, we were finally a family together. Except, of course, for Noah. We went to Century City, where Foumi got her shopping done. And we had lunch at the hotel, where Karl got some fancy eating done. When we came home I called OCC and was told that Noah had been a problem when they took him to the zoo, suddenly lying down on the ground and refusing to move. But otherwise, he was fine.

I have not had a "bust out"—as Foumi calls my temper outbursts—in the past four days. But then I haven't been involved with anything very much either. It seems ephemera make my moods easier for others to take.

Foumi spent the day visiting three of the city's special schools. She liked Marlton, a school for the deaf, best. She is also talking of establishing a special residence for Noah so that he won't be coming back home to Old Heart Disease.

Karl still puts in long hours working on the lights for *The Pajama Game* at the expense of his grades. But what are we to do? He is involved in an activity that he truly seems to like.

We attended our sign-language class last night. Little by little some of it is getting through to me. But not as quickly as to Foumi. She finds time to study it during the week. But I can handle only one compulsion at a time. And these days my compulsion is going to the Cardiac Rehabilitation Center at the hospital to exercise.

When I picked up Noah at OCC this afternoon he was wearing a maroon shirt, eaten away below the neck, as he sat at his worktable allegedly sorting nuts and bolts. I escorted him out of the house. He stood on the lawn near the driveway for several minutes, as if making a decision, before he finally got into my car. On the freeway he repeatedly scratched at my neck and face. But I managed to make it home safely. When he got out of the car he ran into the backyard and was soon sitting on the lawn. From a distance, as he picked at the grass, he seemed to be involved in an activity every bit as legitimate as sorting nuts and bolts at OCC.

When I walked into our house Karl was sitting at the kitchen table, disconsolately poking at an early dinner. He had to be back at school at six o'clock to work on the show. Which still gave him ample time to complain to me that his salmon steak had been undercooked. He was also upset because there was going to be a party after the show and Foumi had set a one o'clock curfew for him. I ignored his petition for redress and went to our room and took care of some phone calls I had to return. When I reappeared he was gone and Foumi asked me to call in Noah.

Noah immediately went for me, burying his long fingernails deep into my wrist. I got the scissors and, wrestling him into submission, pared both his finger- and toenails. Then Foumi saw him through a dinner during which he kept spitting his food onto the floor. He finally settled down when served his dessert, cantaloupe wedges that he speared with his fork, and he then smiled.

And now, after nine o'clock, I hope he's still in a good mood. I've left him with Foumi and come to my office to do some work. Oh how I'd love to come up with something that could make Noah's uncertain future a little more tenable.

Foumi is compulsive and unimaginative. But diligent.

When I returned home last night Noah was standing on his bed and she was trying to brush his teeth. The bathroom, behind them, was a mess. She had bathed him and he had objected to the idea, splashing everywhere, and spitting and pinch-clutching at her. And she was beside herself, crying that she would put him in the state hospital.

I brushed Noah's teeth and cleaned the bathroom. But not to her satisfaction. She mopped up after me. But I did get Noah to bed. Then I chastised her for worrying so much about cleanliness. She seems to assume that if she has not seen Noah for two weeks that he has not been bathed—or for that matter, fed—during that period. Not so. OCC may be a mess in many ways, but I do think his vital needs are being met. The one thing I don't think he's been getting enough of is sleep. He slept from 10:30 last night to almost 9:00 this morning.

Foumi and I did not sleep too well. She was worrying about Karl, so I had to stay up and worry alongside her. He did not come back until 1:20 and I must admit I did worry those last twenty minutes on my own. I know we have to trust Karl but I find it difficult to do so. Foumi finds it impossible. There is another cast party tonight and she does not want to allow Karl to go. But I don't want to deprive him of the wages of his work. What else does he get in the way of reward for serving on the stage crew?

Oh, what a weekend! I've lost control of Noah completely. He no longer listens to me at all. I just cannot deal with him at this time.

I also can no longer deal with Foumi. She will not leave me alone when I want to be left alone. I can't stop her talking when I know it's going to upset me. She does not understand the need for silence.

For example, I am comfortably relaxing in the den. Foumi comes into the room, plants her feet firmly, places her hands on her hips, and announces that she has just spoken with a recently widowed friend of ours. Her late husband had two blocked arteries but would still walk three miles a day and believed in meditation. Also, have I read in the newspaper of the man in Europe who was championing the consumption of mackerel as a deterrent to the development of heart disease?

I try to react calmly but I cannot resist telling her that I do not want any advice from a dead man or an anonymous European mackerel eater. Besides, I can only follow one regimen at a time. And soon we're at each other again. I rage. She cries.

And Noah begins to have a tantrum, banging his head on the floor. Foumi blames me. Says he's catching my bad vibes.

I manage to take Noah for a walk. But when we return he refuses to get into the car for the ride back to OCC. So he is still with us tonight—and I am not. Who is setting whose mood?

It is less than two months since I've discovered my heart disease and I have lots to absorb. I could even become a mackerel eater. But one thing at a time.

June 2, 1980

Noah still did not want to return to OCC this morning. But he was docile enough for most of the ride there. However, when I turned the corner onto the street OCC is on, he reached over from the backseat where I had belted him down and scratched me hard. And he kept scratch-protesting as I drove the four long blocks up the street. When I parked before OCC and opened the car doors, Noah ran onto the lawn and thrust himself down upon it. I had to get one of the aides to help bring him into the house. I watched as Noah finally allowed himself to be returned to the classroom. He was still rebellious and angry. He did not like being back there. Nor did I like bringing him back. But what were my other choices?

June 3, 1980

Foumi sulks. Calls me a dictator because I want to end discussions abruptly. I don't know whether it is the medicine or my diet or the exercising, but I just don't want to talk about my heart anymore. Because when we do talk about it, the words end in arguments.

But, ironically, as I try to ward off bad feelings they only increase. She keeps accusing me of being self-centered and unfair.

Of course I am. She doesn't understand I'm scared shitless and still don't know whether to shake all the time or try to act as if I'm not frightened at all.

Yesterday I was at peace with Foumi. At the heart group, we discovered we are not alone in our intense bickering. Every other couple in our group is undergoing the same problem. The only fault Foumi could find with me since the group meeting is the fact that I talked too much there. Which is true.

For breakfast I ate oatmeal, fruit, a slice of toast, and a glass of apple juice; for lunch I had split pea soup, a pita bread full of lettuce and garbanzo beans and alfalfa sprouts, and a half orange and a half apple. Dinner will be raw fish and rice. I'm doing the best I can to get my cholesterol down.

The mother of Noah's roommate at OCC is trying to set up a residential school. But I know it's going to take her a lot longer to get started than she assumes. I'm afraid we'll have to get Noah out of OCC—or OCC will get rid of Noah—long before her dream is ever achieved.

More immediately, I feel guilty about not having Noah home this weekend. I know how hot it must be in the desert. But I must take care of myself.

I had the courage to walk to work this morning. I was afraid of the long uphill block above Northfield to Sunset. That was where I had my first angina. But I walked slowly and reached my office without missing a beat, so to speak.

But now that I'm here, what do I want to do anyway? Until recently I wanted very little except to be left alone. I still would like my privacy. But I feel ready to reenter the worldly arena. On the one hand I don't want to waste my time doing work of no moment. On the other hand I do need money to make life easier for Foumi and Karl and Noah. My old-age problem, I know, will not resolve my age-old problem. I guess it's time for me to call my agent and get back to work.

Karl has his finals this week. Then another long summer of discontent begins. Already he is talking of learning to drive so that he can get a car of his own in November when he comes of age. He is also talking of going to New York. He is so full of plans. And, so too, if I had a good heart, would I be.

June 9, 1980

Henry Miller died. He was a salty old man, and although I only met him once, his presence here in the Palisades somehow served to justify mine. I mean, this is Bourgeoisiea with a capital B. But if Henry Miller could live here, then so could I.

I also could go more gently into my own good night if I had the certainty that I was leaving Noah in a humane place. I know I cannot allow Noah to stay in OCC much longer because I am always afraid they might mistreat him. Right now it is a treadmill to nowhere for all of us.

23

Every Monday, Wednesday, and Friday as noontime approaches
I walk along the marble-floored halls of St. John's Hospital in
Santa Monica until I reach the Cardiac Rehabilitation Center. At
the entrance, like a parking-lot ticket booth, is a secretarial office.
Farther down the same corridor is a women's dressing room, a
men's dressing room, a day room stocked with heart literature,
and an alcove of nurses' offices. I change into shorts and Adidas
and then go to the end of the corridor, where there is an L-shaped
mini-gym.

I apply sensor circuits to my chest, plug into a telemeter the
size of a transistor radio, and proceed to warm up. Four of us,
heart-disease or heart-attack victims all, are monitored by a
nurse on an EKG machine as we go through our paces. At present
I do four minutes of exercise, a minute cool-down, and then another four minutes, altogether six rounds. I exercise at a "target
rate" of 110 heartbeats per minute. The moment my heart works
faster than that, the nurse tells me to slow down. If I have any
discomfort at all, I stop. Even at lower rates I sometimes experience oxygen shortage. However, starting tomorrow I will increase my rounds to four and a half minutes. And perhaps a
higher target rate will be set for me. I hope I'm not moving up too
fast but the nurses seem to know what they're doing.

At the hospital yesterday I watched a filmstrip describing
"Type A" people, those most apt to have heart attacks or in-

crease their cardiac risk factors: people who have too many projects and too many worries. People, in short, like me.

OCC is not the place for Noah. Nor a place that does its job. It is run by behaviorists without a heart. And I feel guilty about keeping him there. But at this point I do not know what to do other than to sacrifice him on the altar of my own condition. That may be overstating it a bit, but it still does not change the essential truth. I just don't know where else I can leave him at this time.

June 12, 1980

Last night Karl and I went to the theater. To see Henry Fonda in *The Oldest Living Graduate.* It was Karl's idea that we go, and I was expecting him to be more interested in the lights and the scenery than anything else. But he knew how to enjoy the play, laughing at the genuinely funny parts of Henry Fonda's performance.

I'm glad he was able to catch a fine stage actor in action. It is something to enrich his memory bank. I still remember the twenty-eight-cent forays into the balcony of the Flatbush Theatre—to see Frank Craven in *Our Town* and Jane Cowl in *Candida*—I made when I was Karl's age. Our tickets last night cost something like $18.50 each. But they were orchestra seats.

My other son will be coming home tomorrow in celebration of Father's Day weekend. I will bring along a bag of potato chips in the hope that they will deter him from pinching me while I'm driving.

June 15, 1980

I've spent Father's Day wondering how I could kill Noah and hang the rap on Karl.

June 16, 1980

When Foumi and I went to pick up Noah on Friday he was lying out in the OCC backyard in the hot desert sun, shirtless and in his bare feet. As we searched everywhere for his shoes, the Administrative President was telling us that it was impossible to keep Noah in line without aversives. Meanwhile, Noah was upset because his shoes were gone. One of Noah's higher-functioning housemates finally admitted to hiding the shoes, and we were able to get Noah into the car. But he was scratching and pinching so furiously that after a few blocks I had to turn around and take him back.

I went out again on Saturday morning and this time was able to manage Noah sufficiently to be able to drive him home. But he seemed to have a fever and to be dehydrated. With water and Tylenol we revived him.

Karl brought home his final report card. B's in English and Geometry, C's in French and Biology. Not great, but still a comeback, and I praised him for it.

June 17, 1980

Noah didn't want to leave our house and return to OCC. So one of their aides, like a prisoner chaser, came and got him. Even though he pissed on the floor at least once every day that he was home, I still did not want to see him go. But I had no choice.

Yesterday, while exercising at the hospital, I was suddenly dizzy and felt angina. My blood pressure was all the way down to 70 and my pulse beat fell to 56. It was a close call. The nurses wanted me to admit myself to the hospital and stay overnight for observation. I refused to do so, and after resting for a half hour I felt better.

But the incident reminded me what my having heart disease is all about. For both me and Noah. Because of my health, Noah, in a sense, is a hostage at OCC.

June 18, 1980

When we ask the staff at OCC how Noah is doing, they now refer us to the president. When we ask the president he refers us to the staff. I feel as if no one is leveling with us and I do not like that.

June 19, 1980

I had my best exercise day ever. My heart rate was consistently over 110. I was able to go five minutes at each activity. I think that was because I took my medication immediately before the session.

Another worker has left the staff of OCC. I wish I could free the Greenfeld one from the desert too. But the place is comparatively clean and does not abuse him with drugs. Still I do not like his pissing on the floor when he comes home. It's just what an unhappy dog would do after being kenneled.

June 21, 1980
Two of Karl's friends were at our house yesterday evening when the gang suddenly decided they would all go see the Sugar Ray Leonard fight at some restaurant. But it turned out Karl's friends had locked the keys in their car. Still they got into the car faster with a clothes hanger than I can get into my car with a key.

June 25, 1980
Karl announced at dinner the other night that he would be going to the Angel game in Anaheim this Friday evening. Who was he going with? He named three teenaged friends. How would they get there? By car. Who would be driving? David. How long has David been driving? A long time. How long? Since May. What kind of a car would he be driving? A Volks Bug. No way, I said, no way would I allow him to be the passenger of a driver with less than two months of experience in a crowded Volks. What if we get a Mercedes? he asked.

But tonight Karl imparted he would be going to the game in a Pontiac with his friend Steve, who had four years of experience behind the wheel. How could Steve, who is only sixteen years old, have four years of driving experience? I wanted to know. He's from Texas, my resident teenager replied.

Meanwhile, Noah breaks my heart. I still feel guilty as hell for leaving him in OCC. Especially when it's over 100 degrees in the desert.

Noah's home and he's been terrific. We picked him up Saturday night after he had his dinner. He was chirping then and he's still chirping now. Foumi has been working hard, cooking and keeping up with him, but I am glad to have him home. Tomorrow is his birthday.

Yesterday I had some chest pains whenever I breathed in deeply. Foumi wanted to call the hospital. But I insisted that we wait and finally the pains did go away. And today my exercise session went well. I didn't get that burning sensation in the throat, which is my particular angina.

Noah's birthday. Foumi has been serving him the foods he likes and making no demands upon him—just letting him lounge around. And why not? The weather has been hot and just bearable. (In the desert I am sure it *is* unbearable.) The only pressure we put on him was a morning haircut; I washed his hair and Foumi snipped away at it with scissors for as long as he was willing to sit still.

Noah at fourteen wears the expression of an adolescent, as if he constantly has to strain for his own particular brand of oxygen. He is still handsome, though a little long of face, like a Giacometti sculpture. By the time he is twenty he will be lean like the rest of us. But where will he be? I try not to think about it.

I do think when we treat him nicely he treats us nicely. He always responds in kind. Like a cat, a dog, a marriage partner. We are all creatures of response.

We're sending Karl to summer math school again. He hates every minute of it and is letting us know it. He is truly like me in all his bad qualities: Lazy. Frightened. Rebellious. I hope some redeeming qualities will yet come along. Because right now it is difficult to look at him as an unfinished picture—even in my own mirror.

When I took Noah back to OCC the front door was locked and there was a note on it: "Be back in five minutes." We waited in the desert heat over twenty minutes until the teacher returned. It seems she had gone on some errands, taking the other clients with her because she was the only one on duty. And, as I say, it was hot, desert hot. I do not envy Noah his days there.

I had to expect something the way Karl was complaining. Last night the director of the summer math school called. He'd have to expel Karl if he didn't behave properly. I told Karl to shape up. And I am annoyed with him for making me go through the same routine every summer.

July 3, 1980

We've heard that one of the OCC staff had quit because he couldn't abide the hard spankings administered there on orders of the Executive Visiting Adviser. The spankings have stopped, but I have to get Noah out of there soon.

July 6, 1980

It is beastly hot. The temperature near 100. But when Foumi called OCC this morning the staff worker on duty told her the clients were going on a picnic. Foumi told him it was too hot a day for kids to be out of doors and reminded him that if anything happened he would be responsible. But when she hung up she wasn't sure if he had really been listening to her.

July 7, 1980

I read a piece in the newspaper about a regression syndrome that occurs to polio victims as they approach middle age. And the reason for that regression may be too much exercise. Which could place me in a bind. I do have to continue my exercise regime. And I had been thinking, in my more positive moments, that just as I had conquered polio, so too could I persevere with my heart disease. I hate to think that I may not have overcome my polio after all, that it remains instead a threat, waiting to make another pass at me. Especially while I exercise for my heart.

July 8, 1980

Stan Nakao, our counselor at Regional Center, the state agency that deals with the handicapped and disabled, visited OCC. He feels Noah is in worse shape than he was six months ago.

July 9, 1980

My computerized lab test report printout said, "Your chances are 20 percent of having a cardiac problem before age sixty." Nice to know except I have one now, having already brought that 5-to-1 long shot in. My cholesterol count was 236. It should be below 200.

July 10, 1980

Foumi visited two homes that house rather advanced retardates. Neither could possibly accept Noah. His level of functioning—or rather not functioning—is just too low.

July 11, 1980

I had a drink with someone who wants me to write a TV pilot. He's a former network head, full of show-business smarts, who had had a heart attack three years ago. He began to talk about deadlines. I told him that when I hear the word "deadline," I hear the word "dead." I was sure he would understand why I did not want to get involved in any situation that might be stressful. But he didn't understand at all. Instead he laughed puckishly and mentioned a deadline again. If he's a Type A who hasn't learned anything, that's his business. I let him know I would proceed at my own good pace or not at all.

July 12, 1980

Every time the thermometer goes up a degree or the wind dies down in the desert, I feel guilty about Noah's being there. I look forward to having him home—until he is home. Until, in fact, the moment I pick him up when I fear he may be in a viciously scratching mood. Today I will arm myself with a ruler and back-scratcher to fend him off. Foumi will accompany me. We will bring him home and quarrel for two days.

A terrible weekend. When I picked up Noah on Saturday he attacked me in the car. At home he urinated on the floor several times and constantly scratched and kicked. In addition, there were blue marks along his spinal column. When I called OCC, the Administrative President suggested those marks might possibly have come from the pressure exerted in holding him down so that he could receive water squirts. Which, he assured me, were the only aversives in use at the present time.

We can't handle Noah. But we can't deal with the uncertainty caused by keeping him at OCC either.

The teacher running the summer math school called to say he was kicking Karl out because he has a negative attitude and had cursed him under his breath. The real reason, according to Karl, was that there was some group horseplay in which a clock fell and broke. Karl claims he is being singled out for blame.

Karl had really liked the math teacher. He had gone to him for special tutoring throughout the year and had really come to trust him. Now he feels betrayed by an adult. I have warned Karl that adults are often mean and eminently unfair to each other. But having to learn that again firsthand has to hurt. I cannot really get angry with Karl because he is so upset himself.

When I went out to Warner Brothers yesterday to see *Oh, God!, Book II* for the first time, I took Karl with me. Afterward, as the lights came up in the projection room, he whispered fiercely, "This is the worst picture I've seen all year." I didn't think it was that bad. Just almost that bad.

I ran into a friend of mine at the bank. His five-year-old nephew is dying in New York of a brain tumor discovered a year and a half ago. He has had operation after operation in addition to small incisions to clean out infections. But the tumor has doubled in size and the kid is expected to die this week. He sleeps a lot but is lucid when he is awake. I wonder what has been accomplished by having him live for another year and a half. It has been hell on the family, I'm sure. But then when was life anything but a delaying action?

July 19, 1980

Noah's roommate, Willie, has been withdrawn from OCC. His mother is fed up with the place. Especially with the way Willie has regressed. One of the reasons we put Noah there was that Willie seemed to have made so much progress. Now poor Noah is stuck there because of my heart condition. We must find a new place for Noah soon.

July 22, 1980

I have a summer cold. My teeth hurt down to the gums beneath my bridges. But I feel even worse because of my inability to deal with the Noah problem. We should get him out of OCC immediately. But if I were to bring Noah home now, the strain would be unbearable. It could kill me. Leaving him there is also a strain but in no way as intense. Out of sight is out of mind—and out of heart—at least, most of the time.

July 23, 1980

Karl annoys me. His loud voice. His crude manners. His intense self-absorption. He constantly offends me. Only a love object could get under one's skin so.

July 24, 1980

Foumi spoke with some parents in Orange County who are pleased with a group home there. She'll go out to inspect it first chance.

OCC is too committed to a program bent on breaking the kids spiritually through aversives. That is the inherent fallacy of operant conditioning or behavior modification—the need for the constant threat of a deterrent. Theoretically, the aversive is eventually phased out. But it never really happens.

July 26, 1980

Noah is home, down five pounds since February, leaner and meaner, spitting, clutching, scratching. Obviously, we should take him out of there. But where can we put him? We cannot take him home again. Each weekend is an exercise in hysteria for us. I stayed up worrying all last night while Noah sang in his sleep.

July 27, 1980

One of our former baby-sitters in Croton had seemed a lost small-town beauty, an Inge-like character. But then, against her father's wishes, she went off to become an airline stewardess. And yesterday she came to see us, a worldly young lady, married to an advertising executive, who seems to have managed to work out a life for herself. I thought it would be an afternoon sacrificed to the past. It wasn't. It gave me a sense of an adolescent's future. Even Karl's.

He wants to go to New York for two weeks. Foumi is against it. But I think we have to show some trust in him. I also think he could have a marvelous time.

July 28, 1980

Noah was in such a good mood after breakfast that I decided to wash his hair, and he let me get away with it. I think it takes Noah a few days to unwind, to get used to another environment. Here, I hope, we give him a touch of heaven to remember during the rest of the week when he is not with us.

Perhaps we ought to give Noah up to some foster family. There must be a couple somewhere willing to take care of him. Besides, Noah needs a mother figure he can fix on and OCC lacks that.

Karl looks decent, decent enough to send to New York, having finally succumbed to a haircut because of peer pressure. But Foumi is wary of letting him go, feels that he lacks sufficient judgmental ability, and is liable to fall back into his profligate teenage ways of drink and drugs.

July 29, 1980

I won't return Noah to OCC until this evening. I don't want to leave him there for one more minute than I have to.

Karl gave Foumi a hard time all day. Talking back whenever she asked him to do anything, criticizing whatever she said or did. The kid has a nasty mouth and what the NFL would call an "attitude problem." But I hate to stifle him. "Attitude" can also be a sign of individualism, spunk, and intelligence. I hope so in his case.

July 30, 1980

When I drove Noah back to OCC last night he was spitting and scratching and fighting all the way. And Foumi, overreacting, was fearful that I might crash. The desert was an inferno, the OCC house an oven. I felt like a Fagan returning Noah there. Yet I realized we all need the rest. Foumi particularly; her nerves are badly frayed.

July 31, 1980

Foumi called OCC this morning and learned that Noah had gone through a bad night there. Of course, with the temperature at 105 degrees and no air conditioning. We discussed bringing Noah home. I said that might be possible if she weren't such a perfectionist. She immediately defended herself. And soon we were battling each other, raging against each other instead of our fates.

She needs to get away, to have a vacation. Everyone in our family needs a vacation from each other. I can't get away at this time because of my cardiac program. But she can. And she should.

I have angina, that burning sensation in my throat. I assume it's the weather, the intense smog, depriving my heart of oxygen.

August 2, 1980

Even with Noah home Karl is the excited one, anticipating his trip to New York. Foumi is terrified by the prospect. But he will be with friends and I do think that at his age—after all, he's almost sixteen—we have to treat Karl as a mature young man. I just hope he can act like one.

August 3, 1980

In order to get Noah out of OCC I think I will have to buy a house for him and hire someone to live there and take care of him. It is the only way I can survive and he can survive. And it is the only way we can be in control.

I still don't know how to deal with Foumi's concern for my health. What distresses me most is that I find myself treating her the way my father treated my mother before his death—blaming the attendant rather than the illness.

August 4, 1980

At the beginning of the ride back to OCC last night Noah, sitting beside me, probed me repeatedly, spitting and pinching. But his outbursts decreased as I quietly drove on, ignoring him or just calmly reminding him to keep his hands down. When we arrived at OCC I wisely anchored him down by having him carry his own suitcase so that he could not wander off. As usual, I did not like leaving him there. But I only had to recall the afternoon, when I had a few bad moments with Foumi. I guess I am always hypertense when Noah is home. He reminds me that he is an insoluble problem, a metaphysical math course that I am forever flunking.

August 5, 1980

Karl was subdued this morning, nervously fingering his upper lip and brushing across his slight down. I'd made all the arrangements. He has friends to meet in New York, money for ball games and theater tickets. Still he was on edge. It is the first time he's gone on a trip by himself. Foumi and I drove him to the airport and watched him board the plane, his bags in hand, without even a wave back, let alone a kiss or a parting handshake. At times like that I wish I had a daughter.

Tonight we'll go to a CPR class at the hospital and then have a late dinner out. During the next few weeks Foumi may even forget how to cook. How good it will be without kids in the house. And how quiet.

But, damnit, I miss Karl already.

August 6, 1980

Karl arrived safely in New York and he's let us know already that he doesn't like his hostess's cooking. Foumi's talking of bringing Noah home this weekend. And I won't oppose it. I may be at last learning that it's a lot easier to let her have her way, even when she's wrong, than to argue with her.

August 7, 1980

Last night I ran into an old army friend who told me his son is on drugs, hard drugs. About drugs, I've decided, it's like homosexuality. If you think somebody is gay, he usually is. If you suspect somebody is on drugs, he usually is.

August 8, 1980

OCC claims that Noah has been in a bad mood all week. Whether it's because of the weather or their treatment I do not know. They claim it's because of their withdrawal of aversives. They're no longer giving him water squirts or spanks as "consequences." What they call "consequences" I consider rough treatment and I'm glad they've stopped.

August 9, 1980

I made the mistake of bringing Noah home last night. From the moment I picked him up he began to spit, which didn't bode well.

But I managed to keep calm on the ride home, gently telling him to keep his scratching hands off my neck.

For some reason, after Foumi had served him a huge dinner, which he devoured ravenously, he had a tantrum. Still, compulsive Foumi made the mistake of trying to brush his teeth. He then attacked her, grabbing her hair, and after I pried him away I soon felt my angina in my throat. I second-guessed Foumi for wanting to have Noah home this weekend and she defended herself. Noah just continued to claw and spit at us.

This morning I realized again that I cannot afford the luxury of having Noah home. I need whatever respite I can get. Even from OCC.

August 10, 1980

Noah has settled down. Foumi takes care of him and I generally ignore him. I won't even chance taking him back to OCC tomorrow. I've asked a friend to do that.

August 11, 1980

Karl is happy. I have been communicating more with him in the past few days over the phone than I communicated with him in the past few years in person. We really are having conversations beyond the "pick me up at Steve's house" stage. And he surprises me pleasurably. Yesterday, for example, he informed me, he went to the Picasso show at the museum and liked it.

But even from New York Karl is loud. Living quietly together, just the two of us, I'm in love with Foumi again.

August 12, 1980

A bad day. My blood pressure has been low—in the 70s—and my pulse rate down to 50. And I feel dizzy most of the time.

August 13, 1980

No matter how many times the heart and the way it works is explained to me, I'll never understand it. A nurse or a doctor patiently explains, draws diagrams, points to pictures. I nod my head. But I don't understand a bloody thing. Like the theory of electricity, logarithms, quadratic equations, negative numbers, and the piston internal-combustion engine.

August 14, 1980

Karl will spend the weekend in Amagansett, a few days in Westchester, and then he'll complete his metropolitan tour and fly home. So far he's seen the Yankees play three times. Which should be enough. He even turned down a chance to go to the Democratic Convention to attend last night's game. His choice.

My choice: Not to have Noah home this weekend and I don't feel at all guilty about it.

August 15, 1980

Foumi went off to Anaheim to look at a group home there as a possible residential placement for Noah. But she found they didn't deal with behavior problems as severe as Noah's.

August 16, 1980

My mood these days depends upon my exercise performance. A good session can blow away the blues, a bad one plunges me into gloom.

While I was exercising the monitoring machine indicated that my heart was straining for oxygen. And before that I was tired after my morning walk. So I won't try to do any writing today. I find I can't think about my work while I am worrying about my health. In fact, I can't think of anything or anybody but myself. Anyway, I've always said my depressions are my vacations.

August 17, 1980

I am a little disgusted with myself for not writing, for giving up that ghost. But what the hell? These days I need substance. And a good long walk.

Something called the Clients' Rights Committee of OCC wants
to meet with us because of our "refusal to cooperate with OCC."
I'm not sure what that means exactly, but I know it doesn't bode
well. I feel as if the Administrative President and Executive Visiting Adviser are beginning to put pressure on us to remove Noah
by threatening to kick him out.

I saw Howard, my cardiologist, yesterday. He's changing my
medications, putting me on a different beta blocker, to keep my
heart rate down; and a vasodilater, to dilate my arteries so that
my heart can get more oxygen. If I keep having problems, there is
always open heart surgery. But I do want to forestall that alternative as long as possible.

Karl called this morning, angrily complaining. His hostess,
Clarice Imbriano, is a dental hygienist, and she insisted on looking at his teeth. He didn't want that to happen on his vacation. It
was ruining his whole vacation. I didn't tell him that we had
asked Clarice to do so. It was a lot easier, we figured, asking her
to clean his teeth than getting him to our dentist.

Foumi asked me to correct the English in this letter and then send
it off to places like the Ford Foundation:

Dear Sirs:

*I am a mother of severely handicapped boy, that is, he cannot talk
at the age of 14 and on and off has violent temper tanturam and
he is bigger than me. He is now in a residential facility where we
are not happy about. Even we are not happy about the place, we
have to keep him there, because my husband has a heart disease.*

*If Noah come home, our home will be destroied. My husband
might have a heart attack and die and my another normal son
cannot have normal life.*

*About institutions many things really bother me. They give big
dosage of drugs to children unnecessarily and make them like veg-
etables, so that they can save money instead of employing more
people. They are paying a lot of money for professionals who*

claim cure but don't know how to handle children, forgetting about human elements.

Therefore, I want to open myself residential and school. Since I have been operating after school care for these children for four yrs. and as a concern mother of severely handicapped child I think I can operate an Ideal facility and precise care for these children. I don't claim I can cure like those professionals, but I know what these children need realistically.

I want to do according to their brain function and take care of more human basic. I want to do better from nutritional point of view which many places neglect (for instance, we omit all sugar and artificial additives), more physical activities which can improve coordination, more handcraft-work to stimulate brain, music dance, of course academics including sign language. In residential facility they have to learn how to live normally and for that purpose, they will be trained for self-help.

People in the society, those who do not have those children in their family and those who have those children but theirs are still young apt to think the big institution is better, at the same time, the state which is funding institutions think that way too. But in those big institution, when something going wrong and people begin to realize that it is too late. In this case who suffer most? Children who are mute and brain damaged. They will show by regressions. And their families. Small is always better for these severely handicapped children. I want to have four children in one house. That is humanly manageable. And in the future I want to have one more house.

For that purpose we need to have seed money for 5 month operation. Roughly in the amount of $100,000 is necessary, for rent for residential house, school, salaries for workers which is very big, we employ almost one on one basis, foods, furnitures and materials insurance, car for transporting children.

State will reimburse later.

Therefore, I want to ask your help if you agree with me about the welfare of our children, at least you can help eight of them. If you like to help us establish, lend us $100,000 for 6 months for seed money, which we will eventually return you back. In that case we will really appreciate if you can lend us without interest, and that interest will become your donation. Of course, if you can donate $100,000 for our non profit corporation, we will be really grateful.

We want to be very small and well managed.

You will be proud the day this residential and school will start.

I told Foumi I could improve the grammar and the diction but not the effectiveness of this letter if it reached the right party. But, unfortunately, I am not exactly sure who is the right party and at what address. But God she tries. My wife certainly tries. And I'll try to get a list of foundations and corporations and refashion the letter in more professional proposal terms without diminishing the honesty of its heartbeat.

24

Karl is back. He looked like a man and acted like a man from the moment he got off the plane. In the sixteen-day interval he has become taller and he seems light-years more mature. We all lunched in a Japanese restaurant and then came home and talked for hours together. He was a delight, telling us stories about his friend's Communist sister and her Iranian boyfriend, Abdullah; and about one of his hostesses, who fed her cat whenever it meowed no matter what the hour; and about another host's inability to get anywhere on time. How glad we were to have him back, his presence not only immediately filling our lives but also giving it hints of an extended meaning.

But then came morning. He awoke late and came into the kitchen slopping up the sports section of the newspaper. I told him not to eat too much because we would soon be having luncheon guests and that we expected him to join us. He immediately protested that we were ruining his first day home.

Anyway, whatever problems we might have with him are minuscule compared with those involving Noah. Noah is now down to ninety-three pounds from the one hundred he weighed seven months ago when he entered OCC. Yet it remains the only game in town for him at the moment. And now they are threatening to give him the boot because of our "refusal to cooperate with OCC." And they're damned right. We will not cooperate with an aversive program that further victimizes Noah.

We were up late entertaining the Clients' Rights Committee of OCC at our home. The committee is one of those bureaucratic layers that facilities are required to set up to protect their clients from being maltreated. The idea may sound good on paper but it doesn't quite work out. Visiting us, for example, was a behaviorist psychology professor from a local community college who is a friend of the OCC Executive Visiting Adviser; a pharmacist from the desert who is a friend of the Administrative President; and the Administrative President himself. They claimed that OCC could not manage Noah because we wouldn't let them use any aversive other than water squirts; we further tied their hands, they said, by not allowing them to use sweet junk food as rewards. They proceeded in a lawyerly way to build a case against Noah that would justify the use of spanks, permission for which, of course, we refused to grant. Especially after they refused to deal with the point we raised: that in the past, in the case of Noah, their application of spanks seemed to us beyond the simple bounds of common sense.

Which leaves us where we've been: between the same two hard places. We can't take Noah back. We can't leave him at OCC.

Something has clicked in me. My heart problem is over, I have decided, because I have to deal with my heartbreaking one.

I picked up Noah at OCC at ten o'clock this morning. He had not eaten, he was wearing a torn shirt—even though OCC is allotted forty-seven dollars per month for his clothing—but he was in a fine mood anyway and chirped beside me all the way home.

I cannot get over the tall, lumbering Karl. In three months he will be sixteen. In two years he will be out of the house. Off to the college of his choice. Or one that accepts him. Whichever comes first. Meanwhile, we take advantage of his presence. Last night Foumi and I were able to go to a chamber music concert while he watched Noah.

August 25, 1980

Noah has been home three days and has behaved well. I indulge Foumi's overindulgence of him. She feeds him, washes his hands constantly, prepares him for sleep, and takes him for walks. But she'll soon have a vacation, going off to England and France for two weeks. We've offered Karl the opportunity to accompany her but he's turned it down. Which is silly of him. But if he wants to blow it, that's his business.

August 26, 1980

OCC called at 8:00 A.M. today. Some state officials were visiting the facility. Would we mind keeping Noah home until this afternoon? Hell no, Foumi told them, we had other plans for the afternoon. At this point why should we do them any favors?

Karl is a problem again. Foumi has noticed that whenever he returns from certain of his friends he is moody and defiant. He has another set of friends from whom he returns seeming much more mature and mellow. Why doesn't he socialize more with that set? Foumi asked him. Because the parents of those kids don't like him, he replied. Is he so vulnerable or is he simply lying?

August 27, 1980

We continue with OCC in uneasy armistice. And I don't see any immediate resolution. They want permission to spank Noah. They know it won't work but it does give them the only position they know how to take, a party-line ideology. I have no ideology. Just a brain-damaged son.

I wish I could go to England with Foumi. But for our communal sanity she has to get away on her own. We need a separation from each other. She needs a renewal for herself.

August 29, 1980

I have wished a bad weekend on myself. I called OCC and told them I would pick up Noah this evening. Whenever I read about how hot it is in the desert, my Jewish guilt rears up. But I also want him home for another reason. Foumi goes off to England next week and it will be several weeks before he can come home again.

I am pleased with my progress at Cardiac Rehab. When I began going there I could barely do six three-minute rounds of exercise with a minute of rest between rounds. I can now do thirty-six minutes of exercise without a rest. Which means I am nearing the end of my hospital sessions. Soon they'll wean me down to two sessions a week. Then one. And finally, as they say, I will be "sprung."

Exercising can be tricky for me, though. I still have bad days when my blood pressure tends to fall too low. And that frightens me. In fact, anything can frighten me: A cold. A stiff muscle. A bad stomach. I am always afraid that any slight impairment is symptomatic of trouble with my heart.

August 30, 1980

When I picked up Noah he was wearing a clean shirt. I placed him in the rear of my station wagon—something I should have thought of doing months ago—and drove him back as if he were a large child or some sort of an animal. At home he ate dinner while Foumi, Karl, and I watched a TV documentary about the survival instinct in animals. They showed penguins feeding their own young while they slapped away the young of others.

Karl is still a pain but he is also a person who is not without sharp perceptions and keen insights. At lunch he was criticizing certain intellectuals. "Just because they're above average," he said, "doesn't mean they're not beneath brilliance."

September 2, 1980

A Labor Day picnic has left me full of aches. In the baseball game I played a lousy first base and didn't get a decent hit. But along the sidelines I did play with some of the little girls there. Perhaps what I have missed most in my life is not having a daughter, a live, cuddly, huggable daughter.

September 3, 1980

Foumi flew away yesterday for a vacation—a week in London and a week in Paris. Perhaps I should have gone with her. But then I would have missed the farewell at the airport when I realized again, as I looked into her tearful eyes trying not to look into mine, how much we still love each other.

And last night as Karl and I were cooking our own bachelor dinners, I mentioned how quiet the house was with just two people. "It must have been just as quiet when I was in the hospital," I said. "No," said Karl, "Foumi was crying all the time."

September 4, 1980

A producer I know is in the midst of an acrimonious divorce. He has an occluded heart vessel just like me. But, unlike me, he is on coke, has a live-in hooker whom he sends out to procure more hookers, and otherwise lives a Howard Hughes life in a hotel suite.

I can understand his desire to fold his bourgeois cards after seeing the dark man coming. I feel the same way. I could easily give myself to a life spent in the pursuit of pleasure. Only I know, alas, it would not give me pleasure. How many times can one come and in how many ways, and what do you do afterward?

September 5, 1980

Morning—day three of Foumi's absence: When I returned home from shopping last night I asked Karl's help in putting away the groceries. Instead, he gave me the old wait-a-minute routine. I became angry. He called me an "asshole." And we were at each other. Finally we both cooled off sufficiently to have dinner. But I don't think just the two of us together could last for very long.

Evening: The other shoe fell. A registered letter from OCC saying that they would be "terminating Noah's placement in 30 days" because we weren't allowing them to use their "treatment procedures." In other words, the beat-up-on-Noah procedures, which according to law they aren't allowed to use anyway.

I won't tell Foumi about this latest development. Let her enjoy her vacation.

Anyway, I have always regarded Noah's stay at OCC as that of an incorrigible kid sent to a military academy by a household that could no longer manage him. And as it turns out, a very poor military academy. One that is expelling him because his parents, in all good conscience, complained about the conditions there.

I am really overwhelmed at the prospect of Noah's return home. So is Karl. When I told him the news he was very upset.

I can't help but blame Noah's "expulsion" a little on Foumi's inability to wean herself from him, her overbrimming love for him, her perfectionist zeal that he receive the proper foods and be kept clean and neat and sanitary. In other words on her acting like a normal mother.

I love Noah. But not the way Foumi does. Because I am a man. Because of my heart condition. I can be an Abraham only too ready to self-servingly sacrifice my Isaac. Not only can I survive without Noah, but not having Noah around may be necessary for my survival.

Anyway, it's OCC that's to blame. Our differences with them over sweet junk food may be comparatively minor. But when it comes to "treatment procedures" such as spanks they are major. In the long run we will be well rid of them.

I've just spent twenty-four hours alone. Without Foumi. Without Noah. And without Karl—he slept over at a friend's. A life without them has been a life with television and newspapers and books and magazines . . . a life in a motel.

Foumi called from London. She seemed so happy all I could tell her was good news. I lied about Noah. I said he was fine. But I wonder what to do. The time I have played for with OCC is over.

At the age of fifty-two I still ask myself the same question I asked myself thirty years ago: "What do I want out of life?" But now the only answer I can summon up is: "Life itself." Which really, for the alleged sophistication of my brain, puts me in Noah's shoes. So why should his life be worth anything less than mine?

I feel absurd but I am now struggling to keep Noah in OCC. But where else can we place him at this time? I called Noah's former school; they cannot take him back now. I called the L.A. Board of Education; they aren't sure if anything's available at the moment. And I spoke with the OCC president, who said he had to talk to his lawyer before talking to me. I don't know what that's all about. Unless the tension of waiting for us to act has unnerved them. Anyway, as I say, I feel absurd trying to keep Noah there. At first we wanted the best for Noah. Now all we want is the best for us.

But the worst that can happen is that Noah returns home. That's bad. But life hasn't been that good without him either. He is perhaps a talisman of the only real value: selfless love. Without which any life always seems utterly insufficient.

September 9, 1980

I constantly think about having Noah home again. What does that mean? What would it do to my life? I had thought that my productivity would increase once we put Noah in OCC. But, as it turns out, not so; I have done less in the past eight months than ever before.

Karl was supposed to work at some part-time job today. Instead, he went to the beach. So much for my ambitious son. I worry about his future. I fear he's not prepared for it. Nor am I. I'm not even prepared for my own future.

I miss Foumi. But I don't miss all the pointless, repetitious discussions we'd be having about the Noah situation if she were home. Because I don't think we'd be a step further advanced in the way of a solution.

September 10, 1980

I suggested to the OCC Administrative President that perhaps we could still reconcile our differences rather than have Noah tossed out. Because, at the moment, all I want to do with Noah is preserve the status quo. Until I can find a new status for him. But his response was noncommittal.

Karl slept over at a friend's again and will work at his job tomorrow. Foumi? Who's she? I miss her. But Karl and I are quite happy without her. We simply stay out of each other's way. So I do not look forward to Foumi's return. I just don't look forward to anyone's return.

Karl and I had dinner at a fine Mexican restaurant last night. I took him there because I thought he would enjoy it even though I would have preferred Japanese food. As he unenthusiastically pushed his fork around, he suddenly remembered that he had had Mexican food the previous night.

Moral: Whenever I try to anticipate his tastes I make a great mistake. But it would also help if he would try to communicate just a little.

I had dinner last night with a young couple who are planning a class for autistics at a school they run in Lawndale. They seemed nice enough, although it was hard to pin them down on specifics. But I could not help but find off-putting the fact that the woman wore her hair in the same style as the OCC Executive Visiting Adviser.

This morning a doctor I know told me he had faced much the same problem as we are now having with OCC when his father was in a nursing home. Neither he nor his mother could dare complain about the way his father was being treated there. "You have to be political," the doctor advised me. But Foumi is much too pure to play a political game.

Karl's getting on my nerves. He doesn't clean pots and pans properly and I can't stand his booming voice. It's tough living with a teenager for a whole week.

I wish I could be more relaxed. But I have the pressure of Noah upon me. And I am still ever cognizant of my heart problem. Even though I am in good shape. I can now exercise forty minutes without a break. Which is pretty good. These days I wish I could write forty minutes without a break.

A fellow "autistic" parent called me last night. When I mentioned Noah's imminent return he said: "It'll be hard getting back into the trenches, won't it?"

I spent the day shopping with Karl for back-to-school clothing at Bullock's in Century City. I had suggested the Bullock's in Westwood, which is nearer. But no, he insisted on the Bullock's in Century City. He has strong opinons about everything based on absolutely nothing. Is that all part of being a teenager? Or being Karl? Or both?

Foumi's back and I've got her. She looked so tiny coming down the roped-off aisle in the bubble building at LAX where one greets the arriving international passengers. So small and slight and frail. But now that she's been in the house twenty-four hours, she seems a massive presence, like a general resuming control of a command. But I don't mind. I don't want command of this outfit anyway.

A registered package came in the mail from OCC. I wondered what it possibly could be. Something that belonged to Noah? Some important object that I had inadvertently left behind there? It turned out to be a bound volume of material on their theories of behavior and how to apply them. And a long letter from their Executive Visiting Adviser demanding, in effect, that we relinquish all possible controls over Noah if they are to keep him there. To give us time to reach a decision they have extended Noah's stay there until November 5. Their conditions:

They can apply to Noah as many aversives as they wish, including placing him in restraints.
They can feed him as many sweet junk foods as they please.
We cannot visit Noah at all during the next three months.
During the following three months, we can see him only once a month. And after that we can see him once every two weeks—but at their discretion.
Home visits would also be solely up to their discretion.

So there really isn't much to mull over. It would be a complete capitulation on our part. And if we had not experienced OCC firsthand, we might even be tempted to go along with it. After all, it would mean that after November 5 we would finally be free of Noah. We could go wherever we wanted to go and do whatever we wanted to do.

But unfortunately, we know their program. We have finally learned to be as wary of behaviorists as of any other psychologists.

Who knows what Noah will be like when we get him back? But then he was not in such great shape when he entered OCC. But I did not have my heart problem either.

For all my realism—and cynicism—I still dream not of our someday being able to "reach" him but of his being able to "reach" us. In my heart of hearts I have yet to give up hope completely for some miracle cure. Which makes me an easy mark for another OCC. Yes, we still have an interesting future together, Noah and I.

September 20, 1980

"Go away, kid," said the president of the Synagogue of Performing Arts to a tot who had wandered up before the makeshift pulpit on the stage of the Academy of Motion Picture Arts and Sciences Theatre, which had been rented for the Jewish High Holidays, "I only work as a single."

Last night was Kol Nidre—which also happens to be the twentieth anniversary of our marriage according to the Hebrew calendar—but I attended services as a single, too. Foumi, of course, wouldn't come with me for atheistic reasons, and Karl showed no interest either. But I missed his presence beside me, remembering how I used to warm my own father by my presence. At the same time I also remembered how as a child I had hated every minute of enforced *shul*-going. But last night I felt a kind of tranquility, almost a serenity, as I let the nostalgia waft over me. I also had an epiphany: I could keep Noah in OCC as long as I wanted to.

What I mean is this: The Kol Nidre prayer is a denial of the validity of any vows extracted under duress, of any loyalty oaths sworn for pragmatic life-and-death reasons. So I could promise OCC anything until I found another place for Noah. I do have heart disease, and I carry within me a sense of my own doom should I try to live in the same house with Noah.

Does it always have to come down to father and son fighting it out for survival? Noah doesn't know that. But I do and I think it does.

September 21, 1980

One of the endless lures in life is curiosity. We have kids so as to see what our flesh can become. And then we wonder how they will turn out, what sort of adults they will evolve into, who they will marry, and in turn what kind of children they will bear. Curiosity, as much as anything else, motivates longevity. But in the case of Noah, the necessity for a long life—or a longer life—on my part is the desire to keep him as he is: sheltered, protected, and unabused.

I truly loved him this morning as I brushed his teeth. Even when he spit at me. Even when he reached out and pinched me hard. Since OCC's ultimatum, somehow I find Noah more beautiful than ever.

September 22, 1980

The weekend has passed without incident. I stayed out of Noah's hair—other than to wash it—while Foumi took care of him completely, waiting so tenderly and patiently and submissively upon him that I began to wonder if Noah has the Japanese wife I've never had.

September 23, 1980

I was telling a historian friend that I wished Karl could recall irregular verbs as readily as he did batting averages. "Don't worry," my friend advised. "He'll eventually apply his baseball research ability to some other interest."

September 25, 1980

Karl now talks of wanting to leave his high school and transferring to a school back East for his last year or two. It seems he's sick of Pali High. Doesn't think it has much to offer him. I can't argue with that. He's also very anxious to get out of the house. I can't argue with that either.

341

September 26, 1980

Our present plans for Noah: to rent a house and hire a live-in couple to take care of him. But if something in the East is right for Noah, we might have an alternative.

September 27, 1980

Noah has been home since yesterday and what have I done with him? I took him for a car ride today and that's all. Otherwise, I have just ignored him. I guess an autistic child breeds autistic parents. Or at least an autistic father. But even though I'm consciously ignoring him I am forever conscious of his presence just as he, I'm sure, is somehow aware of mine.

September 29, 1980

There is always stress in the house when Noah is home. There is always a long shrug of relief after Noah's gone.

September 30, 1980

Twenty years ago today Foumi and I married. I remember her then as being quiet and strong-willed. She is still strong-willed but she is no longer so quiet. Not within the family.

I wonder about the kind of life I would have had without her. I guess I would have been the traditional Jewish neurotic, married at least twice, constantly griping about how much alimony I had to pay and how little I got to see my kids. I am not sure I would have remained a writer, although I don't know what else I could have done. I like to think that somehow I would have had a more interesting life. But in what way more interesting? And with whom? And for how long? I can't think of anyone else with whom I could have lasted twenty years. Karl says our marriage has endured because of Noah. I like to think there are some other reasons that he's still too young to understand.

We celebrated our anniversary last night, Karl enjoying himself at the festive table, though it was inconvenient having him there.

I should bite my typewriter ribbon's tongue. Who else is there in my life of real note other than Foumi, Karl, and Noah?

25

I've been away for a week on an errand of search and quest. First I went to Atlanta to participate in a symposium on "The Devalued Person." While there I toured the Georgia Retardation Center, a state hospital not unlike Camarillo. The staff was doing the best they could considering their limited appropriations, but most of the clients were just lying around without a thing to do. I saw one patient I shall never forget, a child who had chewed off half of his own fingers.

Then I flew up to Philadelphia and drove out to Camphill, the school run by the Rudolf Steiner Theosophy people. There the clients live within normal family setups, three and four to the house, and have full-day school programs. Several of the kids I saw seemed very much like Noah in their behaviors. In general the atmosphere was serene. Almost too serene. One sensed a Middle European hippie mentality, only without drugs. The chief drawback, as far as I was concerned, was their long summer and Thanksgiving and Christmas vacations when the clients are returned to their parents.

Near Camphill was Kimberton, one of the Steiner group's adult communities. On a thriving dairy farm they had a cheese factory, looms, and a blooming truck garden. Here "normal" families also lived in houses along with the adult retardates. It was a future worth dreaming of for Noah.

In Connecticut I visited Benhaven. The facility had expanded since I had last visited there. Now it included an adult residential setup outside of New Haven. If not as serene as Camphill or Kimberton, it seemed busier and worldlier, with an abundance of workers everywhere. The big problem there from our point of view was that most of the clients were more advanced than Noah. Also, Amy Lettick, the Benhaven director, seemed to change the subject whenever I brought up the possibility of Noah being accepted there.

So with Camphill unrealistic and Benhaven unresponsive, I returned home with the Noah problem still unresolved. Regional Center further informed us this morning that they could not aid in funding Noah out of state anyway. But my trip East was in no way wasted. I have come back convinced there are far better places than OCC. Benhaven keeps its charges busy, Camphill ensures that they are serene. Compared to either, OCC is not worth fighting for. So at this point my only practical option is to rent or buy a house for Noah.

October 10, 1980

I take our cat, T.G., for granted. Yesterday when I came home for lunch I found him ensconced in an open kitchen cabinet near the ceiling, standing like a mini-horse in a model stable. Since he did not belong there, I forced him outside.

I should have then noticed something strange in his repeated efforts to regain entry into the house. Usually when banished to the garden T.G., accepting his fate as if it were an act of choice, goes nonchalantly sauntering away as if that were his very intention. But yesterday was not a usual day. A new roof was being put on next door. The workmen were noisy and there was the smell of tar in the air. T.G. was obviously not happy with the situation.

In the afternoon, when Karl returns from school, T.G. is usually there to greet him. But not yesterday. Nor by dinnertime was he at the door either. By bedtime he still had not reappeared. We all went to bed distraught; I had the additional burden of guilt to bear. After all, it was I who had kicked T.G. out of the kitchen. Foumi claimed she could even hear Karl sniffling in his bed.

This morning T.G. still had not shown up. I spoke to the roofers working next door who had carted to the dump a huge load of the old shakes yesterday evening. No, they had not seen a cat in the debris. But I decided to check it out. I drove out to the dump, off the San Diego Freeway in the Santa Monica Mountains, a pay dump where trucks lined up on the mountainside, waited to be weighed, and then climbed a winding road to dispense their loads. Tractors leveled off the refuse mounds while seagulls hovered overhead. None of the workers there had seen a cat; they all suggested it would be impossible for a cat to have survived there even a single night. Because a cat would instinctively have taken off into the hills only to be devoured by the coyotes. I looked up into the mountains and wept.

I returned home to any empty house and waited for Foumi. Finally, she walked in. She had run over to the school to tell Karl the good news: T.G. had been discovered next door in Smitty's garage. He had been inadvertently locked in there overnight. I got his carrier and retrieved him.

I feel a lot better now. The loss of T.G. would have been a bad omen at a time when I'm so concerned about the fate of Noah. The OCC deadline is less than a month away.

October 11, 1980

I worry about Noah and do nothing. I worry about my work and do nothing. But I don't worry as much as I should. I'm such a terrible procrastinator that I even put off most of my worrying.

I almost could leave Noah in OCC. But Foumi is determined to get him out of there. And she's right. Except I just don't have the strength to handle Noah; I literally don't have the heart for the task anymore.

Yet there is no way we'll find another residence for Noah in two or three weeks. Foumi talks of eventually starting a school and a group home. But I know the burden of dealing with officialdom; all the administrative work and bureaucratic form filling would fall upon me. And I just don't have the energy for the task.

October 12, 1980

I called Amy Lettick, the director of Benhaven. She was most sympathetic. But if we want to place Noah there we first must pay for a trip out here by three of their staff so that they might examine him. Then he would have to get on a waiting list. The wait might be years. And still he might not qualify because of his behavior problems.

I think Noah has to be taught, not to follow orders as they theoretically have been trying to teach him at OCC, but to communicate, whether it's through signing or any other way. He will always be unruly, he will never be calm, until he knows that he can communicate without raging. He still does not know that.

October 13, 1980

I picked up Noah at OCC after breakfast. I drove him home and by lunchtime Foumi and I were really fighting. She had gone to the trouble of cooking specially for him and I thought that was silly. Why couldn't he just have a sandwich? No, she wanted him to have a hot meal. Why couldn't she cook a hot meal for him if she wanted to? And so we battled on through the day.

I suppose I must always let Foumi do what she wants, and I must always do what she wants to do. And I should follow her instincts in regard to Noah. Even though they may lead nowhere. She keeps telling me that she is clairvoyant, that she can foresee the future. I'm not sure of that. The only thing I'm sure of is that she certainly can re-see the past clearly enough.

October 14, 1980

This morning I placed an ad in the *L.A. Times* for a Special Education teacher to live with Noah in an independent residence. This afternoon we will look at some rental houses. Tomorrow we'll visit the Marlton School for the Deaf run by the L.A. School District, which we're told has just started a special class for autistics led by an excellent teacher. We're implementing decisions reached after long discussion at a family meeting last night.

Karl opposed Noah's return to our house because he's afraid he might become too attached to Noah and thus be saddled with him for the rest of his life. "It's easy for you," Karl said to me, "you have just five or ten more years left, and maybe Foumi has twenty. But I have a lot more." He also informed me, parenthetically, that he would not want to live past the point when his body could no longer respond properly to his wishes. "I would hate to become like you," he said.

Foumi argued that as long as Noah was at OCC, we had to treat him as a potential holocaust victim. So how could we knowingly turn our backs on him? He was not someone in Cambodia, an abstraction on the evening news; or a literary figure, a vague personage across the ocean in some ghetto, further detached from us by the remove of time.

The problem never ends, the pain never dies, the quest always continues. So too the dream endures if fueled only by a modicum of reality. Before she got into bed, Foumi was saying that perhaps in Japan, in some paper shack of a building, we'd eventually find the best place for Noah.

In Atlanta, at the symposium on "The Devalued Person," I spoke of my dream for Noah. I said that I wanted him to live in conditions no worse than those of normal people. That I wanted him to get as much happiness as possible out of life. That he was as capable of pain and pleasure as other people, even if on a more primordial level.

The arrogance of some of us to value some lives above others, to reward some people more for the tasks they perform than others. Capitalism, at base, is a very immoral system. Any system that leaves no room for Noah is. Until we actually come up with a way of dealing with Noah we cannot pride ourselves on a moral superiority. Because we ain't moral. We treat those who seem like less as far less.

October 15, 1980

We visited the Marlton School, the L.A. city school for the deaf, which has an autistic class. The teacher, Mark Tajima, is a third-generation Japanese-American from Stockton. There are three students in the class and one aide. When they reach five students they will get an additional aide. So there certainly seems to be enough staff. Willie, Noah's former OCC roommate, is one of the students and he seems to be doing well here, having learned some sign language. But then Willie led us to OCC and that turned out to be a mammoth mistake.

The school has a gym and all sorts of shops and playing fields. Education for the deaf may indeed be the best model for the autistic. All other Special Education models seem to have come out of kindergarten.

October 16, 1980

I enrolled in a swimming class at Santa Monica Community College. My flutter kick is a disaster and I can improve it if I stay with the class. But in the pool I have some angina and despite the sense of muscular youth and strength I get swimming, I'm not sure it's a worthwhile tradeoff.

I finally feel the change of seasons now, the chilly coming of fall. And my clearest, recurrent memory of this kind of weather is skating in the dark one night on East 46th Street in Brooklyn after Hebrew school, gliding smoothly over the black-topped street on the new red-wheeled roller skates my Aunt Lee had just sent me as a gift. I must have been ten or eleven at the time, a kid in knickers, worrying about scraping my knees if I fell.

October 17, 1980

I read one of those Xeroxed booklets that came in that bulky package from OCC. Turned out to be a position paper written by the Executive Visiting Adviser in which she claims her form of operant conditioning is the only way to retrain kids as severely autistic as Noah. She further argues that even the most extreme aversives are ultimately constructive because the removal of them accelerates positive behavior. Which is nonsense logically. Just like her argument that parents of autistics must choose between her program as practiced at OCC and a state institution. There is always another choice. Thus speaketh Greenfeld.

October 18, 1980

An applicant for the post of living with Noah came to the house. He's an overqualified black who seems to have been everywhere and done everything, from playing professional baseball to performing musically. I think he could work out with Noah but Foumi noticed that he seemed more interested in himself than in Noah.

October 19, 1980

I awoke to my perennial dream this morning. Noah was talking, calmly telling me that he would not talk at OCC because he did not like the way he was being treated there. In the next room, of

course, I soon could hear Noah, home for the weekend, half crying, half babbling, but totally incoherent.

October 20, 1980

We visited a center for autistics out in the Valley, set up by a
group of parents I had some disagreements with years ago. The
industrial workshop there really impressed me. Kids and adults
alike were working at sophisticated machines, doing all sorts of
industrial jobs.

We looked at two of their four residential homes. The one for
adults was quite neat. An adolescent house was less so. There
were gaping holes in the wallboards, caused no doubt by head
bangers during tantrums. But the place did seem sufficiently
staffed.

But that's academic. When we met the director he said he had
heard that we were difficult. I explained to him the reason. When
the parent group began talk of starting the present setup, I had
taken the position that the leaders could not just go out, raise
money, and then place their own children there. I felt that was
immoral, that the first children placed could not be those of the
leaders. Otherwise, we would just be rattling tin cups for ourselves. The leaders called me ridiculous, impossible, and, of
course, difficult.

But on our mini-tour of the facility I recognized most of the
client adults and adolescents. They were the sons and daughters
of the leaders.

The director assured me that he was now completely in charge,
that the residents were chosen strictly on the basis of need, and
encouraged us to apply. We will, even though I know better than
to hold my breath for acceptance.

October 21, 1980

I did not get out of bed this morning until after eight o'clock, just
lying there wanting to savor fully the life we are now living without Noah.

He will be back within two weeks. Once more the healers, or
the "healing authorities," will blame the parents for the lack of a
cure. Usually the healers blame the patient. But when the patient
is beyond the pale of reproach, they immediately turn on the next

of kin, the parents. So it is with the Freudians, from the bearded Viennese himself down to the bald Bettelheim. So it is with the behaviorists. Now at OCC they are saying that we imposed too many conditions on them by limiting their use of aversives. They did not complain about those conditions when they accepted Noah. But now they use that as an excuse for blaming us, the next of kin.

October 22, 1980

Foumi and I looked at a possible home for Noah in the neighborhood. But it was way overpriced.

I get depressed when I consider Noah's homecoming. I wonder if I can live under such stress again. What I really would like to do is consider retirement. But a Noah forbids that. Karl forecloses on that possibility too. I am surrounded by a sea of rotten choices. But I will not drown. It will all work out. Life, just as surely as it presents terrible problems, is capable of producing astonishing solutions.

October 23, 1980

Foumi and I looked at four houses today. Our guidelines are simple: We should not buy a house for Noah that we would not be willing to live in ourselves. At the same time the house should be one that could be easily converted into a group home and thus eliminate some of the financial drain. Given the above concerns I have eliminated all four houses we saw today.

October 24, 1980

The plight of Noah threatens to paralyze me. Which house to buy and how to finance it? I am not good at these things. Neither is Foumi. In the meantime we both tend to get on Karl too much for neglecting his schoolwork. Hell, he'll soon be able to drive a car of his own while Noah will never be able to take a bus by himself.

October 27, 1980

We attended a wedding Saturday at "our" church, the church that housed our day-care center. Ruth, the church secretary, married Jack, the choir director, and Spence, the former minister, came down from Oregon to perform the ceremony. So we were there, too. Never in my wildest dreams did I imagine that we could be part of a church community. But then Noah has led us to some very unexpected places.

On Saturday night I brought Noah home for a brief weekend, his final weekend, until he comes home for good—or bad. He was scratching and squeezing, hardly the kind of guest you invite back.

We interviewed a young woman who knows sign language and wants to live with Noah. So now we have two candidates for the job. And this afternoon we saw a house that interested us. It's not the best house we've seen but it's probably the best house we can pick up in this neighborhood. I find myself liking the idea of having Noah just around the corner from us.

October 28, 1980

Being in the market for a house is like having a pregnant wife. Immediately, you notice the condition everywhere. For Sale signs that I once passed without a second thought are now immediate invitations to my curiosity. How many rooms? How much down? What kind of financing? But my curiosity has to stop soon. Noah is almost at term.

October 29, 1980

Last night we went to a reunion of the heart group at the home of the nurse who had supervised it. We were the only patient-couple who turned up. Which shows who are the old softies in the bunch.

We came home in time to catch only part of the great debate. Carter seemed sharper but Reagan came through as being more human and a nicer guy. It is easier to identify with him than with Carter. But I guess I still have to vote for Carter if only because he sends out a better message to the world. And Anderson is still nothing more than an unreconstituted Republican.

When I discussed my decision with Karl he understood it on a sophisticated and knowledgeable level. I liked that. But I did not like trying on a pair of pants that he has outgrown. They fit me.

As a child I had to wear hand-me-downs; now I have to wear hand-me-ups.

We made a bid on a house for Noah. I hate to think what my expenses will be carrying two houses. When I mentioned that fact to Foumi, she pointed out I always get nervous at the expenditure of large sums of money. True. But that doesn't make me any less nervous.

Last night was Karl's Open School Night. All of his teachers but one were absent. Figures: A lazy kid gets lazy teachers. The one we did meet, his history teacher, is a winner, though. A black woman who is articulate, knowledgeable—about both Karl and history—and has a fine sense of humor. So the kid has at least one class he can look forward to.

Noah returns to our house next week, the day after Election Day. Almost perversely, I look forward to having him home again. Somehow my life seemed to have more meaning when we were taking care of him daily. That does not mean it was better. Because it was certainly worse. But our lives definitely had more focus.

In the long run I don't know which is more untenable, Noah's presence or his absence. I do know we're still on some Alice-in-Wonderland golf course, which, unfortunately, is only too real: One has to play every hole but they pop up in no certain order. OCC, for example, was Noah's first institutionalization, and no family is ever happy with the first institutionalization. So we're par for that hole.

Last night as Karl went out Halloweening he seemed in a particularly sullen mood. So Foumi looked in his room. First she found a heap of algebra papers with failing grades. Then she opened his desk drawer: Zig Zig papers. A bong pipe. And hash and marijuana buds.

As we waited for him to return, Foumi suggested that we not

say a word, just throw out the grass and the paraphernalia and wait for his reaction. But I am more direct. I tossed everything on the kitchen table and confronted him as he came in the door.

He immediately confessed that he had begun smoking while Foumi was in England. And then we stayed up till 4:00 A.M. talking. It was one of those mom-and-dad-and-teenager tearful where-do-we-go-from-here postmortems. We did extract from Karl the promise to follow the straight and narrow. And I did admit that some of the problem might be my fault; I tend to obfuscate the signals sent to Karl at a time when he needs very clear ones.

This is the second time we have caught Karl in the drug act. Most distressing was his claim that the hash had been purchased for a friend to whom he would pass it on at a profit after sampling some for himself. In other words, he was cutting and dealing, the new drug morality and entrepreneurial modus operandi. If he has a half-Jewish and half-Japanese business sense, it is not one I want to see applied to the drug trade.

Foumi is convinced that Karl is a wrongo, another bad apple in our genetic bushel. I am confused. I realize the kid must rebel and experiment and that what he has done is not *that* bad. He has not dropped acid or shot heroin or tried PCP.

Still he is starting too early. Earlier than he can handle it. Or than I can allow him to handle it.

He likes the taste of beer, he says. He enjoys the high of marijuana, he admits. How can I argue against his own taste-bud sensations and his own senses of euphoria? I could—and do—try to tell him about the deeper pleasures of deferred rewards and self-achieved highs. But I know he really does not buy that. At the same time I am wary of the consequences of overreacting. But Foumi isn't, and I must go with her instincts. Because mine so far have proven notoriously unreliable.

November 2, 1980

How long will Noah stay in our house? I don't know. I do know at this point Karl's lucky Noah's coming home. Because that will take some of the heat off him.

I really can't understand his thinking, though. For example, he's vehemently against legalizing marijuana, arguing, "Who wants potheads running the country?"

If Portnoy felt that he was trapped into living out a Jewish joke, I feel as if I'm caught in the middle of a Jew-Jap soap opera. A severely brain-damaged kid. A potential junkie. And last night I awoke in a sweat worrying about how I could make the monthly payments on another house.

Perhaps it's best that the drug crisis with Karl came to a head this week? I can't lose sleep over it. I'm too busy losing sleep over everything else I can't handle.

We went to the Marlton School and enrolled Noah. Then we played one last card and failed. So did organized medicine. What happened was this:

We tried to get Noah admitted to the Neuropsychiatric Institute of UCLA for a general checkup, something both necessary and long overdue. The director told us the only basis on which Noah could be admitted there would be for a complete neurological workup. Which sounded fine. Until we met with the neurologist. He said that, frankly, in Noah's case, neurology meant gobbledygook and if Noah were his own son he would not recommend a workup. Because an EEG would just show a few wobbly lines signifying nothing. A scan would involve running the risk of general anesthesia and would mean even less. Foumi and I looked at each other and laughed. The doctors at NPI reminded me of movie executives whose idea of spending a day constructively is to constantly say no.

So today I have two no-choice decisions to make. When to pick up Noah and who to vote for. I know how bad Carter is but I'll vote for him. I know how terrible it will be having Noah home again but I will bring him back from OCC.

I called OCC and bought a few days; I won't be picking Noah up until Friday. I saw the early returns, and a vote for Carter would have been academic; so I tossed my ballot to Anderson to help him qualify for federal help in defraying his campaign debt.

Today I increase my debt: I go mortgage hunting. I am not

good at business and investments. But then the real business of my life is Karl, Noah, Foumi. I am investing in my love for them. Corny but true. So I should not quibble with bankers.

A nasty squabble with Foumi. Before dinner we were talking of Noah's imminent homecoming and I was trying to explain interest rates to her when Foumi suddenly insisted that I be sure to remember to pick up the rice cooker we had taken to OCC. I had just spent a frustrating day mortgage hunting, worrying about tens of thousands of dollars. So I, of the short fuse, immediately exploded. I wasn't about to make a big deal over a lousy rice cooker. Of course, it was more than the cost of the rice cooker that upset Foumi. For the rice cooker represented the promises of OCC in every sense: all the things they did not do, from treating Noah as an individual to respecting his diet. But in the heat of the moment the rice cooker represented just thirty or so odd dollars to me while I was trying to explain that $90,000 at 12 percent was the same as $75,000 at 14.5 percent. Anyway, we went at each other for the rest of the evening. Hour after hour, until bedtime. When Foumi went off to sleep in the den. She slept well there. I had our bed but I didn't sleep at all.

I caught a few moments of our new president's press conference this morning and I must say he handled himself very well. If I were a foreigner I might be afraid that he could be too quick to resort to the use of force. But as a Californian I can relax in the sure knowledge that as a product of the movie studio system Ronnie will be careful not to make too many waves. I also thank my lucky stars that he was an actor and not a director. He'll go with the script.

In a positive way I feel Noah's homecoming will make my life normal again, give it the keel it requires for equilibrium. My health is good and I can handle him now. By being calm. By not being hypercritical of Foumi. By accepting everything as it is.

26

November 8, 1980

After another day in the temples of the moneylenders, I picked up
Noah yesterday afternoon. As I rang the bell at OCC I smelled
the stench that comes from the room of their two older problem
clients. The Administrative President's car was in the driveway;
he did not come out of his office to greet me. Noah was packed,
his suitcase at the entrance. I remembered to ask for the rice
cooker. But I did not check Noah's stuff. Noah, of course, knew
he was going home. However, I do not think he knew that he was
going home for good.

Foumi was happy that I retrieved the rice cooker. But she was
dismayed to discover that a half dozen of his underpants were
missing. Also three pairs of pants plus his bathrobe. Shirts, which
he chews, she didn't count.

And she was still down on Karl for his grass smoking. She was
going to ask him to promise that he would never smoke grass
again. And when I told her that I thought "never" was a very
long time and that Karl would lie anyway about his drug taking,
she was down on me, too. She blamed me again—my leniency—
for Karl's involvement with drugs and said she felt his future was
bleak. I felt her feeling his future was bleak could make it so as
self-fulfilling prophecy. And so we argued back and forth. While
Noah pissed on our bedspread.

November 9, 1980

Noah has behaved better than we had anticipated. Last night I
helped prepare his dinner, gave him his bath, brushed his teeth,

and put him to bed. This morning I rose first to serve him his breakfast and dress him. I think that we will be able to live with Noah.

Karl is the problem. It seems that he has been smoking grass and hash much more frequently than we had assumed—three to four times a week since the beginning of school in September. So today I read him the riot act.

I told him that I have never wanted to throw Noah in his face or give him guilt because of Noah. But that dealing with Noah would now take up all the energies I could muster. That my experience with Noah the past nine months had taught me the truth of "out of sight, out of mind." And I therefore want Karl out of my sight, to move out of the house if he wanted to be a druggie.

He tearfully pleaded that he had no place to go, that I should give him another chance.

Which I did. But I should have sent him packing. If he wants to act like a street kid, then let him spend a few days out in the great cold street. If he does not accept our values, then let him go make his own way. I am prepared to let him fall flat on his face. I am not prepared to have a son smoking grass three, four times a week around my house.

I told my troubles to a friend who was having his own difficulties with his fifteen-year-old daughter. It seems she took their car and went joyriding on Sunset Boulevard—until she rear-ended another car. Fortunately, no one was hurt. Just damages. And a litany of teenage lies. How quickly the kids do lie! It comes to them more quickly than the truth.

I am really upset with Karl. Yet I can't help but notice his return to drugs coincides with the Noah–OCC crisis—the letter from their Executive Visiting Adviser informing us that Noah would be coming home. Either Karl sensed the anxiety I felt at Noah's returning, or he simply took advantage of the fact that my attention was focused elsewhere. In any case, it all boils down to Noah. In our family, somehow, it always does.

November 10, 1980

I got out of bed at 6:20 A.M., the earliest I've been up since standing reveille in the army. But this morning was Noah's first day of school at Marlton. At 6:15 Foumi tried to wake and dress Noah by herself. But to her wake-up entreaties he responded by yelping and then racing into the living room, where he proceeded to sprawl on the floor in a tantrum. After I came to her aid, Noah allowed me to dress him and even went to the bathroom at my request.

The bus, a standard school bus, had just one other passenger, Willie, Noah's old roommate. It arrived at 6:45 as scheduled, with Mark Tajima, Noah's new teacher, riding shotgun behind it on his Honda motorcycle. Just in case, Mark told us, there was any problem on the bus Noah's first day. Noah boarded the bus willingly and Foumi strapped him into a seat. He made the "drink" sign which he also uses for "eat" and we waved goodbye to him. Then off went the bus with its motorcycle escort as if it were carrying a cargo of V.I.P.'s.

November 11, 1980

Noah seems to be holding. This morning when I threatened him with OCC he had a tantrum. I wonder how much he really understands. But Foumi says that when the bus dropped him off from school yesterday it was as if he was relieved to find himself at our house rather than at OCC. And why not? Every kid enjoys coming home from school.

November 12, 1980

Instead of studying algebra in his room last night as he was supposed to be doing, Karl was found playing with some imaginary football league of his own devising. So I gave him my by-now familiar lecture about cutting my losses and getting rid of him. I told him once more in stern Old Testament terms that since I had written off one son I was ready to write off another.

Except I have learned to live with Noah. But a tragedy to Karl would overwhelm me. I couldn't take being a loser with both my kids. What greater curse is there than to have both of one's sons prematurely severed from the future?

Noah is not easy and Karl is harder. I may fall apart trying to keep my family together. I wonder why I struggle so. Foumi wonders why she struggles even harder. Karl wonders what the fuss is all about since he is so unhappy anyway. And Noah rages between smiles.

Karl came to me, tears in his eyes, and said: "I hate Noah." I told him that his feeling was perfectly normal and natural and that Noah was a very easy person to hate these days. And, indeed, he is. Before dinner last night, out of nowhere he suddenly attacked Karl, pulling his hair with a never-leave-go grip. Noah has been a trial and a pain as if he is sick. But he does have an appetite and doesn't seem to be running any fever.

I was able to bathe him and brush his teeth last night but after that it was a strictly no-win situation. First he lay on his own bed banging his hand against his head repeatedly. Then he ran into Karl's room and refused to leave it. I tried pulling him out of there. A mistake. I felt my angina. I became furious with him as if he had caused it. As I got him into his bedroom I swatted him one. Another mistake. Heaven forgive me for it.

I lay down and popped a nitro. Foumi and Karl wanted to call the hospital. I insisted that we all just cool down. The angina went away and I tried to sleep. But it was a bad night for sleeping. Noah was up crying, no doubt against the injustice of my clout. Foumi worried audibly. Finally we all fell asleep.

Waking Noah this morning was a chore. We had to rub his face with a cold wet washcloth, pry him into a sitting position in order to pull his pants up over a bulging erection, while he flailed about wildly, anxious to return to sleep. He finally rose from his bed when I mentioned a car ride and I got him to the bathroom to do his honors. Foumi insisted that he eat an apple—he gets both breakfast and lunch in school—and we argued about that as he took a few slices of one. I put on his shoes and socks. (Why doesn't one put on "socks and shoes," isn't that the logical order?) Then he went outside and stood at the curb, looking for all the world like a normal kid, as he waited for the school bus to come.

He seems to like his new public school. I hope he can flourish in it, I pray we can survive through it. It is not easy for any of us to get up at 6:15 A.M.

I tried going back to sleep. But soon the doorbell was ringing. A repairman for the dryer. Foumi had neglected to tell me that Karl, exploring it in the interests of science no doubt, had broken the belt. Forty-four dollars. I don't know with whom I was angrier—Foumi, Karl, or the repairman who came at 7:20 A.M.

I couldn't sleep. Instead, I just lay in bed musing: With Noah around there's never any rest. We constantly have to be on his case. Making sure that he goes to the bathroom. Wiping him when he does. Checking to see that he has not put any foreign objects into his mouth. Yet somehow the house, our home, feels more like our house, feels more normal with Noah around.

Perversities and infirmities. Infirmities and perversities. Walk around with a pebble in your shoe long enough and eventually it feels right.

November 15, 1980

Noah's reign of terror is worst at mealtimes as he continually tests us. Last night at dinner, for example, he twice tossed his plate to the floor. This upset Foumi, so she ran from the kitchen crying. I salvaged what I could, gave him his fruit dessert, and spiked his jucie with some tranquilizing medication I keep in the house for just such emergencies. We were expected at dinner with friends. Feeling nervous, we finally left the house, with Karl, who was in charge of Noah, firmly implanted before the TV set while Noah bounced on the love seat.

Dinner was a joy. Our friends remembered (I hadn't forgotten; I just hadn't remembered to do anything about it) that it was Foumi's birthday, her big five-oh, and had gifts for her. The other couple present, who are both writers, were as always kissing cousins. It was a warm evening, enhanced by wonderfully prepared Chinese food, and Foumi, who had not slept in thirty-six hours, positively glowed. When we got home Karl reported that Noah had given him no trouble and had dutifully gone to bed at nine.

This Saturday morning I heard Noah chirping around seven o'clock. But I fell back to sleep and lingered in bed another hour, having all sorts of nonsensical dreams. Karl too woke up dreaming—perhaps Noah's keening induces the state—and at breakfast Karl told me his dream:

"You went out by yourself and bought a brand-new car, a BMW, and drove it home. But when you got here Foumi and I noticed that in the backseat was a brain-damaged kid. Not Noah. But a different brain-damaged kid. So you turned around and drove back to the dealer. You wanted to return the car and change it for another one instead. But the dealer refused. 'Buddy,' he said, 'that's the way it comes for you.'"

27

My journal does not end on November 15, 1980. The habit of half a lifetime did not just die suddenly. But I've had to choose a cutoff date so as not to tread on Karl's privileged teenage turf.

However, I do want to sum up what has happened to us as a family and what, if anything, we have learned. And perhaps the best way for me to do that is to begin with my reply to a letter I received from a reader in Minnesota in December 1982.

First, her letter:

December 7, 1982

Dear Mr. Greenfeld,

I hope this letter finds its way to you and that you somehow find the time to write me a short reply. I have just finished reading your two books about your son Noah. I must tell you how grateful I am to you for writing them. I began to read A Child Called Noah, *marking places for my husband to read; places which reminded me of our son Andy and my feelings toward him. After two chapters, I gave up and told my husband to read the whole book; I felt that I could have written it myself. I cried all the way through the book. My son is now four, the age Noah was when you began your book. We too have been from doctor to school to psychologist to nowhere and back again. All your expressions of rage, fear, disgust, exhaustion, anger, guilt, inadequacy are ones that I share. We too face the fear of perhaps ultimately having to send our Andy to an institution.*

I don't suppose I am the first parent who has written to you. I am sure I won't be the last. I wrote for three reasons:

1. To thank you for your books. Just knowing I was not alone has helped so very much. And not too much seems to help some days.

2. To ask what has happened to your family now, since several years have passed since A Place for Noah *was written. Is Noah still with you? Are things any better for you and your wife and oldest son? Is Noah any different?*

3. Because I feel like you are, in a way, living through now what I will probably have to face in the near future, I ask for insights. If you had it to do over, would you have done anything differently? Would you have made the decision to institutionalize Noah earlier or have made a firm commitment to keep him at home? Can you give me any advice?

Once again, thank you. Even if you don't have time to reply to me, you have touched my life and helped me more than you can ever know. I only hope that things are better for you now and for your family.

Sincerely,

[signed] *Barbara E. Roy*

(Please forgive the awful typing. I work full time & my time is at a premium—as I'm sure you can fully understand.)

This was my answer:

December 25, 1982

Dear Barbara E. Roy:

Your letter has just been sent on to me and first let me say that my heart goes out to your family, to you and your husband and your son.

Noah is now sixteen and a half. He attends a Special Education class in a public school for the deaf. (He is not deaf but the deaf schools seem to be running out of students because, thankfully, there have been no rubella epidemics for some time.) He lives in my house with a full-time caretaker—or sitter—whom I've engaged. My wife and I live in another house nearby with our other son, Karl, who is now away for his first year of college.

This is the arrangement I made two years ago out of necessity. Trying to deal with Noah I had come down first with heart disease and then with ulcers. And so far the arrangement has seemed to work out. Previously, I had placed Noah in a small residential school and that had not worked out at all. He was mistreated there and we had to withdraw him. The present setup costs quite a bit but fortunately I have been able to manage it so far. When I run out of money, though, I don't know what I will do.

On his good days Noah functions like a two-year-old. On his bad days like a baby of six months. Like anyone else he can be either happy or depressed. So I seek to give him the same kind of life I want for myself, one that is as pleasurable as possible. And Noah, surely as any other living being, can feel pleasure.

Eventually, Noah will have to go into some sort of institution. I continue to view institutions as places that can only be defined in oxymoronic terms such as "bureaucratic caring." So I treat Noah's eventual institutionalization the way I treat the prospect of my own death—as an inevitability I seek to avoid as long as humanly possible.

As for some kind of scenario for the future of your family, I just don't know what to say except that no two of these children are exactly alike. I have seen children who had displayed similar behaviors to Noah's winding up both better and worse. I think what you must do is follow your own instincts and fulfill your own needs. There is no simple solution, but since whatever you do is wrong, anything you do is also right.

In immediate terms, I would get Andy into a class where he can learn sign language. Sometimes, since signing removes the strain of having to use speech, it actually enhances its arrival. (Noah still does not speak but he can make a few signs.) Signing also seems the first way some children can realize they can actually communicate without having a tantrum. I think I would also test both Andy's hearing and his sight. It is now possible to make such tests without the child's cooperation. But mostly I would try to enjoy Andy for what he is, as much as possible. And if you do find a decent residential facility for him, don't feel guilty about placing him there.

I would suggest you look into the Rudolf Steiner schools and farms. These are places run by the members of a religious cult of sorts who are genuinely dedicated to all sorts of special children. They train them to work on their farms and they have a commitment to them for life. I visited one in Camphill, Pennsylvania, some time back and was quite impressed. At that time I was told that they were planning to open a school and farm in Minnesota.

Another residence that has impressed me is Benhaven in New

Haven, Connecticut. I would place my own son Noah in either facility if they would accept him. I also could be making a mistake in doing so. One truly never knows, no matter how sophisticated one feels one has become, how any residence is until one's child becomes a consumer. And even then it takes time. Our kids can't tell us how they are being treated, which is why they are there in the first place.

Remember that any decision you make is always immediately revocable. If you put Andy in a place you can always change your mind and take him out. And if you are able to find a better place you can always put him there. Your big problem is getting through each day because of the arguments and concerns Andy's presence engenders. Very few marriages can survive such strains. It's one of the ironies of the institution—there's that word again—of marriage that when you need it most it becomes its most tenuous.

If I had to do it all over again I probably would do everything differently—including not have a child in the first place. At the same time I don't know exactly what I would have done instead. Not given my values, anyway. I still live from day to day in terms of Noah and words like commitment and decision mean little to me. Unfortunately, none of our educational systems prepare us to deal with problems for which there are no solutions. Each of us just has to grope in his or her own way.

I do think one must use the same values in dealing with a special child as with an ordinary child. And, in that sense, I have my own idiosyncratic theory that, of course, I have not followed. It is this: I believe money spoils a child. Of course, some money is necessary. But too much money is the ruin of any kid. So as little money as possible should be spent on any kid, special or normal. I don't believe, for example, that schools that charge extravagant tuition fees turn out kids that are any better than those that charge reasonable tuitions or are free. I think the same applies to Special Education schools, programs, and institutions. I resent the people and the groups who make profits out of our afflictions. I question their motivations and dedications. So look for programs and places where the personnel involved are really concerned rather than real avaricious.

Having said all this I must remind you I am presently maintaining two households because of Noah. But then I figure he is the price of the divorce I've never had.

I fear I have made little sense to—or for—you. I know that

with a child like Andy, you will soon discover—if you have not already—that every breath of insight is immediately refuted by the next breath. So again let me urge you to have the courage to pursue your own instincts. Realize that you have unwittingly become the world's greatest expert on Andy. And don't let the professionals grind you down.

I sincerely hope that Andy develops to a much greater degree than you now dream possible. The only thing predictable about kids like ours is their ultimate unpredictability.

A Merry Christmas to you all!

[signed] *Josh Greenfeld*

P.S. Noah, with the help of his companion, laboriously constructed a paste-up Christmas tree for us. This year also, for the second year in a row, he appeared, albeit fleetingly, in his school Christmas play. Last year he was the Jack of Clubs, this year a sailor. And as my son Karl pointed out, "That's progress. From an inanimate object to an animate one."

There are joys, there are still many joys, that we derive from Noah.

From the vantage point of an additional three years of experience there is little I would add by way of advice if I were writing that letter today. Except perhaps to reassure the parent that although having a Noah or an Andy never stops hurting, it is amazing how tough—or desensitized—we all become, both parent and special child, in order to survive.

Noah lived in our old home beginning in February 1981, with a succession of caretaking companions. At first we took our chances hiring locally as best we could: We tried an Arab. Next, a basketball player. Then, a makeup artist. But from September 1982 to April 1984—in a much more successful arrangement— we brought over for a year at a time two native Japanese college graduates interested in teaching, Shinji and Taketoshi, to live and work with Noah. Shinji was able to teach Noah how to use chopsticks and to drink through a straw. Taketoshi got Noah to do push-ups and to run laps with him. They were a great help and Noah loved them both. But there was the continuing problem of having to go to Japan each year to find and interview replacements. In addition, the responsibility of taking care of Noah on weekends, vacations, sick spells, and days off still fell to us. We constantly had to worry about what would happen to Noah if either of us became ill for an extended period.

In April 1984, as Noah approached his eighteenth birthday, the opportunity arose to place him in an adult group residential home for the developmentally disabled. We had visited other homes run by the same people and had been favorably impressed. Still it was not easy to face giving up direct control over Noah's daily regimen. The experience with OCC was never far from our minds. But the move had to be made sometime, for Noah's sake as well as ours, and we decided to place him there.

Since then Noah has lived with five other adult men and women in a ranch house at the end of an ordinary street in a typical Orange County working-class community. He goes to baseball games, movies, Disneyland, and even overnight campouts. He is enrolled in a public school Special Education program. We are in constant touch with both his house mother, Sue McGartland, and his teacher, Jim Hunter, and we visit Noah regularly. And if Sue or Jim is free to come along to ensure Noah's staying in line we take him to dinner with us. I still find it difficult dealing with Noah on a one-on-one basis. Instinctively—or cognitively—he is quick to take advantage of the fact that I am his father.

In many ways, for all the attention and energy expended on him all these years, Noah at nineteen and a half does not appear to have changed significantly in terms of his special behavioral and communication problems. At best his I.Q. still measures at the level of an eighteen-month-old infant. At his worst he is still given to tantrums and sudden rages that include spitting and clutching. But if often a grotesque in behavior, he is still unusually handsome in appearance. When he attends a dance for the disabled, for example, he is a standout. And while both Jim and Sue still labor in the belief that Noah might one day function in a sheltered community workshop, we're not always that sanguine. But Noah does continue to surprise us with new evidences of his capacity to learn. When we recently visited him, for example, I noticed that Noah now could pour ketchup by himself onto a hot dog. I prefer mustard on hot dogs myself. But, as I have long learned, with Noah you take what you can get.

Noah's present placement, Foumi and I both know and fear, is not a permanent solution. But nothing is. Still, after eighteen years of living from day to day with Noah, the past twenty months of living without him have been, to put it simply and bluntly, like paradise. Foumi and I have been able to live like normal people.

Karl, too, is away from home. He has spent the last three and a half years either going to college in the East or living and studying in Paris. He is now conversant with the French language and with the ways of mature and responsible conduct. When I recently mentioned to him all the concerns I had during his teenage years, particularly about drugs, he insisted that I had had a bigger problem with any drug involvement than he ever did. I'm not sure whether I overreacted or he's underremembering. But at any rate—and I don't know how it's happened—Karl, at twenty-one, has developed into a worldly young man whose company I enjoy.

From time to time he makes the preliminary sounds of someone who might want to become a writer. I try to dissuade him, having spent a lifetime stumbling into every pitfall along the literary path. But Noah is not the only son who doesn't always listen to his old man. Meanwhile, my own writing life continues. In April 1984, my novel *The Return of Mr. Hollywood* was published to uniformly fine reviews. Even one from Karl. He told me he was impressed.

However, much more impressive has been Foumi's late-blooming literary career. And if I weren't so damned proud of her I would be downright jealous. But it does reinforce my belief in irony. Somehow my own long-cherished dream has been realized—but by the other side of the bed.

In June 1985 Foumi was awarded first prize in the Newcomer Contests of both *Shincho* and *Bungakai* magazines, two of Japan's most prestigious literary magazines. It was a news event in Japan—the first time any newcomer had won two such laurels. Her two prizewinning short stories, "Passover" and "A Visitor from Afar," both dealing with the parent of a special child such as Noah, were published in book form in October 1985. And her novel, *Tumbleweed*, after all these years, is now scheduled to be published in June 1986.

But even bigger news about Foumi at the moment is the fact that because of "Passover" she has been nominated for the Akutagawa Award, Japan's most important literary prize. We have nothing comparable to it in this country—unless there were a single Pulitzer Prize and it came with a black belt. When I called Karl to tell him the news, there was a moment of awed silence at the other end of the phone. "Gee," he finally said. "I always thought if I had any writing talent it came from you. But maybe it comes from Foumi?" And then he went on to inform me that he was writing something about Noah.

"Welcome to the club," I told him. "Three writers. One subject. No waiting." And we both laughed. But after I hung up I turned to Foumi and said: "There's no way out of it, is there? It's not a matter of choice. It's a matter of fact. Noah has been the central experience of all our lives." Then I smiled and shrugged. "And I would have traded it for anything."

Foumi didn't even bother to peer over her glasses and look up at me from the galleys she was checking. But then she's always been the chief repository of wisdom—both Oriental and Occidental—in our house.

"Of course," she said.

Pacific Palisades, California
December 30, 1985

POSTSCRIPT

On Thursday evening, February 13, 1986, Karl and I were among the hundreds in attendance at the formal ceremonies held in Tokyo to honor Foumiko Kometani, the ninety-second recipient of the coveted Akutagawa Award. Foumi, dressed in a pink-mauve silk gown she had worn only once before—at the Academy Awards ceremonies in 1975 when I had been a loser nominee—looked positively radiant. Her eyes sparkled, her skin glowed as she made her acceptance speech. And Karl and I basked in her happiness—our family at last, somehow, a winner.

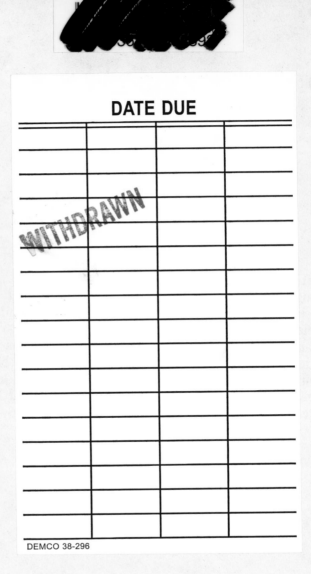

DATE DUE

DEMCO 38-296